Farmers, Kings, and Traders

Farmers, Kings, and Traders

The People of Southern Africa, 200–1860

Martin Hall

With a new Foreword by
Martin E. West

The University of Chicago Press

This book was originally published under the title *The Changing Past: Farmers, Kings and Traders in Southern Africa, 200–1860,* by David Philip, Publisher, Ltd., Claremont, Cape, South Africa, in the series *The People of Southern Africa.* Two maps and a Foreword have been added to this edition.

The University of Chicago Press, Chicago 60637
The University of Chicago Press, Ltd., London

Printed in the United States of America

99 98 97 96 95 94   6 5 4 3 2

Library of Congress Cataloging-in-Publication Data

Hall, M. (Martin)
    [Changing past]
    Farmers, kings, and traders : the people of southern Africa, 200-1860 / Martin Hall ; with a new foreword by Martin E. West.—University of Chicago Press ed.
    p.   cm.
    Reprint. Originally published: The changing past. Cape Town : D. Philip, 1987. Originally published in series: The People of southern Africa.
    Includes bibliographical references and index.
    ISBN 0-226-31326-3 (pbk.)
    1. Africa, Southern—History—To 1899.   I. Title.
DT1107.H35   1990
968—dc20   90-39017
                                                CIP

⊗The paper used in this publication meets the minimum requirements of the American National Standard for Information Sciences—Permanence of Paper for Printed Library Materials, ANSI Z39.48-1984

Contents

Foreword

Southern Africa is a subcontinent with a long history of conflict. The most recent historical manifestation of this has been the colonial experience, where by the nineteenth century Portugal, Britain, and Germany held sway over all the people and resources south of the Cunene and Zambezi rivers—an area larger than Europe itself.

The progress of European conquest and domination was resisted, of course, and colonial settlement was met with rebellion. This resistance has continued through the years, and has led, eventually, to independence from colonial rule for Zambia, Zimbabwe, and Mozambique, and for white South Africans. In Namibia and South Africa itself, resistance to white minority rule continues as apartheid lingers.

In the conventional view, South Africa is an arena wherein clearly defined groups have struggled and fought over time for power and self-determination. While there is some substance to this view, there is an alternative vision which—while in no way denying conflict—has sought to highlight cooperation and interaction between people of different backgrounds and ways of life in the unfolding history of the subcontinent. This historical view stresses the movement of people, changing lifestyles, and the constant shifting of boundaries. In so doing it radically confronts the vision of southern Africans as constituting neatly bounded ethnic entities existing over time as named "tribes," "nations," "peoples," and "ethnic groups."

Professor Hall's book falls squarely within this alternative tradition. The title of the South African edition, *The Changing Past,* captures both the idea of historical process and that of changing *perceptions* of the past. The process of domination is about perceptions as well as about the exercise of force. It is about what people believe about themselves and encourage or coerce others to believe.

In Professor Hall's view, this is a crucial area for the historian and prehistorian. The stereotypes held by the conquerors of the conquered have often been crude in the extreme—we are all aware of the "benighted savages" who were to be brought the benefits of Western civilization by its colonial standard-bearers. The conquerors have generally ignored the early texts, oral histories, and archaeological sites that are evidence for a richly textured past stretching back before colonial settlement.

These stereotypes still pervade much of the writing and general perceptions about southern Africa. The majority of contemporary southern Africans are at best a "people without history"; at worst they are the victims of a prejudiced view that has more to do with the justification for domination than with understanding the past.

This book makes four important contributions within the context I have just outlined. Firstly, it examines and explodes some of the more popular myths about early southern Africa. These include the belief that the ancestors of black South Africans entered the country at roughly the same time as the first white settlers, and the standpoint that the extraordinary Great Zimbabwe complex was a feat that must be attributed to the skills of non-African foreigners.

Secondly, Professor Hall presents the early history of the subcontinent without recourse to simplistic labels. There are no lists of tribes in his book. Instead he presents a rich and intricate tapestry of the movement and interaction of farmers, foragers, and pastoralists. We cannot be certain what the first farmers in South Africa looked like, nor what languages they spoke; and we certainly cannot label them as "Bantu" or "Nguni" or "Sotho." It is a point often overlooked that significant named groupings in contemporary South Africa (from Afrikaner to Zulu) are the recent—and undoubtedly transient—creations of the nineteenth century. Professor Hall concentrates on the underlying processes rather than on groups.

The third contribution is more formally academic. It addresses the models of archaeologists, historians, linguists, and anthropologists, and goes far beyond the simplistic myths of origins and dispersal of the southern African population. Here Professor Hall presents a clear and accessible picture of current wisdom, and builds on this to present his own synthesis and interpretations. There are at least two areas of particular intellectual importance. In the first, Professor Hall examines the prevailing model of an "iron-age package" which sees the first farmers entering southern Africa as a racially, linguistically, and culturally distinct grouping. He convincingly argues for a more complex model, which he labels "incremental," by which farmers entered the region over a lengthy period, interacting in complex ways with people they found there. In the second area he presents his periodization of early southern African history, which includes a new interpretation of the

revolution in economy and society which occurred around 1000 A.D. and an exploration of its implications. When dealing with the past we find that the boundaries between disciplines are sometimes as tenuous as those within the societies analyzed, and Professor Hall's analysis is strengthened throughout by his interdisciplinary focus.

The final contribution of the book is the examination of the links between the past and the present. The current political dispensation in South Africa, for example, is often justified by references to a particular view of the past, and the political geography of the subcontinent—including national, "homeland," and ethnic boundaries—is itself a product of the colonial view of Africa's past. We cannot fully understand the contemporary situation of southern Africa without understanding the past and how it has shaped us all. Professor Hall's book throws new light on both the past and the present, and is recommended to all who would like a fresh look at a troubled subcontinent.

Martin E. West
Professor of Social Anthropology
University of Cape Town

Preface

As with any book of this nature, the author's primary obligation is to those colleagues whose research has provided the basis for synthesis and interpretation. I have benefited from many discussions and arguments, but in particular I should like to thank Tom Huffman, Tim Maggs, John Parkington and Roger Summers for many hours of their time and for their stimulating ideas.

The brunt of my experimentation with concepts has been borne by students, by Athene and Nerissa Hall, and by my colleagues in the Spatial Archaeology Research Unit. To them, and to the University of Cape Town, I owe the privilege of a research environment. Financial support for the collection of material in Zambia and Zimbabwe was provided by the Harry Oppenheimer Institute for African Studies, UCT, while production of the manuscript was aided by a grant from the Mauerberger Foundation Fund. Colin Bundy, Desmond Clark, Janette Deacon, John Parkington, Nigel Penn, Ian Phimister, Chris Saunders, Andy Smith, Roger Summers, Lyn Wadley, John Wright and Royden Yates read parts, or all, of the text and made valuable comments. Tina Coombes and Royden Yates produced some fine illustrations at very short notice and Julia Segar dropped everything for the index. Russell Martin and Martin West were kind, if insistent, editors. After such assistance any remaining errors or omissions must surely be my own responsibility.

Martin Hall
Cape Town
December 1986

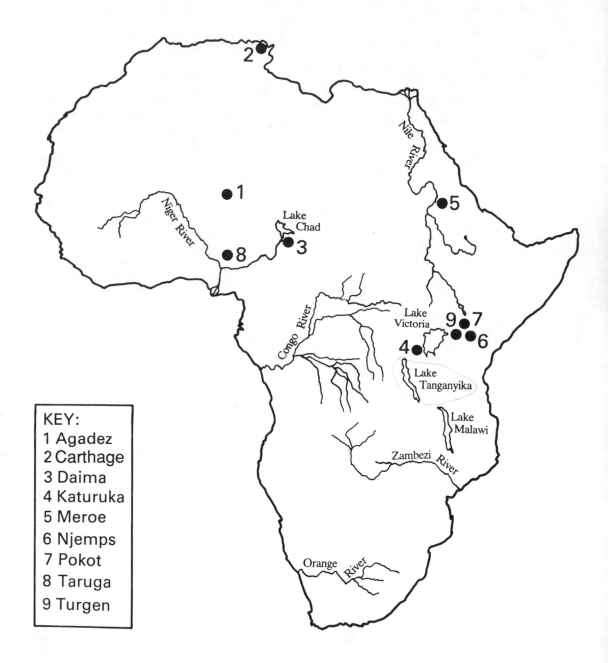

KEY:
1 Agadez
2 Carthage
3 Daima
4 Katuruka
5 Meroe
6 Njemps
7 Pokot
8 Taruga
9 Turgen

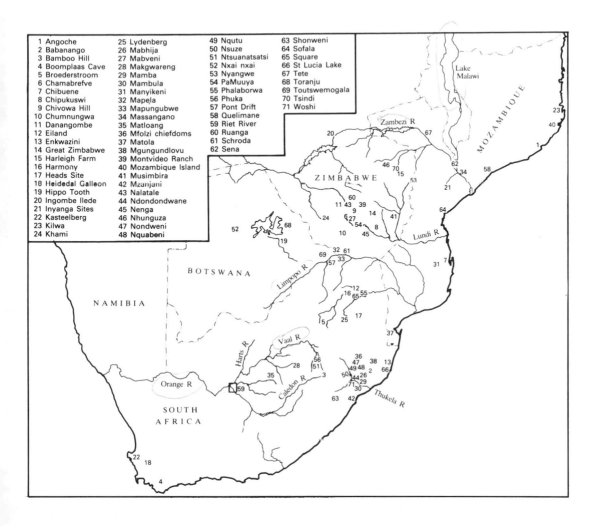

1 Angoche	25 Lydenberg	49 Nqutu	63 Shonweni
2 Babanango	26 Mabhija	50 Nsuze	64 Sofala
3 Bamboo Hill	27 Mabveni	51 Ntsuanatsatsi	65 Square
4 Boomplaas Cave	28 Makgwareng	52 Nxai nxai	66 St Lucia Lake
5 Broederstroom	29 Mamba	53 Nyangwe	67 Tete
6 Chamabrefve	30 Mambula	54 PaMuuya	68 Toranju
7 Chibuene	31 Manyikeni	55 Phalaborwa	69 Toutswemogala
8 Chipukuswi	32 Mapela	56 Phuka	70 Tsindi
9 Chivowa Hill	33 Mapungubwe	57 Pont Drift	71 Woshi
10 Chumnungwa	34 Massangano	58 Quelimane	
11 Danangombe	35 Matloang	59 Riet River	
12 Eiland	36 Mfolzi chiefdoms	60 Ruanga	
13 Enkwazini	37 Matola	61 Schroda	
14 Great Zimbabwe	38 Mgungundlovu	62 Sena	
15 Harleigh Farm	39 Montvideo Ranch		
16 Harmony	40 Mozambique Island		
17 Heads Site	41 Musimbira		
18 Heidedal Galleon	42 Mzanjani		
19 Hippo Tooth	43 Nalatale		
20 Ingombe Ilede	44 Ndondondwane		
21 Inyanga Sites	45 Nenga		
22 Kasteelberg	46 Nhunguza		
23 Kilwa	47 Nondweni		
24 Khami	48 Nquabeni		

Farmers, Kings, and Traders

Farmers, kings and traders in southern Africa

This book is about the people who lived in southern Africa from the first introduction of farming, some two thousand years ago, until the founding of the present industrial economy in the middle decades of the last century.

During this period there was both continuity and change in social processes. Once established in the subtropical coastlands of south-eastern Africa, perhaps as early as 50 B.C., grain farming became the foundation for new ways of living. In place of the nomadic camps of the gathering and hunting groups who had moved with the seasons for thousands of years, more permanent villages were built. Instead of living off the land, communities began to change their environment, cutting and burning clearings in the woodlands for fields. From this more settled way of life, with its new forms of economy, came a need for new technology: iron for hoes and axes, and new implements for preparing and storing food, including large numbers of pots and bowls which were decorated in differing styles. With the later addition of herds and flocks of domestic animals, this farming way of life has provided the basic livelihood for farmers in southern Africa for twenty centuries.

It is wrong to assume that this was some sort of 'dark age' in which generation after generation lived in the same manner as before. The first literate settlers from Europe made this mistake, assuming that Africa had little history, and their journals and descriptions are a heritage of misunderstanding. In recent years archaeological research has revealed a very different story. Villages were built to different plans, and many of the complex architectural styles survive in stone ruins today. Technologies changed and developed. To everyday artefacts such as pots and hoes were added complex terracotta sculptures and ornate metalwork. Economies were transformed as some were able to store wealth and power at the expense of others, and with this came new political orders, including southern Africa's first states on the eastern margins of the Kalahari Desert and in the valley of the Limpopo River. By the time the first European explorers began cautiously to probe the southern African interior, the subcontinent had a history as rich and varied as that of many other parts of the world.

It would also be a mistake to assume, as have

some more recent writers, that the early history of southern Africa was one of isolation, in which chiefdoms and states rose and fell with little influence from the wider world. From as early as the ninth century, traders were establishing a tenuous foothold on the south-east African coast, seeking gold and ivory in return for beads and cloth. Within a few centuries control of this trade, and careful exploitation of the Islamic world's need for gold, had enabled the rulers of the Zimbabwe state to build a magnificent capital more than 300 kilometres from the sea. In the decades that followed, the kings and nobles of southern Africa continued to use the needs of the world economy to buttress their own power, playing Portuguese merchants against their Arab rivals, French against British, and British against Dutch. It was only in the nineteenth century, after a thousand years of political and economic exchanges with the wider world, that the superior military technology of the colonial powers destroyed the authority of kings and chiefs and transformed the peasants and warriors of the southern African states into the wage earners of the new industrial centres.

Encounters: the changing past

But this book also has a second theme, which is intertwined with the factual account of the last two thousand years. It can best be described as a search for the *context* in which history has been written and continues to be written today. It is clear that there are 'facts' about the past which most people would accept, and which can be summarised and set down as a history. But there is also a great deal of subjectivity in the way such information is selected as important or rejected as of little value, and in the opinions and judgements that link together any narrative. For this reason, it is necessary to preface this account of the last two thousand years in southern Africa with a probe into the attitudes and ambitions of the ethnographers, historians and archaeologists who have described communities and their history, or who have excavated archaeological sites. For the past must still be seen through their eyes, and it is necessary to know what coloured and gave structure to the form of their vision. Equally, the far more difficult task must be attempted of searching for the influences on the way history is written today.

The subjective nature of knowledge of the past is well illustrated by one early encounter between a southern African state and a group of would-be traders from Europe. Nathaniel Isaacs – the 17-

One of the collection of terracotta heads found at the fifth-century site of Lydenburg, in the eastern Transvaal. The site is described in Chapter 4. (Photograph by courtesy of the South African Museum, Cape Town.)

year-old nephew of a St Helena merchant – had sailed on the brig *Mary* from the Cape to seek his fortune by trade from the south-east coast. On 1 October 1825 a strong gale drove the ship onto the sandbar across the mouth of the estuary known as Port Natal. Although the sailors tried hard to save their vessel, the damage was extensive and it was clear to Lieutenant King, the ship's master, that the best course of action was to save what was possible and make for the shore.

Isaacs's inexperience at seafaring left him of little use, so he stationed himself on the deck of the wreck and watched the shoreline for signs of life. Eventually patience was rewarded, as Isaacs himself recalled: 'the whole day had nearly passed without my having descried a living creature. In the evening, however, I perceived one of the natives, who I surveyed with an apprehensive scrutiny. He was as naked as a negro on the banks of the Niger, but though he manifested no signs of hostility, I did not feel satisfied that his attentions were amicable.' (Herman 1936) Such was Nathaniel Isaacs's initial encounter with the population of south-eastern Africa – nervous anticipation, suspicion and a degree of hostility.

'A Zoolu warrior and his daughter', based on a sketch by James Saunders King, who commanded the brig Mary aboard which Nathaniel Isaacs sailed to southern Africa in 1825. Keen to promote the establishment of a new colony, the artist has represented his subject in idyllic fashion.

These sentiments persisted during the months that followed, as Isaacs was able to see more of Natal and the court of the Zulu king, Shaka kaSenzangakhona. But at the same time, Isaacs was not suffering hardship and danger for the sake of mere curiosity, for he was keen to establish a colony and make his fortune. In consequence, he also wrote of the richness of the soil, of the wild fruits, game animals and attractions for settlement, publishing a series of articles in the *South African Commercial Advertiser* that were intended to persuade the colonial authorities that Port Natal was worthy of annexation.

Others had visited, and written of, south-eastern Africa in earlier years, but Isaacs's account is the first day-by-day description over a long period. His diary has influenced in one way or another every historian who has studied early co-lonial contact and the history of the Zulu kingdom. Yet Nathaniel Isaacs was young and inexperienced, had little formal education, was often ill and frightened, and was keen to promote a venture that he believed could make him rich. He could only communicate through interpreters, and his descriptions of what he himself did not see were anecdotal and often wildly speculative. Thus Isaacs's diary, fascinating and compulsive reading that it is, can hardly be described as objective.

The inevitable distortions in Isaacs's perception of Zulu life and history can be brought out by considering the image that the Zulu king probably formed from his side of the encounter. Although Isaacs and his companions who visited Shaka often spoke of the power and grandeur of Britain and King George, the reality that the Zulu saw was different. The party of settlers who had preceded Isaacs at Port Natal maintained the imperial symbols, welcoming the shipwrecked party by planting a worn-out Union Jack on the shore. But, as the diarist himself noted, the home to which the new arrivals were taken was hardly a castle, and was 'not remarkable either for the elegance of its structure, or the capacity of its interior' (Herman 1936).

Nor had personal standards of appearance been maintained for long under conditions of hardship and isolation, as is apparent from Isaacs's description of a trader who had been away from Port Natal for some eight months collecting ivory: 'Mr Fynn is in stature somewhat tall, with a prepossessing countenance. From necessity his face was disfigured with hair, not having had an opportunity of shaving himself for a considerable time. His head was partly covered with a crownless straw hat, and a tattered blanket, fastened around his neck by means of strips of hide, served to cover his body, while his hands performed the office of keeping it round his "nether man"; his shoes he had discarded for some months, whilst every other habiliment had imperceptibly worn away. . . .' (Herman 1936) It is unlikely that any Zulu observer could deduce from the appearance of these adventurers that they were the representatives of Regency London and the world of Jane Austen.

Nathaniel Isaacs's record of his encounter with the Zulu kingdom was preceded and repeated, at other times and elsewhere in southern Africa, by traders, missionaries, settlers and others at the frontiers of colonial expansion. The resulting documents that have been passed down to the present are rightly valued as important early accounts of the subcontinent, but they were often the personal views of men and women who, like Isaacs, were in no position to assess and describe what they saw objectively. Similarly, later writers who made use of primary sources from the early stages of contact between African chiefdoms and states and the expanding colonial world have introduced their own selection of evidence, judgement and opinion, creating multi-layered narratives that are as much documents about historians and their times as they are accounts of the past.

Archaeology: 'in small things forgotten'

The chapters that follow will illustrate how ideas about the nature of the past continue to change. These ideas have come from, among others, archaeologists and historians, who have tended to develop rather different approaches to the study of the past.

For many years historians believed that the history of early Africa was, to repeat a notorious and often-quoted phrase, merely the 'unrewarding gyrations of barbarous tribes in picturesque but irrelevant corners of the globe: tribes whose chief function in history . . . is to show to the present an image of the past from which, by history, it has escaped' (Trevor-Roper 1965). But after the middle of the present century more enlightened historians realised that documentary sources were not the only way of gaining access to the past and that, in particular, oral traditions were a valuable source of study (Curtin 1968; Henige 1971; Vansina 1965). As a consequence of new methods of research, historians of southern African societies have been able to work back centuries before the first documents became available (for examples, see Beach 1980; Bonner 1982; Hedges 1978). But traditions that have been passed down through generations are usually not, nor were ever intended to be, comprehensive social histories. Instead, they are almost always focused on the lives and exploits of important leaders, tracing back their ancestry and providing a political charter for their descendants.

Archaeological research can complement and extend the knowledge that can be gleaned from such oral traditions. Thus, for example, the histories of many of the nineteenth-century notables who lived at the royal Zulu capital of Mgungundlovu are known from James Stuart's remarkable archive of interviews (Webb and Wright 1976, 1979), while the layout of the town has been revealed in detail by archaeological ex-

Different disciplines deal with different sorts of evidence, although the overall aim – the study of the past – is the same. Archaeologists learn a good deal from rubbish, and are often interested in the different processes that have interceded between original discard and the final excavation of the site. (Illustration by Mario Maccani.)

cavation (Parkington and Cronin 1979). In contrast, the presence of the early Zimbabwe state is little more than a hint in the oral and documentary sources (Beach 1980), but is well known from the archaeology of its capital and outlying regional centres (Garlake 1973a, 1978; Huffman 1977).

But in addition, archaeological research can tell of the more routine, day-by-day life of the majority of the population of a chiefdom or state, the 'small things forgotten' of which James Deetz has written. 'Archaeology is the study of past peoples based on the things they left behind and the ways they left their imprint on the world. Chipped-stone handaxes made hundreds of thousands of years ago and porcelain teacups from the eighteenth century carry messages from their makers and users. It is the archaeologist's task to decode those messages and apply them to our understanding of the human experience.' (Deetz 1977)

The chapters that follow are an attempt to use such archaeological and historical sources together to provide a synthesis of two thousand years of southern African history, while at the same time taking into account that the reading of these sources has been made through the eyes of people who have brought their own problems, insights and prejudices to bear on their interpretations.

Changing views: from barbarous tribes to Iron Age traditions

The ethnohistorians: from colonial settlement until 1929

Although Nathaniel Isaacs and other early travellers and settlers showed a lively interest in the African past, it was not until the late nineteenth century that writers such as G. M. Theal and G. W. Stow began to give substantial attention to the history of south-eastern Africa (Stow 1905; Theal 1907). These writers had been strongly influenced by Charles Darwin's ideas on evolution, and it seemed to them logical to assume that the same evolutionary processes that lay behind geological formations and the diversity of organic species were also the key to understanding human society. Could not the indigenous occupants of the Australasian, American and African worlds be calibrated and classified on an evolutionary scale in exactly the same way that butterflies or lizards could be ordered, revealing thereby inter-relationships and origins? Was not conquest justified by the principle of 'the survival of the fittest'? (Knight 1981)

These evolutionary views were quite consistent with the politics and economy of the age. During the later nineteenth century more colonies had been added to the empires of Europe, and to some extent the theory of social evolution satisfied the need for an ethic to smooth and justify this process. When the population of an occupied country was seen as stuck on a lower branch of the evolutionary tree, then it could be argued that it was a duty of those higher up to bring the benefits of civilisation to the less fortunate. Because such an outlook involved the running together of contemporary observation with the self-serving reasoning of evolutionary sequences, justifying the inferiority of others, it can appropriately be called 'ethnohistory'.

This practical role of ethnohistoric research within the expanding colonial world is apparent in one of the first archaeological enterprises in southern Africa. From the early years of white settlement in the Cape there had been rumours of riches in gold in the southern African interior. Mashonaland, which has since become part of Zimbabwe, was occupied by Cecil Rhodes's British South Africa Company in 1890, and Rhodes was soon convinced that the site of Great Zimbab-

PRINCIPAL TYPES OF MANKIND. (After Huxley.)

Nineteenth-century evolutionists and ethnographers were preoccupied with classification, whether the subjects were bees, butterflies or mankind. This print illustrates the work of Thomas Huxley, a contemporary of Charles Darwin.

we, which lay within this new territory, had been built by Phoenicians. This interpretation was itself not surprising, and had been suggested by several earlier antiquaries, but Rhodes's interest was more than a passing diversion, for he saw in the Phoenicians a precedent for his own vision of an African empire; a glorious past that could be reincarnated by means of a grand colonial swath from the Cape to Cairo. A writer who was working for Rhodes expressed the relationship: 'What the great British Empire is to the nineteenth century, Phoenicia was to the distant ages, when Solomon's temple was built in Jerusalem.' (Wilmot 1896)

Rhodes set about discovering the treasures of the past with the same practical thoroughness that he brought to his commercial interests. In 1899 he had employed a journalist, R. N. Hall, to represent the British South Africa Company at the London Exhibition. Thereafter, Rhodes instructed Hall to investigate the ruins of Great Zimbabwe and other sites in Southern Rhodesia. Working with W. G. Neal, a local prospector, Hall dug up several sites and left damage which has seriously hindered later research (Garlake 1973a). Hall and Neal divided the occupation of Great Zimbabwe into four phases, which neatly reflect the colonial view of the southern African past. Great Zimbabwe had originally been built by Sabaeans and Phoenicians, and after a transitional phase, it was finally occupied by a decadent 'bastard race' which could be identified with the local population (Hall and Neal 1904).

Thus by the early decades of the present century the combination of ethnographic recording and the limited excavations already carried out had provided settler society with an appropriate ethic, founded on the linked beliefs that African societies were incapable of change and that the continent had a glorious, and long-lost, history of colonisation by earlier civilisations. Peter Garlake (1982a) has appropriately called this the 'settler paradigm'. Although any basis of fact for these and similar interpretations has long been eroded beyond any value, the ethnohistoric approach survives in politically opportune circumstances (Frederikse 1982; Garlake 1973a, 1982a; Hall 1984a, 1984b; Morais 1984).

Carl Mauch's sketch of Great Zimbabwe, which he visited in September 1871. 'Zimbaoe . . . represents a mighty fortress, consisting of two parts of which one, on a mountain of about 400 feet with two very large boulders, is separated by a narrow little valley from the second, which stands on a slight rise . . . the walls, in places still 30 feet high, are completely covered and . . . dangerous nettles ill repay any attempt to creep through them.' (Bernhard 1971: 115)

The beginning of systematic research: 1929–1950

Hall and Neal's elaborate claims for Great Zimbabwe did serve one useful purpose, for they drew international attention to the site, directly promoting the first systematic archaeological research into a farming-based society in southern Africa. Because of the debate that Hall and Neal's publications stimulated, the British Association for the Advancement of Science, which had earlier been associated with Rhodes, came to the conclusion that Great Zimbabwe should be reinvestigated (Hall 1984a). The Association sponsored an expedition by D. R. MacIver, who concluded that Great Zimbabwe was of African origin and that Hall and Neal's opinions should be rejected. But unfortunately, MacIver could not produce firm evidence to date the site and thereby prove it a recent construction rather than contemporary with King Solomon (MacIver 1906).

As a result, the British Association decided to sponsor a second expedition, appointing as its leader Gertrude Caton-Thompson. At the end of January 1929 Miss Caton-Thompson was 'deposited by a strolling Union Castle boat, on a sand-spit called Beira, in time to miss the thrice weekly train' (Caton-Thompson 1931). She had already had considerable experience in unravelling the complexities of large archaeological sites and was not daunted by Great Zimbabwe. In Salisbury, she acquired a second-hand Dodge lorry and met up

with her two assistants: Miss Norie, who was to be responsible for the line drawings, and Miss Kenyon, who took the photographs and maintained the truck.

In her approach to the archaeological problem, Caton-Thompson was systematic and professional. She ignored the temptation to range widely across the rich archaeology of the region, and concentrated on Great Zimbabwe itself and a small set of nearby stone ruins. While on her way to Rhodesia, she had persuaded the Union government to organise air photographs of the sites (Caton-Thompson 1931). These were taken during the clear winter months, and were the first use of what was to prove a very important technique in southern African archaeology.

By carefully excavating deposits, Caton-Thompson was able to classify pottery by its colour, texture and finish – a standard archaeological technique then, as today. From such evidence, it could be argued that the builders of Great Zimbabwe left pottery that was African in style and technique. Equally importantly, Caton-Thompson was able to show a direct connection between the

David Randall MacIver was one of the first archaeologists to describe the controversial, ruined settlements of Zimbabwe systematically, as his careful plan of Nalatale illustrates (from MacIver 1906).

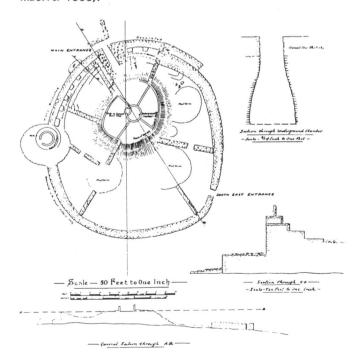

construction of the walls and imported ceramics and other trade goods of known period, thus demonstrating that the age of Great Zimbabwe should be calibrated in centuries rather than in millennia.

Gertrude Caton-Thompson's report on Great Zimbabwe was greeted with intense displeasure by many in the Rhodesian settler community (Hall 1984a). Apart from the fact that she had questioned colonial mythology and thus also shaken, albeit very gently, one of the moral justifications for colonialism, Caton-Thompson's swashbuckling style affronted local sensibilities. She rejected local opinion on Great Zimbabwe, not with any tact, but by announcing in the introduction to her book that the letters of the local 'experts' had been stored in a file marked 'insane' (Caton-Thompson 1931).

Thus began a division between community and scholar that was to persist for many years in southern Africa (Garlake 1973a). But despite opinion in the colony, Caton-Thompson's work marked a watershed for archaeological research. For although the study of skeletal remains and of the Stone Age were already well established in southern Africa, the more recent past had been left to ethnographers who had continued to write in the style of the nineteenth century. Now Caton-Thompson had shown that such communities had also left their artefacts, and that these could be used in addition to the ethnographic record. Although Great Zimbabwe and other sites were still consigned to the 'Bantu Period' – a shallow age of roving tribes – Caton-Thompson had shown that systematic archaeology had a contribution to make in uncovering the past. Her example was followed by a number of amateur archaeologists such as J. F. Schofield (1926, 1937, 1948) and P. W. Laidler (1938). Although these pioneers continued to use ethnographic information in a manner that would not be considered satisfactory today, and certainly imposed the stamp of their own social values on their interpretations (Hall 1984a, 1984b), the principles of careful excavation and recording had been established.

Establishing the Iron Age: 1950–1985

Although Laidler and particularly Schofield collected a considerable amount of archaeological information and put together syntheses that were to stand for many years, it was not until 1947 that professionally employed archaeologists were able to turn their full attention to the archaeology of farming communities. In that year Roger Sum-

John Schofield's classification of pottery from south-western Zimbabwe and the Limpopo River valley: an early attempt at systematic description of ceramics on a subcontinental scale (from Schofield 1948).

mers, who came to Southern Rhodesia from the Institute of Archaeology in London, and Keith Robinson, who soon developed a highly detailed knowledge of pottery and its different styles of decoration, began a long-term programme of research and excavation (Hall 1984a; Summers 1970). In 1950 Summers was able to publish a new synthesis for the recent past in Southern Rhodesia (Summers 1950), a model that attracted many refinements and grew increasingly complex (Summers 1967).

But Summers's original publication of 1950 had an importance beyond its content, for it introduced two significant changes in the way the past was viewed. The first was in the general name he gave to the closing centuries for southern Africa's prehistoric past. Gertrude Caton-Thompson had followed existing practice and referred to the 'Bantu Period', but now Summers, as well as Revil Mason who was working in South Africa (Mason 1951), adopted the term 'Iron Age' instead. This label had occasionally been used before and was not particularly accurate, for it was not an 'age' in

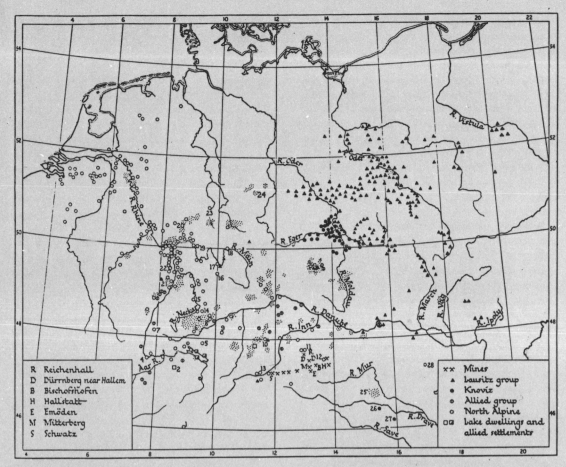

Gordon Childe adopted the concept of the culture as a device to organise the complex prehistory of the Danube valley. (From Childe 1929.)

The concept of culture

Earlier archaeologists, influenced in their work by the study of the fossil record, had been mostly concerned with establishing the *sequence* of the past. They had assumed that particular artefacts could be taken as representative of particular periods, and as a result their interpretations resembled evolutionary trees, with each stage or developing branch identified by a distinctive stone tool or type of pot.

But others had realised that, although sequences were important, in themselves they could tell little about human behaviour – what people were actually *doing* in the past. One way of providing this added dimension was to look at the dispersal of archaeological sites across the landscape, searching for correlations with woodland, rivers, good

farming soils and other factors which may have determined where people chose to live.

Gordon Childe took this geographical approach further by proposing that the one-time occupants of archaeological sites with like artefacts should be considered members of a common society, whether this be tribe, chiefdom or state. As Bruce Trigger has written, Childe 'introduced the systematic use of the concept of the archaeological culture as the basic unit for the temporal and spatial ordering of archaeological data' (Trigger 1980:40).

Childe's suggestion was a hypothesis, a working proposition that he found useful in unravelling the complexities of Danube valley prehistory. In his later writing he became a little doubtful of the value of his suggestion, recognising that there could be many different reasons why people would make artefacts in the same style. But by this stage the 'culture' had become a basic implement in the archaeological tool kit, and many complex interpretations were to be built before people began to ask what the archaeological culture really was.

any universal sense, and many of the communities which it encompassed did not make or use iron. What was important was the shift in meaning that accompanied the new words. The older 'Bantu Period' implied an inertia, a sense of changelessness that was consistent with the Victorian notion of barbaric and savage societies capable of little, or at best slow, change. This attitude was to persist for many years, and some archaeologists still use ethnography in a similarly static way, but at least the concept of the Iron Age allowed the possibility of change – the chance of seeing life a few centuries ago as significantly different from that of the present.

Secondly, Summers and Robinson employed the archaeological notion of 'culture' as a device for interpreting the past. This concept had been propagated in the English-speaking archaeological community more than twenty years earlier by Gordon Childe, Summers's teacher in London. Again, the idea was not entirely new to southern African archaeology. Caton-Thompson, for instance, had interpreted different styles of pottery as representing different tribes, while Schofield had believed that the different Bantu languages of the subcontinent were reflected in the pottery from archaeological sites. But Summers and Robinson made the Iron Age culture a normal part of archaeological practice.

From the early 1960s Summers and Robinson's research was complemented by a number of other Iron Age projects. To some extent, this expansion reflected the increased scope of archaeology as a discipline, but there were also social and political factors that had their influence. Many of the African colonies had been granted, or were about to have, their independence, and this revision of the political map was accompanied by the call for a fresh approach to history that could provide identity for the new states. Historians began to see the possibility of using sources other than the written record, emphasising as well the importance of archaeological research (for example, Hallett 1970; Wilson and Thompson 1969). Although the response in southern Africa to these new political directions was entrenchment of white power rather than concessions to African nationalism, the continent-wide change in intellectual atmosphere certainly spilled over to the south and had the effect of promoting the study of the African past.

Of these new research initiatives, three projects illustrate the diversity of the new momentum in Iron Age studies. In 1966 Tim Maggs began a major study of Iron Age communities of the southern highveld – a vast stretch of grassland that extends across much of the South African provinces of the Transvaal and Orange Free State. Maggs first located stone ruins on aerial photographs and then classified them according to their architectural style, showing convincingly that artefacts other than ceramics could profitably be used in the study of the past (Maggs 1976a). In a second project, Revil Mason returned to his earlier interest in the Iron Age and began to look at the evidence from the Transvaal (Mason 1962). Mason also plotted settlements from aerial photographs, supporting this work with ground survey and excavation of selected sites (Mason 1968). Eventually, this interest led him back to the formative stages of Iron Age settlement south of the Limpopo, which he has continued to study at the important first-millennium site of Broederstroom in the Magalies Mountains close to Pretoria (Mason 1981). A third research initiative occurred in the eastern Transvaal, where Nikolaas van der Merwe began an intensive study of the Iron Age of the Phalaborwa District. This project illustrates the methodological diversity of the new research, for apart from studying the ceramics from his sites, Van der Merwe linked the archaeological evidence to ethnographic data and oral traditions (Van der Merwe and Scully 1971), and also began to examine the chemistry of the local iron-producing industry (Van der Merwe 1980a).

Accompanying this new interest in the African past was the important technical innovation of radiocarbon dating, which was to transform archaeology as a whole. Although radiocarbon dating became available in the 1950s, and was applied in 1953 to the site of Kalambo Falls in present-day Zambia, it was not until the following decade that the method was extensively used in southern Africa.

It is not surprising that with widening research efforts and new methods of dating, came new ways of interpreting the past, for although Summers and Robinson's culture model was a useful way of visualising prehistoric communities, it was not the only method available. Thus in 1974 an archaeologist from the University of Illinois in the United States, Tom Huffman, published a revision of earlier work by Robinson, and in so doing recast the form of the southern African Iron Age (Huffman 1974).

Excavation of an iron-smelting furnace in the eastern Transvaal. (Photograph by courtesy of Nick van der Merwe.)

A carbon-dioxide extraction line at the Archaeometry Laboratory, University of Cape Town. Isotopic analysis of samples is a part of radiocarbon dating as well as a method of establishing prehistoric diet. (Photograph by Mike Herbert.)

The impact of radiocarbon dating

The impact of radiocarbon dating is demonstrated quite clearly through the fortunes of the classificatory scheme for Iron Age pottery in the south-eastern coastal region of South Africa. In 1948, John Schofield had defined three groups of pottery for the Natal coast: NC1 which he saw as the oldest, NC2 which was an intermediary group, and NC3 which Schofield believed to be quite recent (Schofield 1948). But in 1973 Tim Maggs, taking advantage of the emerging radiocarbon chronology, argued that the sequence should be reversed, with NC3 as the oldest (Maggs 1973). A few years later new collections, with new radiocarbon dates in association, necessitated another change, for it now emerged that a sub-category of NC2 had the claim to the earliest date, followed by NC3 and lastly NC1 (Maggs 1980a). Thus Schofield's scheme was completely rearranged, not because he had been wrong in the basis of his categorisation, but because he did not have adequate means for placing his categories in the correct time sequence.

In order to appreciate the full implications of Huffman's contribution, it is again necessary to refer back to the formative years of archaeology, this time in the Americas. Childe's (1929) seminal work in the Danube valley had been matched by parallel developments in Mesoamerica and the American south-west, where archaeologists had also been compelled to find devices to interpret complex changes in pottery and other artefacts through both time and space. But unlike Summers's mentors in Europe, who had divided their pottery into sharply defined 'boxes', American archaeologists emphasised connections and continuities through time. Such interpretations could often be drawn as if they were trees, with lines of origin and subsequent divisions, or 'branches'. In emphasising connections rather than divisions, these 'traditions', as they were called, were subtly different from the 'cultures' of European archaeology (Binford and Sabloff 1982; Hall 1983).

These two ways of seeing the past had contrasting practical connotations. For in order to decide to which cultural 'box' a new collection of pottery belonged, the archaeologist would find a few typical examples, match these to specimens definitive of existing boxes, and then write out the appropriate label. In contrast, assigning a position in a tradition was a more exacting task, demanding the close examination of attributes such as decorative motifs and their positions on the artefact. Consequently, it is not surprising that Huffman was attracted to one of the more richly varied Iron Age pottery assemblages in seeking to rearrange the cultures of southern Africa into traditions.

Traditions and cultures: the Iron Age synthesis

The re-ordering of southern Africa's 'cultures' into 'traditions' marked almost fifty years of systematic Iron Age research. During this time, the chronology of the Iron Age had been completely transformed, for where earlier interpretations had the 'Bantu' moving southwards over the Limpopo River at much the same time that colonists from Europe arrived in the Cape, archaeological research demonstrated conclusively that Iron Age communities had been settled in southern Africa since at least A.D. 200. (For recent reviews of radiocarbon dates, see Maggs 1977; Hall and Vogel 1980; Parkington and Hall 1986.)

But although this outline has been boldly drawn, the finer details are still a blur. To the confusions in interpretation that have followed from the different implications of 'cultures' as against 'traditions', has been added the preliminary and parochial nature of many of the published results. In consequence, there is no one summary of the Iron Age on which archaeologists would agree.

One point that most writers have conceded, however, is that there are no antecedents in southern Africa for the shape and decoration of Early Iron Age ceramics. Consequently, origins have been sought to the north by tracing 'streams' of movement across the map of the continent. Although several different schemes have been put forward, a major debate has developed between David Phillipson (1977), who has argued for two distinct streams, and Tom Huffman (1979a, 1982), who sees three. Phillipson and Huffman's disagreement is an interesting example of different perspectives on the past. Most of Phillipson's archaeological experience has been in eastern and central Africa, and he gives considerable attention to the archaeology of Kenya and Zambia, and little to the Iron Age south of the Limpopo River. But Huffman has worked almost entirely in Zimbabwe and South Africa, and his account of the Iron Age in the south is particularly full. Consequently, Huffman's synthesis is the more useful here.

Huffman sees in his first stream a close connection between the pottery of eastern and southern Africa, including ceramics known as 'Urewe' and 'Nkope' from eastern and east-central Africa, and the 'Matola' (or 'Silverleaves') Tradition south of the Limpopo. The radiocarbon dates from sites in the eastern Transvaal, in southern Mozambique, and from the coast slightly to the north of Durban range between about A.D. 200 and A.D. 400.

The second stream is distinct from the first. It passes through Zimbabwe early in the first millennium A.D., represented by pottery known as 'Bambata', and then on across the Limpopo River and into the Transvaal lowlands, the Natal and Zululand river valleys and coastlands, and Transkei. Pottery from this large cluster of assemblages has been named the 'Lydenburg Tradition', after a site in the eastern Transvaal. The radiocarbon dates fall between about A.D. 400 and about A.D. 900. This second stream is seen as replacing the first stream and is the most widespread and long-lived form of the Early Iron Age south of the Limpopo.

Huffman's third stream comes into Zimbabwe to replace Bambata pottery. These new ceramics have been named the 'Gokomere Tradition', which likewise lasts through to the end of the first millennium, and is therefore contemporary with the Lydenburg Tradition, forming the Early Iron Age between the Limpopo and the Zambezi rivers.

Thomas Huffman's model for the origins of the Iron Age in southern Africa. An eastern stream (A), the Matola Tradition, first spread southwards along the coastlands of Mozambique and northern Natal. A second, western stream (B), the Lydenburg Tradition, moved through Zambia and Zimbabwe a few centuries later, overrunning the eastern stream along the south-east coastlands. Finally a western stream (C), the Gokomere Tradition, moved southwards into Zimbabwe, filling the space left by the southward-moving Lydenburg Tradition.

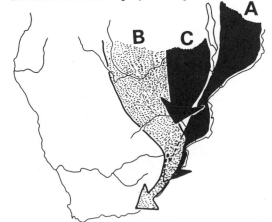

There have been equivalent disagreements concerning the transition from the Early Iron Age to the Late Iron Age. One view is that there was a complete break at the end of the first millennium, with new pottery again coming in from the north (Oliver and Fagan 1975; Phillipson 1977). Huffman (1978a, 1982) has argued against this interpretation, pointing out that the ceramic evidence suggests a far more complex situation. Instead of a simple movement from north to south, Huffman has argued that, because of a population build-up in the south-east, the successors to the Lydenburg Tradition moved back to the north, recolonising Zimbabwe and leaving pottery which Huffman has called the 'Kutama Tradition'. Huffman includes in Kutama a basket of ceramic cultures, including Leopard's Kopje, material from the Limpopo valley, Great Zimbabwe and Khami. He also argues that the people who made Kutama pottery spoke the Shona language, introducing it into modern-day Zimbabwe.

The Kutama Tradition has been matched to the south by the 'Moloko Tradition', which has been proposed by T. M. Evers (1981, 1983), although in this case an origin has not been identified. At the core of the Moloko Tradition are the different types of pottery associated with the numerous stone-built sites of the high grasslands of southern

A model for the origins of the Late Iron Age in southern Africa. It has been argued that people moved northwards from the south-east African coastlands about A.D. 900, speaking the Shona language and making pottery which has been named the Kutama Tradition. A few centuries later there was a second movement westwards of Sotho–Tswana speakers, taking Moloko pottery and stone-built settlement onto the southern highveld.

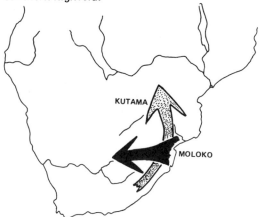

Africa. Just as the Kutama Tradition has been linked to Shona, so Evers has suggested that the Moloko Tradition represents the origin and dispersal of the Sotho–Tswana group of languages.

As yet unexplained by recent syntheses are the second-millennium ceramic traditions of the south-east: the pottery of Zululand, Natal and Transkei, which is sharply distinct from the ceramics of the Early Iron Age and yet apparently unconnected with the Moloko or Kutama Traditions (Maggs 1980a).

Although the combination of the 'three-stream model', the Kutama Tradition, and the Moloko Tradition leads to a fairly coherent pattern, many other archaeologists would criticise this synthesis. Firstly, it has been pointed out that the pottery which defines two of Huffman's Early Iron Age streams – Matola and Lydenburg – is very similar, and that many of the motifs were used to decorate ceramics throughout the first millennium. Maggs (1984a) suggests continuity throughout this period, arguing that pottery from the site of Lydenburg itself attests to the gradual transition from Matola to Lydenburg-style ceramics.

Maggs's model avoids one of the weakest links in Huffman's synthesis: the interpretation of Bambata pottery as evidence for the migration of the makers of Lydenburg pottery through present-day Zimbabwe (Huffman 1982). Maggs has pointed out that, although the more than twenty Bambata sites that are known from south-western Zimbabwe have pottery of an Iron Age character, they are all rock shelters which have assemblages in other respects characteristic of the Stone Age (Maggs 1984a). The two collections from open sites that Huffman (quoted in Hall and Vogel 1980) believes to be evidence for Bambata farming villages could easily belong to the Gokomere Tradition (Walker 1983).

In 1980 N. J. Walker re-excavated part of Bambata Cave itself in an attempt to gain more evidence relevant to this problem. He has suggested that Bambata pottery was obtained by trade as early as 200 B.C. by gatherer-hunters from immigrant Iron Age pastoralists whose archaeology is as yet unknown, but who preceded the makers of Gokomere pottery (Walker 1983). The wider implications of Walker's proposition have yet to be followed up, but his suggestion serves to demonstrate that a conclusive synthesis of Iron Age ceramics in southern Africa remains an ambition rather than an achievement.

Equally controversial are the Moloko and Kutama Traditions, the link between the Early and

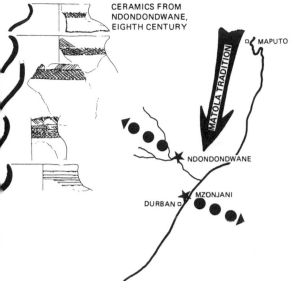

CERAMICS FROM
NDONDONDWANE,
EIGHTH CENTURY

MATOLA TRADITION

MAPUTO

NDONDONDWANE

DURBAN   MZONJANI

Most authors agree that the earliest phase of the Iron Age in southern Africa was the Matola Tradition, and that it spread southwards through the coastlands. But there is disagreement about subsequent events. Some writers have argued for local continuity, with Matola-style ceramics from sites such as Mzonjani developing into Lydenburg-style ceramics at sites such as Ndondondwane. Others have suggested that the Lydenburg Tradition originated in a later, separate migration down the south-east African coast.

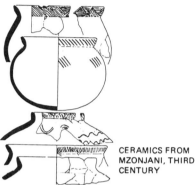

CERAMICS FROM
MZONJANI, THIRD
CENTURY

Late Iron Ages. Mason (1983), arguing against Evers's suggestion of a Moloko Tradition, has maintained that the ceramic evidence from the Transvaal indicates a continuity from the earliest settlement at Broederstroom through until colonial contact, and that Sotho–Tswana-speaking communities therefore have a direct ancestry within their present areas of distribution which can be traced back to the first Iron Age migration. Others have objected to the direct connection between the Lydenburg Tradition and the Late Iron Age, which is the key to Huffman's Kutama Tradition. The statistical basis of the connection, which rests on the characterisation of ceramics from poorly described assemblages, has been criticised (Hall 1983), while Maggs (1984a) has pointed out that there is evidence for continuity in ceramic style within the Limpopo River valley – an area where the Kutama model demands a complete break. Maggs has suggested a more complex interpretation, in which Late Iron Age ceramics developed from Early Iron Age traditions in some areas, while in others there was the complete break widely recognised by earlier archaeologists.

Finally, Phillipson (1985) has restated his earlier two-stream model, although in a different guise. He now suggests that the entire Early Iron Age of eastern and southern Africa should be renamed the 'Chifumbaze Complex', after a site in Mozambique from which characteristic first-millennium pottery was first excavated. Within the Chifumbaze Complex, Phillipson identifies a 'western facies' – which includes ceramic collections from western Zambia, Zaire and assemblages that Huffman and Maggs would place within

their Lydenburg Tradition – and an 'eastern facies' – subdivided into a coastal group which is synonymous with the Matola sites, and an inland group which appears to include Gokomere pottery. Phillipson makes no attempt to reconcile his interpretation with any of the debate that followed his earlier (1977) two-stream model.

Pots or people?

Thus, despite the amount of research that has been carried out in southern Africa since Gertrude Caton-Thompson's pioneering excavations at Great Zimbabwe and despite the general agreement on chronology that is now well supported by a framework of radiocarbon dates, there are almost as many interpretations of the ceramic sequence as there are archaeologists of the Iron Age. This rather surprising situation seems to demand explanation in terms of the general place of archaeology within southern Africa – the 'world view' that must invariably affect the attitude of archaeologists to their discipline.

The root of the problem in Iron Age studies seems to be an over-extended concern with classification. The history of archaeology in most parts of the world shows that the first tasks to be tackled are invariably those of ordering artefacts into typo-

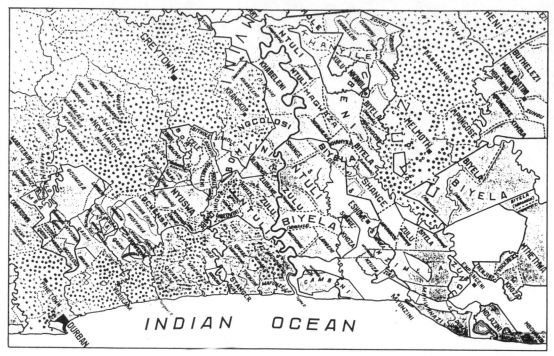

logical schemes and developing some system of dating the resultant categories (Clarke 1968; Daniel 1975; Willey and Sabloff 1980). But in most other regions, such 'typological phases' of research have long been accompanied, and sometimes almost completely superseded, by aims such as analysis of the interaction between human communities and their environments, the study of prehistoric economies, or investigation of the symbolic role of material culture. Although some archaeologists in southern Africa have now turned

to these problems, this re-orientation has only taken place comparatively recently.

The reason for this delayed response to international trends, and the consequent proliferation of competing classificatory schemes, may lie in the social and political environment in which most archaeologists of the southern African Iron Age have worked, and particularly in the ambiguity of their political and social position (Hall 1984b). On the one hand, rewriting the chronology of the Iron Age has been an inherently political action, for it has been to oppose the 'official' histories of colonial and post-colonial minority governments (Cornevin 1980; Frederikse 1982; Garlake 1973a). But on the other hand archaeologists, like others who live and work in southern Africa, have been continually assailed by the emphasis on tribal diversity, characterisation and classification that has become such an important part of political management by the minority governments of the subcontinent (Hall 1983, 1984a, 1984b). As a result, issues such as tribal and linguistic origins, 'ethnicity' and cultural classification may have been emphasised at the expense of broader questions about the nature of past human behaviour and the pre-colonial history of southern Africa. Simply stated, half a century of Iron Age research has produced a lot of information about pots, but relatively little about people. The chapters that follow are an attempt to correct this bias.

3

Origins: unwrapping the Iron Age package

The package

The concepts of ceramic culture and tradition, which have so dominated the study of the southern African Iron Age from Gertrude Caton-Thompson to Tom Huffman, have often carried with them a major assumption about the identity and behaviour of the people who made the pots. This is that the pottery, the sherds of which are found in such quantities on archaeological sites from the southern Transkei to the Zambezi valley, was made by people of the same human physical type and language, with the same metallurgy, agriculture and animal husbandry, who came into southern Africa early in the first millennium.

This proposal was eloquently argued by Huffman (1970) and has since been restated by a number of authors including Phillipson (1977, 1985) and Tim Maggs, who has written of the first farming communities in the subcontinent that 'the main archaeological markers of this are semi-permanent villages which produced ceramics, metals, crops and domestic animals. This cultural and economic package was certainly complete by A.D. 500 . . . .' (Maggs 1984a: 331) But Maggs goes on to point out that some components of this 'package' may have arrived before others and that, indeed, this whole diffusion model must be regarded as controversial (Maggs 1984a). In this chapter, the Iron Age package is unwrapped and reassessed – a review that will necessitate drawing together evidence from many different parts of Africa.

Race against time

Fundamental to the idea of an Iron Age package is the notion of the immigration into southern Africa of a new race, which replaced or absorbed earlier races. But developments in the theory and methodology of physical anthropology in recent years suggest that there is little to support this concept. The idea of race has become a victim of time.

The description of human races goes back at least to Linnaeus who, in 1735, made a distinction between *Homo europaeus*, *Homo asiaticus*, and *Homo africanus*, the last being the black-skinned people of Africa. Linnaeus's purpose was to classify humankind, and his scheme was geographic, as the

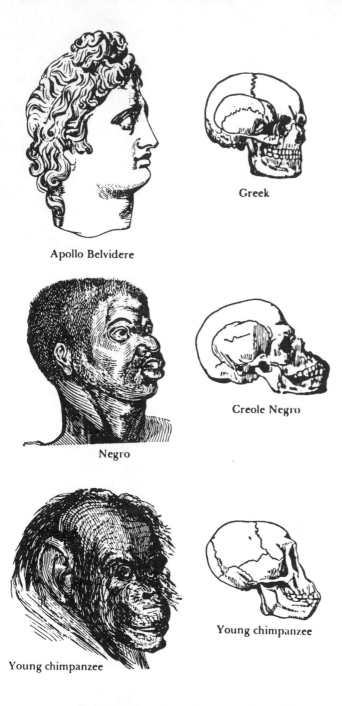

Apollo Belvidere

Greek

Negro

Creole Negro

Young chimpanzee

Young chimpanzee

A nineteenth-century interpretation of the evolution of human races. The illustrator has falsely inflated the chimpanzee skull, and extended the 'Negro' jaw, to imply that the 'Negro race' might in fact rank lower than the apes. These views are discussed further by Gould (1981). (Illustration from Nott and Gliddon 1868.)

specific names that he suggested indicate. But later writers became more interested in assessing the relative superiority of the different classes, and by the late nineteenth century Darwinian evolution had provided the spur for anthropological disciplines such as craniology and eugenics – the physical counterpart of the classificatory ethnography described in the last chapter (Hall and Morris 1983; Gould 1981). In keeping with the world view of the ethnohistorians of the time, it was assumed that race and culture were mutually dependent; thus language and customs might be inferred from the classification of a skull.

But in the years since the Second World War, when the Nazi enthusiasm for the idea of race put eugenics and related disciplines into disrepute (Gould 1981), physical anthropological studies have developed in a different direction. It has been widely realised that the idea of type, which allowed Dart and others to define southern African races from a single specimen, subjects the full complexity of human physical variation to the emphasis of a few 'obvious' characters such as skin colour, hair form and the various cranial indices that have been devised. Instead of searching for elusive conformity, physical anthropologists now generally prefer to study the geographical distributions of individual traits, and search for their genetic causes (Baker 1967; Jones 1981; King 1981; Weiss and Maruyama 1976). In a particularly instructive study, Latter (1980) found that only about 10 per cent of humankind's genetic variability lies behind the 'racial' characters upon which earlier classifiers had completely depended.

This new direction of research has been followed by many physical anthropologists working in southern Africa. The emphasis has been on 'breeding populations' rather than races; groups within which marriages frequently take place and which consequently share a common 'pool' of genes (De Villiers 1968; Tobias 1966; Nurse 1983). As a result, the term 'South African Negro' has become a loosely defined convenience rather than a racial epithet – a broad set of gene pools, from the same part of the world, which have a certain number of elements in common as a result of intermittent flow between them (Hall and Morris 1983).

The realisation of the complexity of human genetic structure and inheritance leaves the question of physical origins open, and there is now little basis for asserting that a 'Stone Age' race, found once over much of Africa and still represented today in the Kalahari and other remote areas, was replaced by a 'Negro' invasion from the north.

An example: the 'Boskop race'

The earlier approach to the concept of race is well illustrated by the concept of a 'Boskop race' which, it was proposed, was 'once widely distributed in South Africa from the Transvaal to the remotest south-eastern corner of the subcontinent' (Dart 1923: 625). Cranial fragments from a small number of archaeological sites were used to reconstruct a 'typical' skull and identify a set of 'Boskopoid features'. This race was believed to be the maker of the Middle Stone Age tools which had been found at many localities in southern Africa. In time it was replaced by the immigration of a new race responsible for the Late Stone Age (Dart 1923; Galloway 1937; Hall and Morris 1983). By the middle years of the present century more than seven races had been identified as ancestral populations of southern Africa (Tobias 1955), each believed to have a distinctive set of traits, and a specific culture associated with it. One of these was the 'Negro' race which was assumed to be inexorably linked to the Iron Age. Such an approach to the study of human physical variability is now completely outdated.

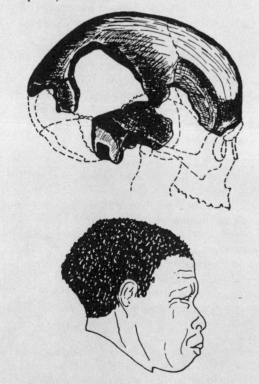

Fragments of the Boskop skull and an attempt to reconstruct a racial type (from Hitzeroth 1972).

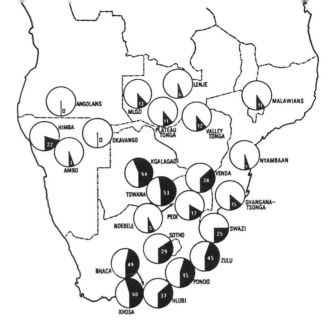

Today, physical anthropologists identify breeding populations by tracing genetic markers, and acknowledge that the distributions of such populations are often determined by social factors. This example shows variation in the frequency of the serum protein allele Gm 1,13 (from Tobias 1974).

Although the San populations of Namibia and the Kalahari (once refered to by the derogatory term 'Bushman') have been more genetically isolated than other groups for a long time, they still share many characteristics with other breeding populations. In addition, it has been suggested that some of the genetic markers that are characteristic of southern African gene pools are evident in skeletal material from archaeological sites in the subcontinent far earlier than they are to the north, thus turning the old migration account of physical origins on its head (De Villiers and Fatti 1982).

Given the present state of knowledge, it can reasonably be concluded that human origins are complex and that there is no definite evidence one way or the other for the migration of a 'Negro' race through Africa, coinciding with the spread of new languages, economies and technologies. Although physical anthropology can provide very valuable information about the past, this must come from the reconstruction of the distribution and dating of gene pools, which in turn demands the careful statistical examination of large collections of human skeletal remains – material which, with only a few exceptions, has yet to be excavated from southern African sites (Hall and Morris 1983).

If only pots could speak

The study of the languages of Africa, like the study of human physical variability in the continent, started in the last century and, in now-familiar fashion, incorporated many of the assumptions of the late Victorian world view. Indeed, as Jan Vansina has argued, interests in language and race were closely connected, for 'the late nineteenth century was . . . obsessed with origins. The similarities among languages [it was argued] stemmed from their differential growth from a common ancestral language . . . . But a common ancestral language meant a common ancestral community of speakers, a "people" – and for nineteenth-century minds this evoked the notion of "race".' As a result 'Bantu soon became a pseudo-ethnic term applied indiscriminately to race, culture and language' (Vansina 1979: 295). This concept persisted well into the present century and, as Vansina has pointed out, was restated by Seligman (1930) in his overview of the 'races' of Africa. Seligman's concepts of ethnicity strongly affected De Villiers's approach to physical anthropology (De Villiers 1968; Hall and Morris 1983). Furthermore, Seligman's notion of a Bantu 'mode of thought' (Vansina 1979) finds an echo in Huffman's use of the idea of 'cognitive system' and his statement that 'within central and southern Africa, Iron Age archaeology is Bantu archaeology' (Huffman 1982: 148).

The general distribution of the Niger–Congo language family, as classified by Joseph Greenberg (1963).

A model for 'Bantu expansion', based on Malcolm Guthrie's linguistic research. From a nucleus in the Katanga woodlands, it was suggested that Bantu-speakers expanded steadily through the southern woodland belt from coast to coast (1). Following the introduction of Asiatic crop plants, populations expanded into areas of higher rainfall (2), later to settle the remaining areas of the subcontinent which are today occupied by speakers of Bantu languages (3). This early attempt to synthesise archaeological and linguistic evidence is now seen as speculative and an over-simplification (see Oliver 1966).

But, as with physical anthropology, there have been methodological changes in linguistic studies, involving the discard of most of the extraneous baggage of ethnic and cultural assumptions, and a concentration on the problems of classification and connection. A watershed was Greenberg's (1963) general survey, which placed the Bantu languages in the larger Niger–Congo family, with an area of origin in the far north-western part of their area of distribution, probably within present-day Cameroon. Greenberg's scheme was followed a few years later by a competing classification and the counter-argument that the Bantu languages were derived from a nucleus in the central savanna belt that lies to the south of the equatorial forest (Guthrie 1962). Since the early 1960s there has been debate as to which of these two proposals best serves the synthesis of early African history.

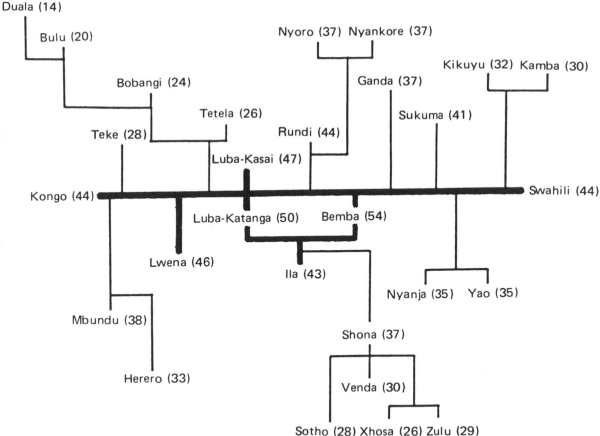

Duala (14)
Bulu (20)
Bobangi (24)
Nyoro (37) Nyankore (37)
Kikuyu (32) Kamba (30)
Tetela (26)
Ganda (37)
Teke (28)
Rundi (44)
Sukuma (41)
Luba-Kasai (47)
Kongo (44)   Swahili (44)
Luba-Katanga (50)   Bemba (54)
Lwena (46)
Ila (43)
Nyanja (35)   Yao (35)
Mbundu (38)
Shona (37)
Herero (33)
Venda (30)
Sotho (28) Xhosa (26) Zulu (29)

A simplified version of Malcolm Guthrie's Bantu language classification. Guthrie drew up a list of more than 500 general Bantu 'roots' – word components which have a widely shared meaning and therefore may be residues of the original ancestor language. Languages with a high proportion of roots (shown in the figure as percentages of the total set of general roots found in each particular language) were taken as members of the original Bantu language nucleus, argued to have spread through the southern savannas from west to east coast. To the north and south, the proportion of general roots in each language lessens (after Guthrie 1962).

At first it appeared that Greenberg's and Guthrie's proposals complemented one another and agreed with other evidence. It was suggested that there was an initial expansion from Greenberg's West African area of origin as a result of population expansion induced by early cultivation of root crops. These first Bantu- speakers moved through the equatorial forests by river to eastern Zaire – the nucleus suggested by Guthrie. This savanna zone was seen now as a secondary area of expansion, across which Bantu- speakers expanded, adopting domestic cereal crops from Cushitic-speaking communities in eastern Africa, as well as Malaysian crops at the coast, allowing a further expansion into south-eastern Africa (Oliver 1966; Vansina 1980). The apparent concord between the different sources of evidence strongly supported the idea of an Iron Age 'package'.

But other linguists argued that Guthrie's classifications, and the inferences of genetic connections between languages, were not necessarily valid. Henrici used Guthrie's data to devise a different classification, and Heine argued that intense borrowing between languages had led to strong convergence and the loss of characteristic features other than vocabulary, giving false impressions of relationships (Heine 1973 and Henrici 1973, cited by Vansina 1980). Although the cradle of the Bantu languages was still seen as Cameroon, as Greenberg had originally suggested, these later interpretations of spread did not agree with the ceramic evidence.

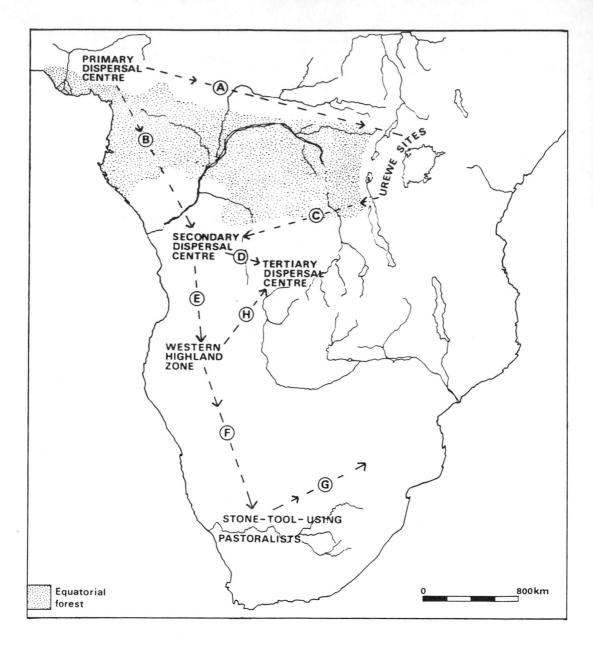

PRIMARY DISPERSAL CENTRE

(A)

(B)

UREWE SITES

(C)

SECONDARY DISPERSAL CENTRE (D)

TERTIARY DISPERSAL CENTRE

(E)

(H)

WESTERN HIGHLAND ZONE

(F)

(G)

STONE-TOOL-USING PASTORALISTS

Equatorial forest

0   800km

David Phillipson's interpretation of the spread of the Bantu languages through Africa. This model compromises between conflicting explanations by postulating two movements outwards from Greenberg's primary dispersal centre: the one (A) eastwards to the area where the early, Urewe Tradition ceramics are found, and the other (B) southwards through the equatorial forest to Guthrie's secondary dispersal centre in north-western Angola. Phillipson suggests that these two streams were re-united as Iron Age farmers moved south-westwards (C) through the savanna lands. He argues further division occurred from this secondary dispersal centre. One group moved southwards again (E), forming the Western Highland group of Bantu languages, and providing the domestic stock and ceramic technology used by Khoisan-speaking pastoralists who moved southwards (F) before introducing cattle to the Transvaal Iron Age in about the fifth century A.D. (G). Elements from the secondary dispersal centre (D) and the Western Highland zone also recombined in a tertiary dispersal centre, bringing the Iron Age to Zambia.

The new analyses of the linguistic evidence have led David Phillipson (1977) to put forward a new synthesis – a rescue attempt for the notion of an Iron Age package of traits of which his 'two-stream' model for Iron Age ceramics, described in Chapter 2, forms a part. Phillipson argued that the archaeologists and historians who earlier had tried to accommodate Greenberg's and Guthrie's competing theories made a simplistic correlation between pottery cultures and language spread, and that a successful model must take into account the full complexity of both sources of evidence.

Phillipson suggested that Bantu-speakers moved out of Greenberg's area of origin in two directions. The first group moved along the northern and then eastern edges of the equatorial forests, obtaining cattle and cereal crops from speakers of Central Sudanic languages, and entering the interlacustrine region where they made the Urewe pottery ancestral to Early Iron Age ceramic traditions. Phillipson suggests that the Bantu languages spoken by these (and indeed all the makers of Early Iron Age ceramic traditions in eastern and southern Africa) have now been lost but that their early Sudanic contacts are preserved in relic loanwords.

The second ancestral Bantu-speaking population travelled from Cameroon through the equatorial forest to Angola and northern Namibia, where they established a 'western highland' group of languages. Towards the end of the first millennium these communities began to expand eastwards, bringing with them Late Iron Age pottery and the 'eastern highlands' languages, which include Shona, Sotho–Tswana and the Nguni languages spoken today.

Support for Greenberg's original model, although with a different set of archaeological implications, has come from Christopher Ehret's (1973) study of the distribution, and phonological and morphological characteristics, of loanword sets in the Bantu languages. Ehret's proposition is simple: contact between communities speaking different languages leads to the adoption of sets of words, and, consequently, sets of 'loanwords' held in common by now-separated languages indicate earlier contact. Ehret (1982a) rejects Phillipson's suggested routes around the forest and restates Greenberg's earlier proposition that the Bantu languages spread through the tropical zone, with a sustained period of local differentiation in the woodland savanna regions before the final expansion to the east and south-east.

But Ehret has also added a more radical suggestion to Greenberg's model, proposing that parts of central and southern Africa were populated by pastoralists speaking Central Sudanic languages at least several centuries *before* the arrival of Bantu-speaking communities. By establishing sets of loanwords and tracing their distributions Ehret (1973) has reconstructed three such groups, which he has called the Interlake people (living around the southern end of Lake Tanganyika), the Batoka group (in southern Zambia) and a Zimbabwean population which was also implicated in the origin of the Khoikhoi languages (to be discussed in Chapter 4).

Ehret believes that Bantu-speakers, arriving in the central African savanna lands after the Sudanic-speaking pastoralists, saw their languages differentiate into three branches while at the same time adopting common sets of Sudanic loanwords. One of these branches, which Ehret names Tuli, split further into two subgroups, which then adopted additional loanwords from different Central Sudanic-speaking communities. Spreading still further south, one of these subgroups was ancestral to the present-day Bantu languages of Malawi, Mozambique, eastern Zambia and south- eastern Africa.

The scenario outlined by Ehret is a complex kaleidoscope of differentiation, borrowing and parallel loans between daughter languages of now-lost ancestral forms. The model does, however, have several weaknesses. Although the distribution of loanwords in languages must contain a considerable amount of information about the histories of past communities, there can be methodological problems in identifying phonologically comparable vocabularies and in accounting for the various forms of 'interference' that may have obscured the historical relationship (Borland 1982, 1986). In addition, Ehret relies heavily on glottochronology – the dating of language change – asserting, for instance, that 'the lexical variance between the most distantly related Bantu languages, with cognation in basic vocabulary dropping into the low 20 per cents and occasionally even lower, cannot be accounted for by any shorter period unless one supposes Bantu Africans to be somehow different in their linguistic behaviour from other human beings' (Ehret 1982a: 58). But glottochronology has long been viewed with distrust, particularly when, as in Africa, there are rarely texts which can be dated to provide fixed markers for language change (Hymes 1960).

Thus the concordance between archaeological and linguistic data that seemed evident in the 1960s has proved a chimera. There is consensus that the Bantu languages originated in Greenberg's nuclear zone and spread southwards, that many of the languages in eastern and southern Africa are closely related, and that their comparative lack of differentiation indicates that they spread rapidly. But there is no longer any unequivocal case for associating this spread with a particular 'people' (in either the racial or cultural sense) or, indeed, with a specific economy. Detailed studies of restricted areas have tended to show a lack of fit between ceramic and linguistic data (see for example Nurse 1982 and Soper 1982), while even David Phillipson, who so confidently argued for a linguistic distinction between the Early and Late Iron Ages in 1977, has more recently retracted his proposition and suggested instead that the ceramic change be attributed to women taking over the craft of pottery manufacture (Phillipson 1985).

This lack of fit between the different sources of evidence also has implications for the explanation of the spread of the Bantu languages. Earlier writers almost unanimously agreed that the new languages were carried southwards by migrating populations, and, indeed, as long as the ceramic evidence buttressed the linguistic evidence this was a reasonable suggestion. But the more recent linguistic models allow for the possibility of other mechanisms of spread, such as drift, the development of *linguae francae* used by traders, the emergence of new languages accepted over an area as 'standard intercommunity speech' and reflecting the preferences of elites, and the occurrence of language shifts as earlier communities abandoned their speech in favour of a Bantu language. As Vansina has argued, 'any and all of the forces sociolinguists have discovered may have operated at different times in different places and with different intensities. It is not certain at all that any population explosion was ever needed to account for this spread, nor is the contrary – the extinction of aboriginal populations – a necessary implication of the Bantu language spread. Moreover, language did not necessarily spread with any of the more "advanced" arts such as agriculture and metallurgy, let alone with new pottery styles. . . .' (Vansina 1980: 312–13)

Domesticating crops and animals

Just as more recent work in African language studies has revealed a complexity that demands models of explanation more sophisticated than the old 'Iron Age package', so the archaeology of metal-working and plant and animal husbandry is more complex now than when writers such as Roland Oliver (1966) presented simple models of population build-up and expansion. But unlike reconstructed proto-languages, which can only be dated by means of very tenuous assumptions about the rate and nature of language change (see Ehret 1984, for instance), early metallurgy and domestication of crops and animals have left more definite, and datable, evidence. Although this is not substantial, some patterns are clear.

It was long believed that both farming, and the skills of iron-working, were brought to Africa after their initial development in south-western Asia. In the case of agriculture this spread was seen most frequently as the result of diffusion – ideas and techniques from outside the continent that were applied with African crop plants (Stahl 1984). Domestic cattle and sheep, it was believed, were more direct introductions from the Mediterranean basin, while, many centuries later, iron-working was introduced along the Nile valley to Meroe – from the seventh century B.C. the capital of an extensive Sudanic kingdom. Here, large mounds of iron slag have led to the description of the city as the 'Birmingham of Africa' (Shinnie 1967; Trigger 1969).

But although it is clear that there were early connections between Africa and the Mediterranean (it is improbable, for instance, that sheep were domesticated independently in Africa), it is also apparent that economic and technological changes were related to African circumstances and involved many adaptations that were unique to the continent. Rather than trying to trace lines of connection across the maps of Europe, Asia and Africa, it is more useful to ask *why* new economies and technologies were adopted, and what were the circumstances of human communities before they adopted the new ways of living.

In 6000 B.C. the Sahara was not the desert of today, but was rather a semi-arid land with lakes and rivers containing fish, crocodile and hippopotamus, and surrounded by grasslands that were adequate for the sustenance of grazing animals (Williams 1984). Human communities made full use of these resources, hunting game, grinding wild grasses, and manufacturing a range of elaborately designed harpoons for fishing. In comparison to modern gatherer-hunters of southern Africa, the Saharan communities may have moved over restricted ranges, spending sustained periods in river and lakeside camps where they stored food in underground pits and manufactured pottery, dec-

The concept of domestication

For many years there has been considerable debate about what constitutes plant and animal domestication, and how this process began and took place. Domestic species are distinguished from their wild relatives and progenitors by a number of attributes, including higher productivity and greater tractability. Generally, domestication seems to have taken place through a process of selection: individuals with favourable genetic mutations such as larger grain size or improved milk yield were propagated by incipient farmers, thereby increasing the frequency of the mutation in the plant or animal population as a whole and in this way changing the morphology of the species. Thus domestication can be seen as active human intervention in natural selection. Although the range of major plant and animal domesticates is today quite narrow, there are many minor domesticates and evidence for considerable experimentation in the past with different species.

People have experimented with many different species as possible domesticates. These early Egyptian paintings show wild cattle and oryx being hunted by lasso, and gazelle, oryx and possibly Barbary sheep being led back from the hunt. (See Clark 1971.)

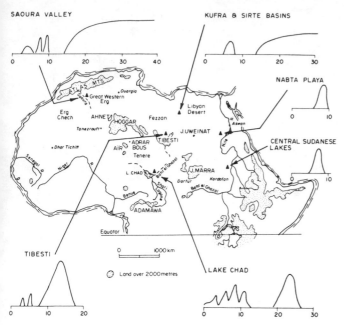

SAOURA VALLEY

KUFRA & SIRTE BASINS

NABTA PLAYA

CENTRAL SUDANESE
LAKES

TIBESTI

LAKE CHAD

The changing environment of the Sahara has been traced by studying changes in river and lake levels. In the figure (from Williams 1984), the peaks represent wet phases, dated in thousands of years before the present time.

orated with designs from woven fish baskets and perhaps used for boiling and extracting fish oil (Clark 1980, 1984; Smith 1980a).

Shortly after 6000 B.C. a series of climatic fluctuations began that must have made life far more difficult for these early Saharan communities. Although different areas of the Sahara were affected in different ways (Williams 1984), and there is still debate about the precise chronology of these environmental patterns (for example, see Close 1984), it seems that the adoption of a pastoral way of life was closely connected with these changes. The bones of short-horned, domesticated cattle have been excavated and dated, showing that by 3000 B.C. herding was widely practised from the Upper Nile valley in the east to modern-day Niger and Mali in the west (Smith 1980b, 1984a). It has been suggested that keeping livestock was a way of coping with the deteriorating environment of the Sahara, for 'the acquisition of stock would . . . have made it possible to maintain and even to increase population densities by providing a "stored" source of animal protein that would have significantly reduced the problem of the famine season, not only through the regular supply of meat it made available but, also, through the use of milk and blood' (Clark 1980: 567).

Most archaeologists now agree that cattle were domesticated independently in the arid regions of Africa, although there is still discussion about exactly how this took place. Andrew Smith has suggested that the area of origin was on the northern fringes of the desert, where sheep were first brought from the Near East after 6500 B.C. and used as a 'model' for domesticating cattle. This pattern seems to be reflected in the successive levels of Capeletti Cave, where, from 4500 B.C. onwards, cattle steadily become a more important part of the pastoral economy (Smith 1980b). Fred Wendorf and Romuald Schild, on the other hand, have argued that cattle domestication in the eastern Sahara began in the centuries after 8000 B.C., well before knowledge of herding could have spread from the Near East or before the general desiccation of the Sahara could have led to the wider spread of pastoralism (Wendorf and Schild 1984). The test of these, and other, hypotheses must be the statistical analysis of larger samples of animal bones, which will show more precisely when and where animal domestication took place. Such samples have yet to be excavated.

Although the origins of African animal domestication may still not be clear, the widespread impact of the pastoralist way of life is very evident, for herding soon spread from the Sahara to the savanna lands of both West and East Africa. By about 2500 B.C. the increasing desiccation of the southern Sahara, which had first led communities living by hunting, gathering and fishing to adopt domestic stock, now began to force people to look beyond the desert for new areas of settlement. At the same time, the reduced rainfall in the grasslands around the desert may have caused a southerly movement of the tsetse belt – the area infested with trypanosomiasis, usually fatal for livestock.

Excavation of the skeleton of an early domestic cow from the Saharan site of Adrar Bous. (Drawing by Tina Coombes.)

26

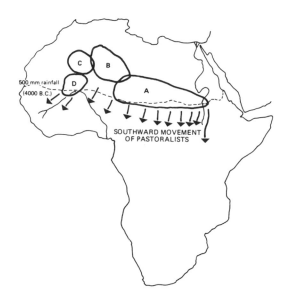

Prehistoric pastoralists and their movement out of the central Saharan region, 4500–1300 B.C. Stylistic variations in stone tools suggest that four groups of pastoralists occupied the Sahara between 4500 and 2000 B.C. (A–D). After the Sahara became more arid (about 4000 B.C.) pastoralist groups moved firstly into the southern Sahara, and then southwards again into the Sahel region (see Smith 1984b).

Taking advantage of this combination of circumstances, pastoralists moved southwards into areas such as Niger's Lower Tilemsi valley (Smith 1979) and south-eastwards into northern Kenya where livestock were herded from about 1300 B.C. (Ambrose 1984).

Ann Stemler has suggested that in this movement by pastoralist communities from desert to savanna lay the cause of the domestication of sorghum, a cereal that was to be central to the origins of farming in southern Africa. She has suggested that the desert nomads introduced herding to savanna gatherer-hunter communities, encouraging population growth and causing further pressure on resources: 'as population levels around the Sahara rose and wild plant food supplies decreased with desiccation, indigenous savanna hunter-gatherers began sowing and harvesting native wild grasses in their efforts to provide more food. In so doing, they began the process of cereal domestication.' (Stemler 1980: 523)

But domestication does not follow automatically from the intensive use of a narrow range of wild grasses. Indeed, it is evident that Saharan pastoralists, and before them the lakeside hunters and fishers, had been collecting wild cereals for several thousand years before herding spread to the savannas. The crucial link in the domestication process is the selection by the harvester of plants with characteristics favourable to human use, and the cultivation of such mutants with the result that distinct species emerge from the stock of the wild progenitor. Stemler has pointed out that as long as harvesters stripped the grain from tough-stemmed wild cereals such as sorghum, domestication could not take place, because the human plant-gatherers would merely be mimicking the natural seed dispersal of the wild grass. But once the tough stalk of the sorghum plant could be *cut*, harvesters would select those heads of grain that were most suited for preparation as food, in this way starting in motion the domestication of the wild species (Stemler 1980).

Thus in looking for the origins of mixed farming in sub-Saharan Africa – the combination of livestock husbandry with cereal cultivation – attention must be directed to the technological innovation that allowed the tough African grasses to be harvested and the soil turned for cultivation: metallurgy (Stemler 1984).

Metal-working

As with studies of plant and animal domestication in Africa, recent research has shown that, although the diffusion of techniques of metal-working from the Near East may well have had an important role, innovations and developments within the continent were probably more important.

Although small-scale iron-working was practised in the sixth century B.C., more recent work at the Sudanese city of Meroe has shown that the furnaces which produced such quantities of slag were used in the early centuries A.D. and were Roman in design. They were probably serving a Mediterranean rather than an African market (Shinnie 1971, Tylecote 1975).

A second possible route for the diffusion of metallurgy from the Mediterranean to Africa south of the Sahara was through the Phoenician trading stations and city-states that were built along the North African coast from about 800 B.C. The Phoenicians were not concerned with territorial settlement on any large scale, but rather used their sea power to maintain a monopoly over commodities from the west, which they then traded to the Mediterranean world. Gold was obtained from

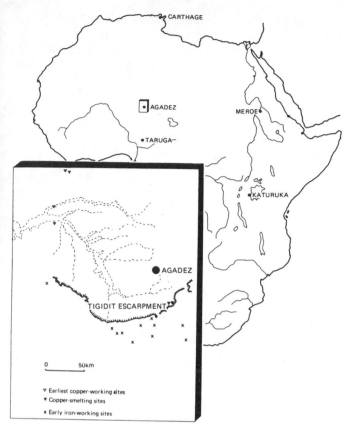

Early sites of copper- and iron-working in Africa.

West Africa across the Sahara, probably through the agency of Berber tribes such as the Garamantes. Knowledge of the techniques used in working iron could easily have travelled along these lines of commerce (Law 1978; Mauny 1971; Van der Merwe 1980a). There is as yet no definitive evidence for iron-working in sub-Saharan Africa earlier than the establishment of settlements such as Carthage, and all could therefore have originated in Phoenician innovation and expertise. But there are indications that future research could change this picture.

Firstly, several sets of radiocarbon dates from iron-smelting furnaces suggest that iron may have been produced across a wide swath of the savanna lands south of the Sahara at very much the same time that Phoenician traders were laying their first tentative claims to parts of the northern coastline. Such a chronology suggests an almost impossibly rapid rate of spread across thousands of kilometres. The most controversial of these dates comes from the smelting site of Katuruka, east of Lake Tanganyika, where a sustained iron-working

industry may have started as early as the sixth century B.C. (Schmidt 1978). All the early dates come from charcoal in one small part of the site, and may in fact indicate the age of the heartwood of a tree which had lain in the area for six or seven hundred years before being used for iron-smelting (Soper 1982). But Peter Schmidt has also pointed out that a study of fossilised pollen grains from nearby lake sediments shows a decrease in tree cover in about 500 B.C. – precisely the environmental impact that could be expected from extensive burning of the charcoal essential to the smelting process.

Taken alone, the Katuruka dates would not amount to sufficient basis for a revision of the metallurgical history of Africa. But they are matched by equally early sites in Niger, also far from the Phoenician settlements (Calvocoressi and David 1979). Furthermore at Taruga, in the high savanna of northern Nigeria, 13 furnaces have been dated back to the fifth century B.C. (Van der Merwe 1980a).

But techniques such as iron-working can spread rapidly, particularly if they satisfy urgent technological needs and when knowledge can be carried along trade-routes. One of the main reasons that persuaded earlier writers that diffusion of this nature may well have been the source of metallurgical skills in Africa was the apparent absence of earlier, experimental stages in metal production. If, it was reasoned, iron-working first occurred as a fully formed set of techniques, then it was improbable that it represented an indigenous innovation (Tylecote 1975).

The results of recent research in the remote Agadez region of Niger have shown that arguments such as these may no longer be valid, and that sub-Saharan Africa may well have been the scene of many centuries of experimentation in metal-working. In 1976 a team of French archaeologists found a number of copper-working furnaces near the source of the Azelik River deep in the Sahel. The earliest of these have now been firmly dated to between 1000 and 2000 B.C. (Grebenart 1983) and are evidence for the melting of 'native copper' – a phase of metallurgy which is known to precede copper-smelting in many parts of the world (Tylecote 1982). After 800 B.C., these Sahelian communities were able to smelt copper ore, using their furnaces up to five times a year to produce several kilograms of copper, which was then worked into weapons or ornaments. The rest of the material culture from these archaeological sites suggests that these copper

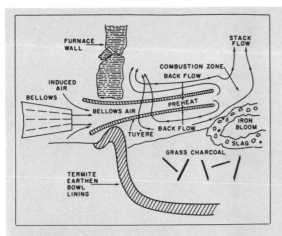

The iron bloomery process. Air is injected at high velocity into the tuyère. From the combustion zone, some of the blast goes up the stack of the furnace, but the rest flows back along the tuyère, heating its walls which in turn preheat subsequent injections of air from the bellows. This process achieves high temperatures for smelting the iron in the furnace. (Illustration from Avery and Schmidt 1979.)

An iron-smelting furnace in preparation for firing in Malawi. The technological process was re-created as part of an ethno-archaeological study. (Drawing by Tina Coombes from a slide provided by Nick van der Merwe.)

Techniques of working iron

The most common form of iron production in the pre-industrial world is known as the 'direct', or 'bloomery', process. A cake of iron particles and entrapped slag was produced in the furnace at a temperature of about 1200 degrees Celsius. By reheating this 'bloom' in a forge, and hammering it while still malleable, impurities were removed and iron implements with a relatively low carbon content produced. This method was common throughout the Medieval world until it was replaced in late-fourteenth-century Europe by the indirect process of steel production, which is the basis for modern commercial practice (Van der

Merwe 1980b).

But although the direct process was, and still is, widely used in Africa, at some time before the fourteenth century a highly innovative method of producing high-carbon steel was developed. In this new process fluid, iron-rich slag was produced at temperatures of up to 1500 degrees Celsius in tall furnaces which induced a natural draught, and the resulting bloom was subsequently decarburised by forging until it was sufficiently soft for the manufacture of implements. As Nikolaas van der Merwe has remarked, 'African metallurgists invented the only direct method for the production of steel known in metallurgical history' (Van der Merwe 1980b: 334). Thus iron-working in sub-Saharan Africa was not a simple primitive response to a superior innovation from the north, but was rather a technology with long-founded antecedents in the continent.

smiths were nomadic pastoralists, moving their settlements frequently with the shifting availability of grazing and other resources (Grebenart 1983).

Some time after 500 B.C. more permanent settlements were established to the south of the Tigidit escarpment. Villages were larger – up to a hectare in extent – and people now made harder and far more durable implements of iron. It has been suggested that, for some centuries, the nomadic copper smiths obtained iron implements

from the Tigidit villages by trade (Grebenart 1983).

These Agadezian archaeological sites indicate a long history of metallurgical experimentation within the Sahel – the sort of situation that could have led to the development of iron-working with little stimulus from beyond Africa. When the results of Grebenart's research are set alongside Stemler's botanical reasoning, the probable motivation for both early metallurgical experimentation and the rapid spread of iron-working through

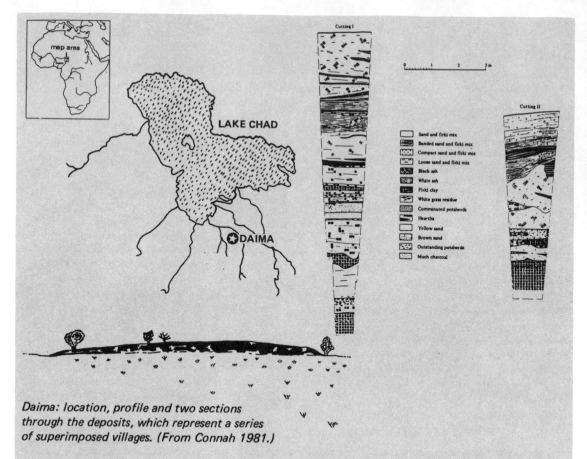

Daima: location, profile and two sections through the deposits, which represent a series of superimposed villages. (From Connah 1981.)

Legend:
- Sand and firki mix
- Banded sand and firki mix
- Compact sand and firki mix
- Loose sand and firki mix
- Black ash
- White ash
- Firki clay
- White grass residue
- Comminuted potsherds
- Hearths
- Yellow sand
- Brown sand
- Outstanding potsherds
- Much charcoal

Daima

The changing interaction of technology and economy is well illustrated by the remarkable site of Daima – a large mound some 45 kilometres from the present shoreline of Lake Chad – which was built up by successive human occupation from about 550 B.C. until A.D. 1150. For the first five hundred years of its history Daima was occupied by herdsmen who fished in the lake and collected cereals – a pattern of living that was probably typical of the Sahel at this time. But by about A.D. 50 the Daima villagers had learnt to make tools of iron, and as a result there occurred a series of connected changes in their style of living. Ground stone axes and bone harpoons were replaced by iron tools, which also allowed more effective digging in the heavy clay soils near which the village was sited. As a result, more substantial clay houses could be built and deep wells excavated, thus allowing the people of Daima to remain in their village throughout the year, rather than moving closer to surface water supplies during the dry season. It is also possible that the new tools permitted construction of the low dams used to retain water in the 'falling flood' technique of cultivation, perhaps making possible the start of the dry season cultivation that is practised in the area today (Connah 1981).

the Sahel are apparent. Thus instead of the Bantu-speakers equipped with iron tools who, it was suggested, 'burst through the forest barrier into the southern woodlands' (Oliver 1966: 367), it seems probable that nomadic pastoralists, faced with the steadily deteriorating environment of the Sahara and moving southwards into the Sahel, experimented for many centuries with the technological improvements necessary to increase their yields of plant foods. With iron came the opportunity of domestication, cultivation and the propagation of sorghum beyond the zone in which it occurred in the wild.

The origins of farming in southern Africa

Recent research in the fields of African languages, physical anthropology and archaeology has shown that explaining the origins of farming in southern Africa is a complex problem. What conclusions can be drawn from these conflicting interpretations?

Firstly, there seems to have been a *necessary* connection between agriculture and metallurgy. Although many farmers probably used implements made from wood and stone, iron tools allowed hard and heavy soils to be turned, fields to be tended, and crops to be harvested more efficiently. The new archaeological evidence from the Sahel suggests that the spread of iron-working and cereal cultivation was connected, and it is probable that, by the time the farming way of life came to be adopted further to the south, iron tools, crop plants and agricultural methods were part of a closely connected set of techniques.

But there is *no* necessary connection between farming technology and the other components of the old Iron Age package. For although the Bantu languages of Africa are closely related, and originated to the north of the Zambezi, there is no longer any consensus about routes of dispersal, methods of spread, or times when this took place. There is similar confusion about the physical appearance of the first farming communities, for although there must have been variation between the many different gene pools in sub-Saharan Africa, there has not been sufficient research with statistically acceptable samples of skeletal material to determine how much of this variation is inherited or where the lines of connection and movement were.

Similarly, there is no necessary connection between the spread of farming and styles of pottery manufacture and decoration. Farmers clearly made and used pots for a variety of tasks including storage, cooking and transportation, but then so did the gatherer-hunters and nomadic pastoralists of the Sahara several thousand years earlier (Smith 1980a, 1984a). The suggestion that pottery decoration can be equated with language (Huffman 1982) is an untried proposition which, even if true, would be unhelpful, as the chronology of language spread in southern Africa remains unestablished. It is more probable that pottery decoration was part of a complex code that meant different things in different circumstances (Hodder 1982; Hall 1985a) – a problem to be investigated in its own right.

If sense is to be made of the ceramic, linguistic and physical information, a fresh archaeological approach is required in which the datable evidence for agriculture, as well as assessments of what was possible and probable within the environmental constraints of Africa, is used to set up propositions about the origins of the farming way of life south of the Zambezi. Such propositions can then be tested against the linguistic and skeletal data, and abandoned and modified as necessary.

The most reasonable hypothesis is that farming spread steadily southwards from the Sahel. In the savanna and woodland environments of southern Africa the most effective form of agriculture is swidden cultivation (discussed in Chapter 4), and this can demand slow movement as old fields are abandoned and new plots cut. In addition, availability of crucial resources (such as iron ore or shellfish to supplement the diet) or the presence of barriers (such as woodlands infested with tsetse fly or environments beyond the range of conditions tolerated by domestic plants and animals) may have circumscribed the choices of new lands open to farmers and therefore have accelerated their dispersal. Adding complexity to this pattern would have been the interaction between those with the farming technology and those without: the gatherer-hunter communities who will sometimes have reacted with hostility to the incursion of farmers into their territories but in other cases will have adopted some or all of the new techniques for themselves.

The suitability of this incremental model for farming origins south of the Zambezi is further explored in the next chapter, but the wider task of setting this, or other hypotheses, against the linguistic and skeletal data remains. Indeed, as Jan Vansina (1980) has argued, it is probably better that archaeologists, linguists and physical anthropologists concentrate on the problems and possibilities of their own sources of information for the time being and set the task of grand synthesis on one side.

4

Pioneers

Frontiers

The reassessment of the evidence for the Iron Age 'package' (Chapter 3) shows that contrary to the belief of many earlier historians of southern Africa there is little evidence to support the idea of a rapid invasion of the subcontinent by farmers. Instead, the pattern is more likely to have been a combination of local movements by farmers seeking new fields and pasture, and the adoption of new techniques of making a living by indigenous gatherer-hunters – the sort of 'incremental' pattern of spread suggested in the last chapter.

Such 'frontiers' between economic systems are by no means unique to southern Africa (Alexander 1977). A good comparison is with the dispersal of wheat and barley cultivation across Europe from the Near East, where they were first domesticated. It has been concluded that these crops were dispersed by a combination of local population movement and wider diffusion of the techniques and technology of agriculture, resulting in a steady 'wave front' of advance (Ammerman and Cavalli-Sforza 1973).

Although at least one archaeologist has tried to use similar techniques to model the dispersal of agriculture through Africa (see Collett 1982), there are at present too many areas with inadequate evidence to make the exercise feasible, and it is still necessary to rely on more hypothetical reasoning. In this respect, John Alexander (1984) has drawn a useful distinction between 'moving frontiers', where farming societies or their technologies are still spreading into new areas, and 'static frontiers', where the process of advance has ceased, and long-term relationships are developing between farmers and gatherer- hunter communities. Alexander further distinguishes two phases of the moving frontier. In the first of these, small groups settle in new areas and have a wide influence over indigenous gatherer-hunters. Later, denser farming occupation follows, usually with the development of long-term relationships with gatherer-hunters.

A crucial variable that serves to define the character of different frontiers in Alexander's model is the degree of population movement. For early wheat and barley farmers in Europe this must have been quite small, probably because rich soils and temperate climates provided many potential fields, which could be cultivated for a comparatively long time before being left to lie fallow. As a result the 'wave of advance' of agriculture spread through Europe at about one kilometre every year (Ammerman and Cavalli-Sforza 1973). But in Africa soils are generally poorer and climates less equitable, and the wave of advance must therefore have been more in the order of five kilometres a year, given the distance between the areas where food production began in the Sahel and southern Africa.

But, despite the tendency of archaeologists and historians to draw bold lines and arrows across the map of Africa, farming did not spread in a uniform, featureless environment of equal opportunity. For while some areas were suitable for cultivation and stock-keeping, others either lacked crucial resources such as adequate soil nutrients or water supplies, or else harboured species inimical to farming, such as the tsetse fly. This – the ecological context of early farming – served to channel, accelerate or decelerate the different phases of the moving frontier. Thus before considering the archaeological evidence for the first farmers and herders south of the Zambezi River, it is important to identify the most important features of the environment that they found before them.

The southern African environment

A basis for reconstructing the environments of southern Africa before the advent of food production is provided by geological and geomorphological structure. This has been much the same throughout the last ten thousand years, for the processes that form mountain chains, plateaus and coastlands are extremely slow and the changes over two millennia have been fractional. Thus we can surmise that southern Africa once consisted of a vast interior basin of low relief, peripheral mountain chains, and continental margins falling away sharply to the coasts. This configuration can best be simplified as a shield, the interior in contrast with the perimeter (Wellington 1955).

Climate, on the other hand, is more variable, and recent work has shown that significant short-term changes are taking place all the time. The climates of the recent past in southern Africa are still poorly understood, although studies of rainfall records (Tyson, Dyer and Mametse 1975) and, in a very preliminary fashion, of variations in tree-ring widths (Hall 1976) do suggest regular oscillations. But in more general terms, there is still every reason to assume that southern Africa two thousand years ago would, as today, have had dry, cool winter months and hot, wet summers in the central and eastern areas, and a Mediterranean climate of winter rainfall and dry summers in the south-western region.

In contrast, the vegetation two thousand years ago was in some areas very different. More than eighteen centuries of farming have transformed the living environment, and present patterns of vegetation cannot be taken as representative of the past. Again, there has been little research on past floras and faunas, but it seems likely that the lower-lying, subtropical areas to the east and

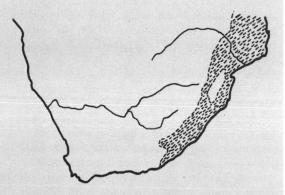

Areas in southern Africa with climate suitable for the existence of forest. (After Granger 1984.)

south-east of the peripheral mountains would have been mantled by woodlands and forests (Granger 1984; Hall 1984c), while the higher watersheds and interior of the 'shield' would have been grassland plains (Tainton and Mentis 1984). The more arid western areas were probably as they are now, and the unique heathland vegetation of the south-western extremity of the continent was already established, although there may have been more trees in some areas (Huntley 1984; Kruger and Bigalke 1984).

Thus the hills and valleys of southern Africa two thousand years ago, as well as the general course of the seasons, were probably much the same as they are at present. But although the broad sweep of the highveld grasslands, the arid lands to the west, and the Mediterranean flora and fauna of the south-western Cape have also seen little basic change through the centuries, the lower lands between mountains and ocean in the south-east were mantled by a woodland canopy, beneath which woodland-adapted animals would have lived.

The moving frontier: the spread of pastoralism in southern Africa

Techniques of early food production in southern Africa fall into two divisions, which coincide with the possibilities and restrictions of the environment. In the western and south-western regions livestock herding, supplemented by gathering and hunting, was established about two thousand years ago and continued until Dutch settlement in the mid-seventeenth century (Deacon *et al.* 1978). Such economies were well suited to the arid regions where crop plants would not grow, and to the south-western Cape where the dry summer months are unsuited to the cultivation of the African cereal plants. In the central, eastern and southeastern areas summer rainfall allowed crop cultivation and mixed farming economies (Maggs 1980a).

But there is still some doubt whether these broad geographical divisions have always applied to food-producing societies in southern Africa, or whether mixed farming in the central and eastern regions was preceded by a herding phase. Earlier interpreters saw a straightforward migration of pastoralists from eastern Africa into the southwestern part of the continent, where they remained independent of contact with farming communities to their east (Stow 1905). This view was elaborated by Cooke (1965), who envisaged a movement from the north-east across Zimbabwe and Botswana and into northern Namibia, and then southwards along the west coast and finally eastwards from the Cape. But this relatively simple

Map of rainfall distribution in southern Africa. (Map drawn by Daniel Maggs.)

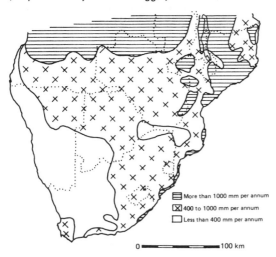

More than 1000 mm per annum
400 to 1000 mm per annum
Less than 400 mm per annum

0 ▬▬▬▬ 100 km

model was complicated by Westphal's (1963) re-classification of the languages spoken by pastoralists and gatherer-hunters in southern Africa, which he called the Tshu-khwe group and traced to an area of origin in northern Botswana. Since the publication of Westphal's conclusions, debate has centred on two issues: firstly, the source of the domestic livestock obtained by speakers of the Tshu-khwe languages, and secondly, the areas within southern Africa over which early pastoralists dispersed.

Some writers, and in particular Phillipson (1977, 1985), have maintained that the western pastoralists obtained their livestock from the first immigrant farming groups of the Iron Age. But the chronological evidence tends to militate against this interpretation, for bones of domestic sheep have been dated to the first few centuries A.D. at a number of sites in the southern and south-western Cape (Deacon *et al.* 1978), some two thousand kilometres south of the probable area of Tshu-khwe language origin. Even with an improbably rapid rate of migration, these dates would demand the exchange of livestock from farmers to putative herders a half millennium or so *before* the earliest date yet known for an Iron Age farming settlement in the eastern Botswana–western Zimbabwe area.

A further difficulty with a simple contact-and-exchange model lies in the distinctive Bambata pottery which has been found in 26 rock shelter sites in south-western Zimbabwe, and which has already been discussed in Chapter 2. Although Huffman (1978a) has claimed that Bambata pottery formed a part of the second stream of Iron Age movement into southern Africa, Walker's (1983) re-excavation of Bambata Cave itself has provided a date of about 150 B.C. for sheep bones and Bambata pottery – again, too early to be explained as simple contact with the Iron Age and at about the latest possible date for the Tshu-khwe dispersal from nearby northern Botswana. Ehret's (1982b) linguistic extrapolations provide some independent support for Walker's chronology although, as with other glottochronological hypotheses, the problems involved in arguing from assumed rates of language change must always be taken into account.

Walker has suggested that the occupants of the Bambata group of rock shelters obtained their pottery and livestock from a yet-to-be-identified group, who formed a 'vanguard of the Iron Age' (Walker 1983: 90) several centuries before mixed farming was established. Such an interpretation conforms well with Alexander's (1984) first phase of the moving frontier, in which food production

34

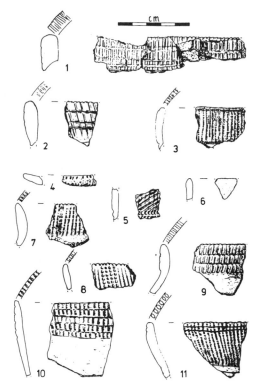

Bambata pottery from south-western Zimbabwe.
1-8: Bambata Cave. 9: Maleme Dam Shelter IV.
10: Broadlees Cave. 11: shelter near Bambata.
(From Walker 1983.)

has a wide sphere of influence, and it would seem to be the best interpretation of the admittedly inadequate archaeological evidence.

The second issue – that of the pattern of dispersal of pastoralism into southern Africa – has also hinged on chronological considerations. Although Cooke's (1965) derivation of pastoralism directly from East Africa was largely discarded on linguistic grounds, it did seem that his proposed route of spread was the best way of accounting for the scatter of early dates for domestic sheep and pottery through Namibia and the western and southern Cape. Robertshaw (1978a) refurbished the old interpretation, arguing for dispersal from the nuclear Tshu-khwe area westwards into northern Namibia and then southwards along the western margins of the continent. This, of course, emphasised the separateness of western, Stone Age pastoralism and eastern, Iron Age farming.

But Christopher Ehret and Richard Elphick have argued for a very different pattern of spread – an interpretation that has implications for understanding the origins of food production in southern Africa as a whole. By tracing items of 'core vocabulary' through dialect chains, Ehret (1982b) has reasoned that 'proto-Khoikhoi' moved southwards from northern Botswana until they came to the upper catchments of the Orange–Vaal River system. Here they divided into a 'pre-Nama' group which travelled westwards along the Orange, and a 'Cape Khoi' group, which spread to the south and then westwards and eastwards along the Cape coast.

Given the problems of glottochronology and the use of core vocabulary (Borland 1982), Ehret's interpretation could not be taken as conclusive in itself. But his model is supported by other evidence as well, as Elphick (1985) has shown. Pastoralists encountered in the south-western Cape after the mid-seventeenth century saw their affinities with communities to the east rather than the north; indeed, they regarded people in Namaqualand as completely different to themselves. Elphick has pointed out that this is not consistent with the idea of a dispersal southwards down the west coast. In addition, archaeological research has not resulted in the discovery of pastoralist sites in Namibia earlier than those in the south-western Cape (Dea-

Two different models have been proposed to account for the origins of nomadic pastoralism in southern Africa. Both acknowledge that dispersal was from a primary area in north-western Botswana, but one argument (A) is that pastoralists first moved southwards through the highveld and Karoo, splitting westwards and eastwards to settle the coastlands. Alternatively it has been suggested (B) that pastoralists moved westwards and then southwards and eastwards through the coastlands. Both interpretations fit the available archaeological and historical evidence, and more research will be necessary to determine which explanation is the more probable.

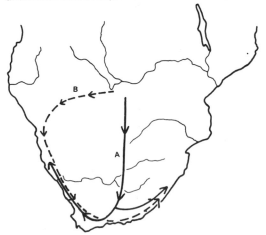

con *et al.* 1978), while sheep and pottery are now known from the northern Cape by at least the fifth century A.D. (Humphreys and Thackeray 1984). Finally, the arid western continental margins have never been favoured lands for any form of food production, while the northern Cape and the heathlands of the southern and south-western coasts would have been far more attractive (Elphick 1985).

The weight of evidence supports the suggestion of Walker, Ehret and Elphick that early pastoralists made a living in parts of the central basin and the peripheral coastlands of the southern African shield at least several centuries before mixed farming became established in the subcontinent. In some areas, there must have been overlap and interaction between the two economies. The way of life of these pastoralist communities will be considered in the next chapter, but first it is necessary to turn to the evidence for early mixed farming in southern Africa.

The moving frontier: early agriculture in southern Africa

Just as early pastoralists must have been discriminatory in their choice of places to live, searching for adequate grazing, water, and suitable plant and animal foods to supplement the yield of their flocks, so early agricultural communities clearly chose favourable locations for their villages. Such a pattern of site location is illustrated clearly at St Lucia Lake on the south-eastern coastline, the only area where a detailed distribution study of these first farming villages has been carried out (Hall 1981).

Although the lake itself is unique in its size and in its ecology, the coastal landscape of the St Lucia area is fairly typical of the subtropical Indian Ocean littoral. The coastal plain has a low relief, and the rivers which have cut such deep gorges inland now meander across the gentle topography. But this monotony is broken at the shoreline by a cordon of high dunes which have prevented easy drainage through to the sea. In consequence, there are strings of lakes and pans, of which St Lucia is the largest, that extend along the inland margin of the dunes.

It was argued earlier in this chapter that pioneer farmers would have found a wooded landscape in these coastal regions. But these forests were not necessarily uniform in their distribution. Remnant stands which have survived to the present day, or

The first farming settlements in the region of St Lucia Lake, on the south-east African coast. Villages were built between the lake and the coast, and on the inland margins of the coastal dunes: ideal locations to take advantage of both agricultural soils and the rich shellfish beds of the shoreline. (After Hall 1981.)

which have become re-established over a long period, show that the trees and bushes on the dune cordon grow closely together to form a dense forest. But at the foot of the dunes, where the water-table is higher and the land flooded in summer, this closed forest gives way to open patches of water-tolerant grasses and bushes. Inland again, on the drier coastal plain, the woodlands are more open, likewise with clearings and patches of swamp.

Although the St Lucia area has been searched carefully, sites with the distinctive pottery of the third and fourth centuries A.D. have been found only along the boundary regions between the dune cordon and the lake shores. Pottery dating to the second millennium has been found higher on the dunes and inland of the coastal lake system, but there is nothing to indicate that the first farming communities chose to live in these other regions.

Sites are typically quite limited in extent, although there is usually a considerable density of broken pottery, often evidence of iron-working and broken shells of the mussel, *Perna perna*. One site, known as Enkwazini, has been excavated, and although the finds were disappointingly scarce, there was enough carbon closely associated with decorated pottery to confirm that this set of sites dates to the third–fourth centuries A.D. (Hall and Vogel 1978).

No plant or animal remains were found at Enkwazini, and so the actual components of the economy remain unknown. But the numerous fragments of large, heavy pots, as well as the evidence for iron-working, indicate at least semi-sedentary villages and the practice of farming. The settlement pattern reinforces this interpretation, for the area between the marshlands and the dune forest would have provided a good location for villages, from which fields could be cut back into the lush vegetation mantling the higher slopes. At the same time, fruits and other forest and marshland produce would have been important resources to supplement crops.

The place of domestic livestock in this initial farming economy is less clear. No excavated sites from this pioneer period have yielded any faunal remains, either wild or domestic, although this may be due to problems of preservation and sampling. While some archaeologists believe that the earliest farmers would have moved southwards with domestic stock, it has also been suggested that the surroundings of the villages would have been unsuited to cattle. The open strip of land between marsh and dune must have been narrow, with grazing for livestock available after only several generations, when the dune forests had been opened up somewhat by fields. In addition, the combination of subtropical climate and dense vegetation must have favoured parasites inimical to livestock – in particular, trypanosomiasis. On balance, it would seem more likely that, although farmers knew of domestic stock, it was only after more favourable conditions had been created that they were brought into general use.

An absence of livestock and the persistent presence of shellfish on archaeological sites of this period may be a clue to the reason why these pioneer villages hugged the southern African coastline. Cereal agriculture provides a diet high in carbohydrates, but without proteins from domestic livestock, through either milk or meat, other food sources are needed. Shellfish are particularly rich in protein and are a dependable source of food when tides and weather conditions permit their collection. Settlement along the inland margins of the coastal dune cordon would have been a satisfactory compromise between the needs of agriculture and access to essential foods from the sea.

It is difficult to say to what extent the settlement patterns of the St Lucia area are typical of other parts of the coast. Pottery with the same distinctive style of decoration is found southwards for as far as the combination of dune cordon and coastal plain persists. This is consistent with the St Lucia evidence, for the favoured environment between dune forest and marshland was not present further to the south. One of the southernmost sites, Mzonjani, has been excavated. It has been dated to the third century A.D. and, like Enkwazini, lies behind the dunes. It is marked by scatters of shell as well as of pottery (Maggs 1980b).

Sites with ceramics similar to those from Enkwazini and Mzonjani, and also located on the inland margins of the dune cordon, have been

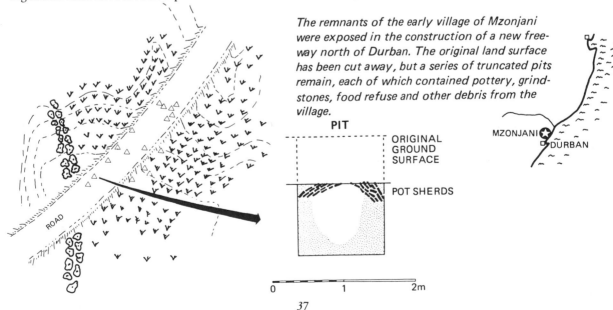

The remnants of the early village of Mzonjani were exposed in the construction of a new freeway north of Durban. The original land surface has been cut away, but a series of truncated pits remain, each of which contained pottery, grindstones, food refuse and other debris from the village.

ROAD

PIT

ORIGINAL GROUND SURFACE

POT SHERDS

MZONJANI
DURBAN

0   1   2m

37

noted to the north of St Lucia, although they have yet to be formally described. Beyond this, in southern Mozambique, is the coastal shell midden of Matola, which again has the distinctive ceramics that are the mark of this first farming phase, but which are here dated to the first century A.D. or earlier (Hall and Vogel 1980). These radiocarbon determinations may prove to be inaccurate, but on the other hand they may be an indication that farming settlement in south-eastern Africa was earlier than is currently believed.

The second phase: 'subduing the wilderness'

There seem to be many similarities between the agricultural communities of the south-eastern coastlands and the gatherer-hunter bands who had lived in these and other parts of southern Africa for millennia. Both made use of marine resources, wild plant foods and animals, and lived in ephemeral settlements (Deacon 1984). Elphick (1985) has made the same point about pioneer food producers in the western regions of southern Africa, noting that they made use of many of the skills of the gatherer-hunter in making a living. Such patterns are, again, quite consistent with Alexander's model for the first phase of the moving frontier in which 'small groups or individuals from established farming communities move out into a wilderness inhabited, if at all, by hunters and gatherers, and exploit some of its resources, often using the strategies of the hunters and gatherers they meet' (Alexander 1984: 12).

But Alexander has also pointed out that this first phase of expansion is followed by a second, in which more substantial farming villages are established as part of the process of 'subduing the wilderness'. This is clearly evident in the archaeology of early agriculture in southern Africa, for within a few centuries of the first villages along the coastlands larger settlements had been built in other parts of the woodlands.

Between the Zambezi and Limpopo rivers lies the Zimbabwe plateau, an area with fertile soils and an equitable climate particularly favourable for farming (Wellington 1955). A number of archaeological sites are evidence for early farming in this area, but in most of the reports the emphasis has been on the description of pottery, and there is little information about the nature of settlement. An exception is the village of Mabveni, which, if the radiocarbon dates are correct, has preserved the earliest structures built by farmers in southern Africa.

Mabveni lies sheltered between two granite hills, on a small watercourse not far west of Great Zimbabwe. The site was discovered by Keith Robinson, who excavated there in 1960. Two heaps of plaster above the surface of the ground marked the position of former structures, and impressions on the plaster showed that it had once covered a framework of 'stout sticks averaging 2 inches in diameter' (Robinson 1961a). Beneath this heap of fragments were the broken remains of a clay floor, resting in turn on a thin, ashy soil. Pottery from the pile of plaster, the floor and the midden beneath was similar, suggesting that all belonged to the same period of occupation. Robinson felt that this structure was too small for a house, and was more likely to have been for storage. Burnt plaster indicated that the building was destroyed by fire.

A little to the east, more fragments of plaster were exposed in the side of a cutting made by a track. When fully cleared, these proved to be the edge of the irregular remnant of a clay floor, similarly destroyed by fire. Robinson felt that this had been a circular house, with a roof consisting of a plastered, light wooden framework. The same distinctive pottery indicated contemporaneity with the first structure.

There is no direct evidence for agriculture at Mabveni village, although this is not surprising considering the shallowness of the midden deposits and their exposure to the elements for many centuries. But as with the coastal sites, the numerous sherds from heavy clay pots, coupled this time with the remains of buildings, strongly suggest a sedentary farming community. This interpreta-

Sites discussed in Chapter 4.

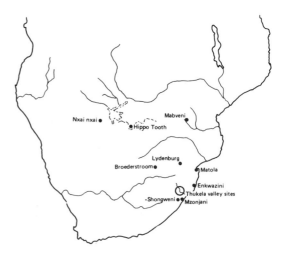

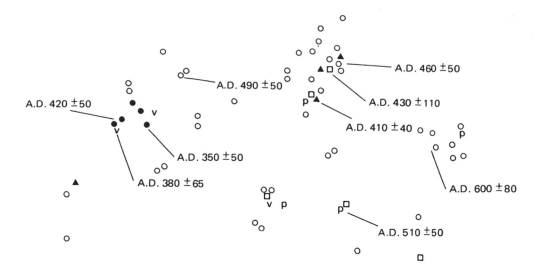

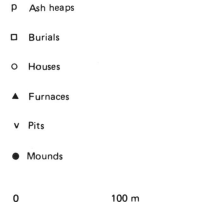

A.D. 420 ±50

A.D. 490 ±50

A.D. 460 ±50

A.D. 430 ±110

A.D. 410 ±40

A.D. 350 ±50

A.D. 380 ±65

A.D. 600 ±80

A.D. 510 ±50

p Ash heaps

□ Burials

o Houses

▲ Furnaces

v Pits

● Mounds

0   100 m

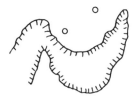

Map of Broederstroom. This site is a complex palimpsest of villages, built on top of each other over several centuries. The map shows the excavated areas, houses, and the places from which dated radiocarbon samples were obtained. (From Mason 1981.)

tion is reinforced by the animal bones from the site, which include domestic cattle, sheep or goat and some wild species (Huffman 1975). Robinson wrote his report before radiocarbon dates were available for his site, but he nevertheless estimated a date early in the first millennium on the basis of the style of the pottery. This interpretation has been confirmed by two radiocarbon dates, although these are several centuries apart (Huffman 1975). Thus the cattle and buildings from Mabveni are the earliest yet known south of the Zambezi (Huffman 1982).

In contrast to the Zimbabwe plateau, the country to the south of the Limpopo River is more varied in character. Numerous tributaries fall away from the highveld shield, breaking up the landscape into drainage basins and watersheds.

Soils are equally variable, with some comparatively infertile but others particularly suited to farming settlement (Wellington 1955). One such favoured area comprises the gentle slopes of the Magalies River valley, which forms the upper catchment of the Crocodile River and lies just beneath the boundary between the savanna woodlands and the high grasslands of the southern African interior. This area has been the scene for more than a decade of intensive research by Revil Mason and his colleagues. In particular, Mason has concentrated on a complex of houses, furnace areas and middens known today as Broederstroom (Mason 1981).

Broederstroom consists of a series of villages, apparently built one after the other and slightly overlapping in plan, that date to between A.D. 350

A house floor from Broederstroom excavated by R. J. Mason, J. Houmoller and R. Steel in 1973 as part of a research project carried out by the Archaeological Research Unit at the University of the Witwatersrand. The site has been radio-carbon-dated to the fifth century A.D. The house was about three metres in diameter. (Photograph by courtesy of Revil Mason.)

and A.D. 600. Houses were circular and up to six metres in diameter. As with Mabveni village, the complete collapse of the structures at Broederstroom makes it difficult to deduce what they would have looked like. Likewise, there are the extensive and durable remains of iron-working, although none of the furnaces have survived intact.

Mason was not able to recover plant remains from the middens at Broederstroom. As with other early village sites, it is difficult to accept this negative finding as conclusive, for other factors strongly suggest that agriculture was practised. Certainly, domestic animals were husbanded by the village's occupants, for the bones from the rubbish heaps indicate, in Mason's words, that

'Broederstroom supported a pastoral economy based on the raising of sheep and, more probably, goats, with cattle being acquired only rarely, over a century after the establishment of the village' (Mason 1981: 411). The faunal remains also suggest that hunting was important.

To the east of Broederstroom, the margin of the highveld is far more sharply defined, for the escarpment plunges some one thousand metres to the lowveld and the Mozambican coastal plain beyond. As would be expected with such gradients, the landscape is often spectacularly rugged and little suited for human habitation. But there are also deep, broad valleys with rich soils suited to farming, and these disclose evidence for settlement early in the first millennium. In one, the Lydenburg valley, there has been considerable archaeological research, and the sites that have been discovered there provide a case study of early village settlement in this part of southern Africa.

The base of the Lydenburg valley is some twenty kilometres wide, and along the lower slopes at its side rich soils have washed down from the peripheral highlands. Five first-millennium villages have been found, all along the eastern side

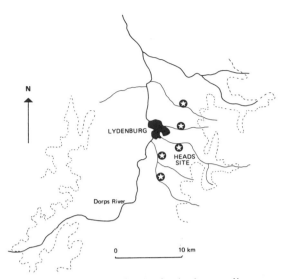

Early farming sites in the Lydenburg valley.

of the valley, close to tributary streams of the major river and all in sheltered locations (Marker and Evers 1976). Clearly, pioneer farmers in this area also had very specific requirements when it came to choosing a place to live.

The best known of these villages has been called the 'Lydenburg Heads site' after the unusual set of terracotta heads that was discovered there in 1962

(Inskeep and Maggs 1975). Unfortunately, this important site has been badly damaged by erosion and, despite careful excavation, it has not been possible to discover any details of village structures (Evers 1982). All that now remains are the lower parts of pits containing pottery, animal bones and other rubbish. Fragments of wall plaster indicate that there were once buildings on the site, and slag indicates that iron-working took place. The small sample of animal bone shows that although there was some hunting, domestic stock and in particular sheep or goats were important. Radiocarbon dates indicate that the village was occupied in the sixth century A.D.

Continuing along the edge of the southern African shield, the landscape again changes as the abrupt transition from highveld to lowveld is replaced by a steadier gradient on which there are large midland areas. Here in the south-east the major rivers flow from their headwaters in the

Excavations at Ndondondwane, a typical first-millennium village in the valley of the Thukela River. Large sherds of pottery, as well as numerous animal bones, can be seen in situ beneath the level of the topsoil, which has been disturbed by ploughing. (Photograph by courtesy of Tim Maggs, Natal Museum.)

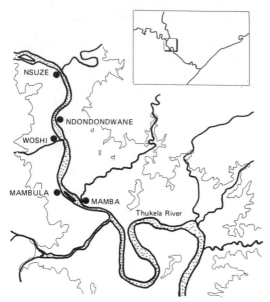

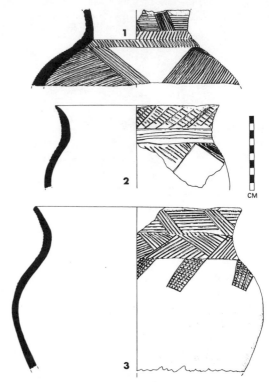

Ndondondwane and other first-millennium farming villages in the Thukela River valley. Rich sediments have accumulated along the meandering course of the river, and these were particularly favoured by early agriculturalists. (From Maggs 1984b.)

Lydenburg Tradition pottery from the basin of the Thukela River. (From Maggs and Michael 1976.)

Drakensberg, more than 2 500 metres above sea level, to the Indian Ocean some two hundred kilometres away (Wellington 1955). These rivers have cut deep valleys, within which more than 150 first-millennium villages have now been discovered, conforming to a distinctive pattern of settlement (Maggs 1980a). The results of excavations by Tim Maggs at two villages in the Thukela River basin illustrate what is known of pioneer farmers in this area.

Msuluzi Confluence is an archaeological site on the tongue of land between the converging Thukela and Msuluzi rivers. As with the Lydenburg Heads site, the landscape is now badly eroded and there is little evidence for the form of the village. However, there is pottery in abundance and evidence for iron-working on a large scale, while bones dug from the ubiquitous rubbish pits show that the village's occupants hunted, fished and kept domestic stock, mostly sheep or goats. Carbon samples have been dated to the seventh century A.D., and Maggs considers the village to have been one of the earliest in the Thukela valley (Maggs 1980c).

Ntshekane village was also located on a confluence, this time the meeting of the river after which the site is named and the Mooi. The ceramics found at Ntshekane are particularly important, for they are the most developed form of the Lydenburg pottery tradition in the south-east (Maggs and Michael 1976), bringing to an end a trend that began at Msuluzi Confluence. But likewise, the erosion at the site has destroyed most of the evidence for the way of life of the villagers, although radiocarbon dates place occupation in the ninth century A.D., and small stock and cattle were both important elements in the economy.

One of the most distinctive characteristics of these early south-eastern villages is their association with the deep fertile soils along the major river courses (Maggs 1980a). Again, this settlement pattern, along with the presence of the suite of artefacts associated with farming, is strong circumstantial evidence for crop cultivation. More direct confirmation for agriculture in this region in the first millennium comes from the protected deposits of Shongweni Cave, in a narrow gorge some thirty kilometres inland from where Durban stands today. Here, plant remains excavated by Oliver Davies (1975) included finger and bullrush millet, *Eleusine coracana* and *Pennisetum americanum*, sorghum, and the bottle gourd and tsamma melon, *Lagenam sicerana* and *Citrullus lanatus*. Interpretation of the radiocarbon dates from Shongweni is a complex problem, but it would seem most likely that the plants were left in the shelter by farmers (Maggs 1980a), perhaps during a temporary stay away from their village.

Although there are still few areas in southern Africa where there has been enough archaeological research to gain more than an outline understanding of the way of life, the locations of villages in places such as the Lydenburg valley and the Thukela basin show definite patterns of preference that must reflect economic needs. Comparison between these areas suggests further points which, although tantalisingly vague, may prove to be the shadow of past behaviour.

Firstly, all these communities seem to have had domestic livestock – a point of immediate contrast with agricultural settlement along the coast during the first phase of the moving frontier. If the argument that the coastal farmers had to remain close to the shore because of their need for animal protein from the sea is correct, then it follows that the acquisition of domestic livestock may have been the economic development that allowed this constraint to be broken.

This is not to suggest the sort of second migration that has been implied by the 'stream' models for southern African ceramics, in which farmers who previously had only crop plants suddenly acquired livestock (Thorp 1979). The transformation is more likely to have been ecological, with farmers using 'slash and burn' (also called swidden cultivation) to open up the woodland environment, thus providing the grazing lands which livestock require, and which were not present in the coastal regions in the first phase of the moving frontier.

Although such comparisons can be misleading, the pottery scatters that mark the earliest villages at the coast do tend to be significantly smaller than the extent of debris at inland sites. The St Lucia site of Enkwazini, for example, was limited enough to suggest a short-term occupation by a small group of people (Hall 1981), while in contrast Broederstroom village was occupied over several centuries (Mason 1981), and Maggs has estimated that several hundred people may have lived at Msuluzi Confluence during the seventh century (Maggs 1980c). Within a generation or so, farmers at these inland villages would have transformed the woodlands surrounding their villages into a patchwork of cultivated fields, virgin savanna, and formerly cleared areas in different stages of regen-

eration. These latter clearings would have provided the grazing needed by livestock.

Consistent with this possible transformation from crop cultivation to mixed farming are the faunal assemblages from those sites that have been excavated. For at the earlier villages in different parts of southern Africa – whether the Magalies, the Lydenburg or the Thukela valley – sheep and goats seem to be more numerous than cattle. Thus at the sixth-century village of Magogo in the Thukela basin small stock outnumber cattle (Voigt 1984), as they do at the eighth-century site of Ndondondwane which falls within the same river catchment (Voigt and Von den Driesch 1984). But by the time Ntshekane was built in the ninth century cattle had become more important than small stock (Maggs and Michael 1976). This pattern is repeated to the north, in the Limpopo River valley, where in the centuries before the rise of Mapungubwe cattle became progressively more important (Voigt and Plug 1981).

Although much more evidence is needed before this can be seen as a general pattern, a trend in which sheep and goats were important at the pioneer stage, gradually to be replaced by cattle, would be quite consistent with the changes that were being made to the vegetation. While the woodlands around villages were still comparatively closed there would have been more opportunity for browsing species; but once more open areas had been established, cattle herds could be allowed to increase in numbers.

Interactions across the frontier

By the end of the first millennium food-producing economies were well established in the western and south-western parts of the subcontinent, where they were based on nomadic pastoralism, and also in the the eastern and south-eastern woodlands, where villagers had been 'subduing the wilderness' with swidden agriculture for many generations. But what of the interactions across these farming frontiers with gatherer-hunter communities; the initial phases when farmers adopt indigenous techniques to supplement their domestic resources; and the later stages when food producers develop long-term alliances with gatherer-hunters (Alexander 1984)?

One of the particular features of early pastoralism in the western parts of southern Africa is the general *absence* of technological change. Although herders made small quantities of pottery, such sherds are often all that distinguish the sites of their settlements from those used by gatherer-hunters. This in itself suggests that early food producers were making use of many long-standing aboriginal techniques. Elphick (1985) has suggested that this very similarity between gatherer-hunter and herder lifestyles would have led to conflict over resources. This proposition is supported to some extent by Manhire's (1984) study of settlement patterns in one part of the western coastlands, where gatherer-hunter groups may have moved away in the face of the expanding herder frontier.

But Elphick has also pointed out that such a rigid division between the two lifeways was *not* encountered by the Dutch in the seventeenth century. They recorded a confused variety of situations which included obvious examples of clientship and cooperation between pastoralists and gatherer-hunters. Elphick has argued that such interaction developed after the initial phase of conflict, for 'the transformation of the hunters' hostility into cooperation permitted the peaceful growth of Khoikhoi herds and flocks, as did the acquisition of reliable herdsmen. Increased herds meant a secure food supply, and human population consequently grew. As wealth was a very important basis of political power in Khoikhoi society, prosperity favoured the emergence of more prestigious rulers and the formation of larger political units.' (Elphick 1985: 35-6)

The settlements used by early food producers in the east of the subcontinent also show evidence that gatherer-hunter technology was utilised. Stone tools have been found at a number of early farming villages, including Broederstroom (Mason 1981), the Lydenburg Heads site (Evers 1982) and Msuluzi Confluence (Maggs 1980c), where Tim Maggs has been one of the few archaeologists to try to deduce the nature of this interaction. Maggs has noted correlations in the distribution of pottery and stone tools across the Msuluzi Confluence site, suggesting that both classes of artefact came from the same occupation. Further evidence of possible interaction are bone 'arrowheads', grooved stones and perhaps the practice of making shell beads. Maggs has suggested that gatherer-hunters visited the farming village to obtain iron implements – indicative of a close and regular economic relationship.

Equally interesting evidence comes from far to the north, along the northern margins of the Kalahari. Here, rock paintings in the Tsodilo Hills show cattle, either being herded or being stolen (Campbell 1982), and recent archaeological excavations on the Kalahari margins at the sites of

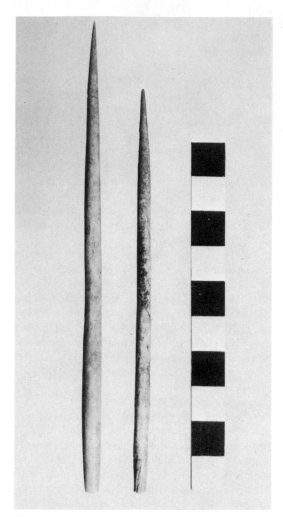

Bone arrowheads from a first-millennium farming village in the Thukela valley. These may have been obtained by trade with gatherer-hunter communities, perhaps in exchange for iron goods. (Photograph by courtesy of Tim Maggs, Natal Museum.)

Nxai Nxai and Hippo Tooth have demonstrated a long-standing interaction between the two ways of life (Denbow and Wilmsen 1983). Indeed, it is rapidly becoming apparent that gatherer-hunters in the Kalahari have not been isolated from contact with farmers as some earlier ethno-archaeological work had implied. Indeed, archaeological evidence now suggests that 'foragers and food producers have been enmeshed in networks of interaction and exchange for 1 000 years longer than was previously suspected. Over 1 200 years ago, these networks reached into the heart of the Dobe area and into other presently isolated parts of

Detail of a rock painting in the Tsodilo Hills, Botswana, with human figures and cattle. (Tracing by Tina Coombes from a photograph by Alec Campbell.)

New ways of living: San gatherer-hunters resettled at Tshumkwe, Namibia. (Photograph by John Kramer, courtesy of the South African Museum.)

Botswana. Although the archaeological evidence does not point to complete displacement of foragers, it does appear that population groups in Botswana have been more opportunistic and open to changes in subsistence strategies and, likely, social systems than the standard anthropological categories of hunter gatherer or herder farmer would suggest.' (Denbow 1984a: 178–9)

Thus the introduction of food production into southern Africa was a complex process which began with the 'migratory drift' (Elphick 1985) southwards of pastoralists in the last few centuries B.C.; continued with the tentative probing of the south-eastern woodlands by agriculturalists some five hundred years later; and was followed by the founding of long-term interconnections between food producers and gatherer-hunter bands. Indeed, in some parts of southern Africa the farming frontier is still expanding, as Kalahari gatherer-hunters adopt new ways of living in changing circumstances (Yellen 1984).

5

Taking stock

Livestock and the village community

It is probable that the people of the frontier villages and camps described in the previous chapter lived precariously, with periodic shortages of food which forced them to look for other sources of sustenance. Such fluctuations in supply tend to be a natural consequence of agriculture, for by concentrating their efforts on a narrow range of food plants, farmers place themselves at risk if crops fail. This is particularly so in southern Africa, where the climates of the summer rainfall area tend to prevent storage of grain for more than a short period (Sansom 1974). In the west of the subcontinent early herding economies were equally precarious, for the regular fluctuations in rainfall made the availability of pasturage unpredictable.

Managing risks such as these was probably one of the prevalent concerns of the earliest food producers (Bronson 1975), and remains an issue with farmers today (Wolpert 1964). One solution is to accumulate food supplies, both as protection against possible future shortages and as a means of gaining the indebtedness of others, thereby creating obligations that can be claimed in times of need (Bender 1978).

Farmers in southern Africa gained this enhanced economic security by increasing their holdings in domestic stock. In the west and south-west, the possession of larger herds allowed their owners to build up wide-ranging networks of alliances with other herders and with client gatherer-herders. Small groups of animals could be moved to widely separated areas, the farmers taking advantage in this way of the highly localised variations in rainfall (Elphick 1985; Jacobson 1984). In the east and south-east segments of herds could, in similar fashion, be moved to areas with better resources, or they could be used in transactions between villages, creating reciprocal obligations (Kuper 1982a; Hall 1985a).

The use of livestock to secure transactions between people – binding them together with commitments – was a *qualitative* change from simple food producing, for, as Barbara Bender has emphasised (1978), there was more to the farming way of life than merely growing crops. Thus whereas the communities that comprised the first

phase of the frontier in southern Africa shared much in common with their gatherer-hunter contemporaries, later farmers were organised differently. Some aspects of these changed circumstances are evident from archaeological sources, and form the subject of this chapter.

Agro-pastoralism on the southern highveld

It is possible that the extensive grasslands that cover much of the Orange Free State and the Transvaal were settled by herders during their early expansion southwards from the Tshu-khwe language nucleus early in the first millennium, although there is at present no archaeological evidence for this (Elphick 1985; Maggs 1976a). But it does seem that the area was *not* settled by first-millennium pioneer agriculturalists, for no trace of their distinctive pottery has been found in these high-lying areas (Maggs 1984a). This is not surprising, since the largely treeless environment would have been of little value for economies prin-

The grasslands of the southern highveld. The cone-shaped hill to the right of the photograph is Ntsuanatsatsi, which is linked in myth to the creation of man. (Photograph by courtesy of Tim Maggs, Natal Museum.)

cipally dependent on swidden agriculture. But once farmers had increased livestock numbers to the point where their animals formed a principal resource, they were able to move onto the high grasslands and take advantage of their extensive, open grazing lands. This they did early in the second millennium, building numerous stone enclosures which still stand today.

At first sight, the topography of the southern highveld may seem monotonously even, but closer examination shows that a complex network of dolerite sills and dykes marks those places where volcanic lavas pushed their way through the sedimentary rocks of the Karoo series many millions of years ago. Very often, these dolerites have broken into convenient, if irregular, blocks which are ideally suited for use as a building material. For

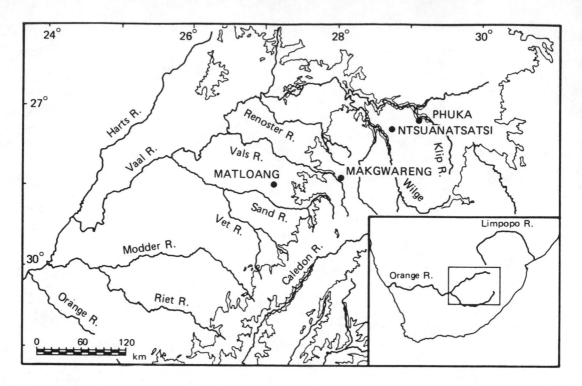

this reason, but perhaps also because the ridge crests are commanding locations above the surrounding plains, the dolerite intrusions were favoured places for farming settlement from first occupation.

The ruined settlements of the highveld were described in writing by the first explorers from Europe who made their way across the interior shield of the subcontinent more than a century ago, but it was not until Tim Maggs began extensive research that there was any systematic description of the architecture and some understanding of the people who once lived there (Maggs 1976a). Maggs made extensive use of air photographs, recognising different styles of architecture, which he termed 'types' and named after notable and characteristic examples of the group. Excavation of sites representative of each type revealed details of construction technique and something of the style of life of the people themselves.

Maggs called the earliest architectural style Type N, after Ntsuanatsatsi, a prominent, flat-topped hill in the north-east highveld which is also the subject of a common creation myth. 'The Basuto say they come from a place named Ntsuanatsatsi, a kind of big hole with a rock overhanging it, full of reeds, where voices from under the ground may be heard' (Maggs 1976a: 140). Type N settlement units have at their centre a group of primary enclo-

Location of excavated sites on the southern highveld. (Illustration by Tina Coombes.)

The different types of stone-built settlements on the southern highveld (after Maggs 1976b).

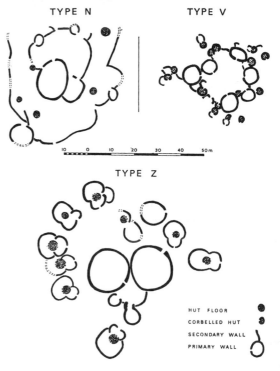

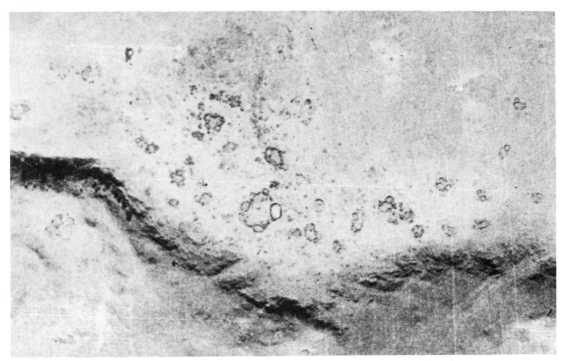

Air photograph of Type V settlements on the southern highveld. The walled enclosures of numerous settlement units are clearly visible. (Photograph from Maggs 1976a, by courtesy of the author.)

sures, linked by secondary walling to produce a larger, secondary enclosure. Houses and other features surround the central enclosures, and the entire settlement unit is enclosed by a low wall.

Type N sites are only found in the north-eastern part of the highveld. Usually, settlement units occur in clusters of up to one hundred, indicating quite sizable groups of people. Guessing population density is one of the more unrigorous archaeological pursuits, but Maggs has suggested that such 'towns' may have housed as many as 1 500 people (Maggs 1976b). However, these clusters of units are widely spaced in comparison with later architectural styles, suggesting that the overall farming population was still relatively small.

Some idea of the nature of life at Ntsuanatsatsi in the fourteenth century (a date obtained from a radiocarbon sample) has been revealed by detailed research. Careful examination of the landscape around the settlement units (of which there are here about one hundred in close proximity) showed that there was probably a more luxuriant environment in the past than today, perhaps with some low trees on the hill slopes and pools con-

nected by small streams, fringed with reeds and rushes. Plaster fragments with telltale impressions suggest that these reeds were used to build houses in the town, although few details survive of structures other than the ubiquitous stone livestock enclosures. Rubbish heaps – always a profitable source for the archaeologist – contained broken pottery, some rough clay models of cattle, some iron and bone tools, and a small collection of animal bones that confirmed the presence of domestic stock and showed that the community also hunted the animals of the surrounding plains (Maggs 1976a).

Maggs excavated a settlement unit in a second Type N town, some forty kilometres to the north-east of Ntsuanatsatsi, and although many of the features are merely confirmatory, there are additional details that add further knowledge of the way of life during this period. Phuka (or OU2) is one of about forty adjacent settlement units strung along a ridge overlooking a tributary of the Klip River. This valley has soils suited to agriculture, and Maggs has argued that the small stone platforms found between the livestock enclosures and the perimeter wall were used as grain bin stands. Two small impressions on potsherds may have been made by sorghum seeds, although this has yet to be confirmed. At Phuka, there is slightly more evidence for the form of the houses, which had paved floors, perhaps covered by a layer of plaster.

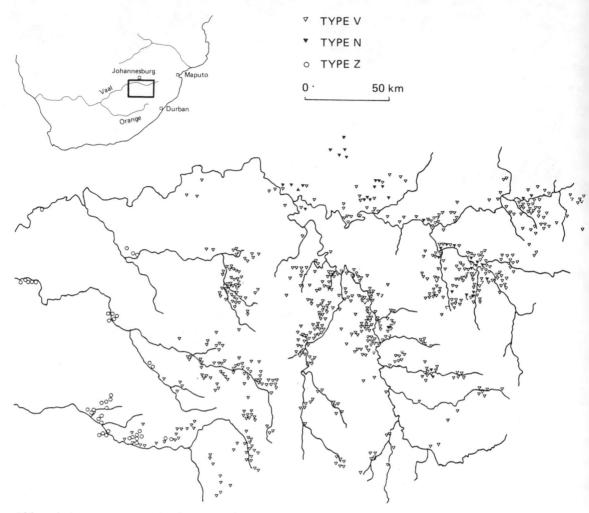

Although the superstructure has long since disintegrated, chunks of plaster with reed impressions suggest a dome-like structure (Maggs 1976a).

After perhaps two centuries, the Type N architectural style was overtaken by new preferences in building. The characteristic combination of primary and secondary walling for livestock enclosures was still retained, but the surrounding wall was abandoned and, in many cases, the reed and plaster houses were replaced by structures of 'corbelled' stone. Although there is no evidence for the reason for this transition, Maggs feels that this new style, which he has called Type V, was most probably a development out of Type N, rather than the consequence of a fresh immigration of distinct communities (Maggs 1976a).

Type V is by far the most common and widely distributed architectural style of the highveld. As Maggs himself has commented, 'Type V is a true Highveld expression of the Iron Age, occurring

Distribution of Type N, V and Z settlements over part of the southern highveld (after Maggs 1976a).

almost exclusively between the altitudes of 1 450 and 2 000 metres [above sea level] . . . which restricts it to the zone between the Drakensberg escarpment to the east and the minor escarpment of the central Free State to the west' (Maggs 1976a: 29). Type V sites are found across and beyond the distribution of the Type N style, and in many cases the older sites have been robbed of their stone to allow building in the new fashion.

Following the custom of their predecessors, the builders who used the Type V style placed individual settlement units quite close together to form towns of up to a hundred units. But there was less distance between these larger clusters, indicating that the population density of the southern highveld was now considerably higher. Towns were characteristically placed on spurs and other prominent features of the landscape above the valleys of the larger rivers and their tributaries.

Now and again there are larger settlement units within towns, suggesting a difference in wealth and status. Maggs has summed this evidence up as follows: 'it is worth mentioning that on some sites one settlement unit is appreciably larger than the others and probably reflects the hierarchical structure of the society . . . . But more often this is not evident and the component units of the settlement are undifferentiated.' (Maggs 1976a: 32) Of the same order are the 'elongated Type V' settlement units that were found in a limited area around the Klip and Upper Vaal rivers. In these the ring of primary enclosures has been stretched into a long irregular belt, creating an altogether larger settlement unit. Maggs found 35 towns that had such elongated units within their boundaries, and commented that 'their size and shape, and their occurrence usually as a single unit among a number of smaller Type V settlement units suggest that their inhabitants were an economically and politically powerful group within the settlement' (Maggs 1976a: 33).

But what of the daily life of these highveld farmers? Unfortunately there is not the evidence to unravel day-by-day activities, although Maggs did

carry out extensive excavations at one town, which he has called Makgwareng (code OO1), after the ridge of that name on which the settlement was built.

The first people to live at Makgwareng did not use stone, building livestock enclosures and partly plastered houses some two metres in diameter from reeds set in trenches that served as foundations. This initial phase seems to have continued for at least half a century, during which Makgwareng may have been either successively abandoned and reoccupied, or else occupied continually with houses and enclosures replaced as they fell into disrepair. But after a while, the townspeople decided to replace their buildings with more substantial stone structures. The site was levelled, and fine pebbled floors were laid where houses and some other structures were to stand. Then five large primary enclosures were built and linked to form a secondary enclosure around which stood six houses of corbelled stone. In this initial form, the Makgwareng settlement unit was probably the home of between 18 and 45 people and was, in Maggs's words, a 'family

The settlement of Makgwareng after excavation. (Photograph by courtesy of Tim Maggs, Natal Museum.)

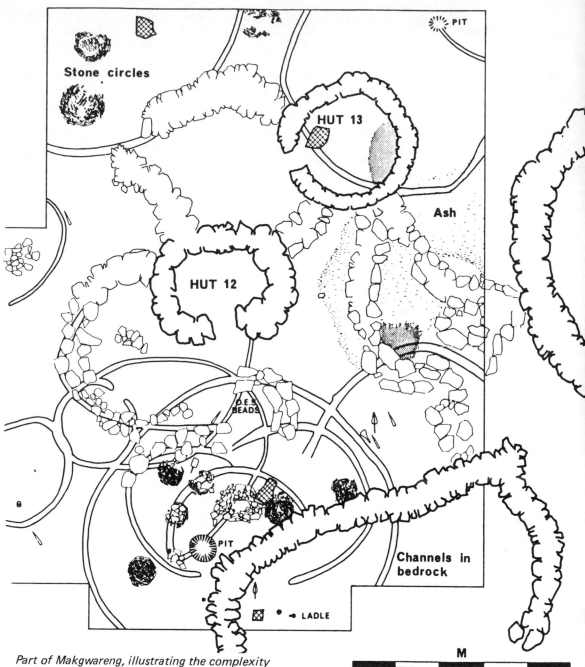

Stone circles

HUT 13

Ash

HUT 12

O.E.S. BEADS

PIT

Channels in bedrock

PIT

⊠ ●→ LADLE

M

Part of Makgwareng, illustrating the complexity of building and rebuilding within the excavated area. The channels cut into the bedrock beneath the site are all that remains of the first occupation of the village. Later, stone-walled houses were built (marked on the plan as huts 12 and 13), linked together by secondary walls. Abandoned artefacts found during excavation included ostrich eggshell beads, iron hoes and spearpoints. (From Maggs 1976a.)

homestead' typical of many others in the area (Maggs 1976a).

In the years that followed, births, deaths, marriages, emigrations and immigrations would have changed the numbers and interrelationships of members of the household, and buildings were accordingly abandoned or constructed. Four of the six original primary enclosures were altered and no longer used to pen livestock. By the number of grindstones found, one of the abandoned enclosures seems to have been used as a work area for grinding corn, perhaps by women. In addition, the position of the main entrance to the secondary enclosure was changed and additional stone houses were built, suggesting that the number of occupants increased.

The end of the Makgwareng settlement appears to have been sudden and violent. Abandoned stores of valuable iron tools, including two hoes, show that the occupants did not have the opportunity to salvage their belongings. More evidence comes from around the entrance to a house, where a cluster of spear heads suggests an intense battle, while a human jaw bone found in the main entrance indicates a desperate defence of the stock pens. Maggs has suggested that, in common with many other Type V sites, Makgwareng was laid to waste by armies from the south in the early years of the last century.

Maggs has identified a third style of highveld architecture, which he has called Type Z. The distribution of Type Z settlement units is far more restricted than that of the ubiquitous Type V and is confined to the valleys of the Sand, Vals and Renoster rivers in the north-west of what is today the Orange Free State. In addition, the style of building is distinct. In the centre of each settlement unit is a compact group of large primary enclosures: the stock pens. Surrounding these, and looking from the air rather like the petals of a flower, are usually between eight and twenty distinctive houses, often with front and back semi-circular courtyards. Maggs has called these 'bilobial dwellings' (Maggs 1976a).

Maggs carried out survey and excavation work at one particularly large group of Type Z settlement units, which he named Matloang (or OXF 1). Houses and animal byres were packed tightly for more than a kilometre along a ridge, perhaps housing a population of more than a thousand people. Maggs has estimated that Matloang and other Type Z settlements were occupied a little before the beginning of the nineteenth century, although the length of time over which each settlement was used, and whether or not all the settlement units at Matloang were contemporary, remain unanswered questions (Maggs 1976a).

By and large communities such as that of Matloang, which have been studied and reconstructed by archaeologists, remain faceless. Thus although individual actions and identities are occasionally perceived – the symbolic clay heads from Lydenburg or the townsman who died defending his herds at Makgwareng, for instance – the story is mostly of environmental influences or the outlines of economy and social organisation. But for the more recent past, the evidence of archaeology overlaps with other sources, in particular oral traditions. Although such marriages of evidence may not be easy, they do begin to provide a more definite identity for the men and women who tilled the fields and tended the herds.

Tim Maggs has used such sources of information to suggest links between his architectural styles and the corpus of recorded oral tradition (Maggs 1976b). He has pointed out that almost all the major Sotho-speaking groups on the southern highveld trace their origins to the north-eastern margins of the grasslands and the headwaters of the Limpopo River – traditions which parallel the spread of farming inferred by the contrasting distributions of Type N and Type V architectural styles. In particular, two sections of lineages, known as the Kwena and Kgatla, are remembered as having moved into the area around Ntsuanatsatsi, and it is possible that these were the communities that built the Type N towns. Oral traditions relate that, after this first move, the Kwena lineage divided into several further groups, which in turn moved southwards, reaching the Caledon River valley in the mid-seventeenth century and building, in at least one case, the corbelled houses often found on Type V sites. The Kgatla lineage seems to have subdivided in similar fashion, with groups such as the Tlokwa and the Sia moving southwards by the early nineteenth century. To the west, Type V sites are associated with areas occupied by a further seminal lineage, the Taung (Maggs 1976b).

In the case of the Type Z settlements, the connections are clearer for, by carefully fitting together archaeological and historical sources, Maggs has shown that settlements such as Matloang were occupied by the Rolong, a southerly Tswana group who moved into the north-western Orange Free State sometime before the seventeenth century (Maggs 1976a, 1976b).

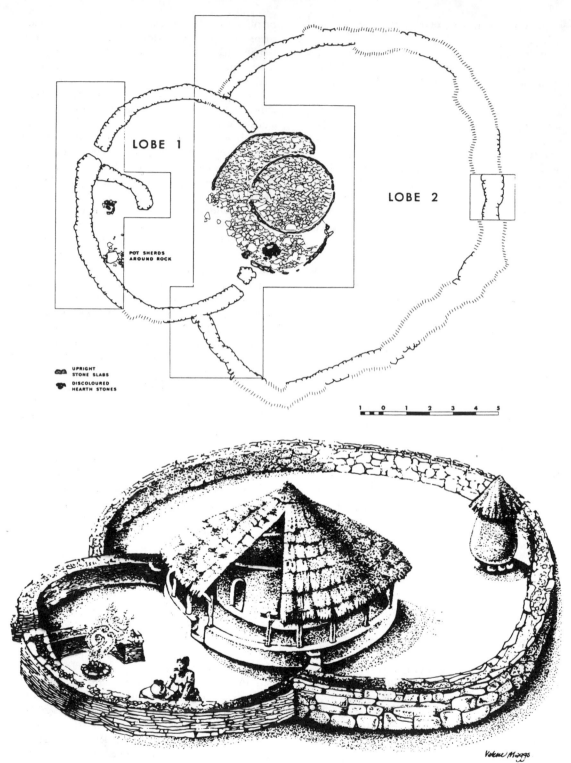

LOBE 1

LOBE 2

POT SHERDS
AROUND ROCK

UPRIGHT
STONE SLABS

DISCOLOURED
HEARTH STONES

1 0 1 2 3 4 5

An artist's reconstruction of a typical 'bilobial
dwelling' at the Type Z site of Matloang, on the
southern highveld (from Maggs 1976a).

54

Agro-pastoralist communities of the south-eastern grasslands

In common with the vast plains of the highveld, the watersheds to the south-east of the Drakensberg seem to have been grasslands throughout the Holocene, and remained unoccupied by farmers during the first millennium. Similarly, numerous stone ruins of varied architectural style attest to a richness of occupation that has only recently been appreciated, and is still imperfectly understood. One area – the Babanango plateau – serves to illustrate second-millennium farming settlement in this region.

The Babanango plateau stands between the valley and tributaries of the White Mfolozi River to the north and the complex Thukela drainage system to the south. As on the highveld, extensive dolerite sills have capped the Karoo-series sedimentary rocks, in this case protecting the softer formations from weathering, and forming flat-topped spurs and gently undulating uplands that stand above the deep river valleys on either side (King 1982). Although the climate of the plateau is markedly seasonal, its elevated location beneath the Drakensberg ensures, in most years, good summer rains and generally cooler temperatures than the valleys and coastlands (De Jager and Schulze 1977).

As on the southern highveld, the open environment coupled with the practice of building in stone provides an excellent opportunity for the archaeologist to scan a large area using standard air photographs. In almost 900 square kilometres more than 800 stone structures were plotted and classified in a simple scheme based on their shape (Hall 1981). Many of the sites were of the ubiquitous designs common to both past and present, but one distinctive architectural tradition could be easily picked out from the air. Following the same system of naming that Tim Maggs has used for the highveld, this group was called 'Type B' (for Babanango).

The design of Type B sites is in many respects similar to the Type V sites known from the highveld. Stone primary enclosures are arranged in a roughly circular plan and linked by secondary walls to form a secondary enclosure. But the entrances to these Babanango enclosures are distinctive: carefully cobbled passages that are invariably placed to lead up the slope of the hill, however gentle this may be, or whatever special architectural arrangements are necessary to achieve this result. In addition, there is no evidence for the corbelled stone houses that are so characteristic of

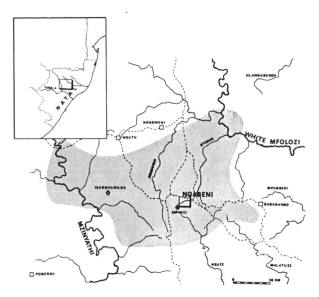

The distribution of Type B sites across the Babanango plateau (from Hall and Maggs 1979).

the highveld, although some of the Babanango enclosures do seem to have remnants of paved stone platforms that might have been foundations.

So far, excavations have been carried out at only one Type B site, and little is known about the lifeways of its occupants. This settlement, known today as Nqabeni, was built to overlook the headwaters of the Ntinini River, which in its turn runs into the White Mfolozi. Six primary enclosures

Detail of the entrance into the secondary enclosure at Nqabeni. The carefully laid dolerite stones (lightly shaded in the plan) line the entrance through the perimeter wall and fan out into the secondary enclosure. This architectural feature is typical of Type B sites. (From Hall and Maggs 1979.)

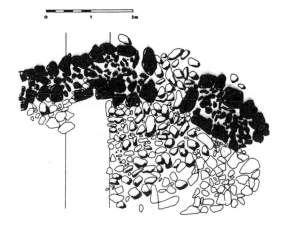

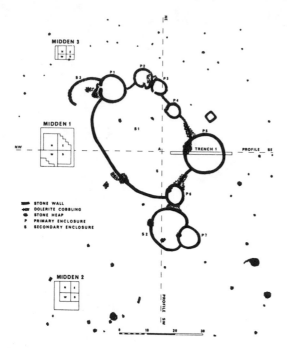

Plan of Nqabeni. Although there are some broad similarities with stone-built settlements on the southern highveld, there are important differences in architectural detail. Entrances were built to face up the slope (at the bottom of the illustration) and were carefully cobbled with rounded dolerite stones. No trace was found of houses: the numerous stone heaps shown on the plan are probably the result of clearing the site for cultivation once it had been abandoned. (After Hall and Maggs 1979.)

ments of metal showed that iron tools had been used, although there was no evidence for actual iron-working on the site. Bones from the middens reveal that both cattle and sheep and goats were kept, although the size of the sample is far too small to build up any accurate picture of the relative importance of the different species. Carbonised seeds indicated that sorghum, cow peas (*Vigna unguiculata*) and maize (*Zea mays*) were among the crops grown near the village. The presence of this last crop, which seems only to have been introduced in Africa in the last few centuries, coupled with the late radiocarbon date, suggests that people were living at Nqabeni in the eighteenth century (Hall and Maggs 1979).

But perhaps more revealing of the nature of farming settlement on the Babanango plateau is the arrangement of Type B settlements relative to one another. For this, the regional scale is too coarse, and it is better to focus in detail on one smaller area. The Upper Ntinini valley, in which lie Nqabeni and almost one hundred other sites, many of them belonging to Type B, is typical of the headwater basins that together create the rolling topography of the Babanango plateau. Once stone ruins had been plotted from the air photographs, the Ntinini valley was carefully searched on foot and all the architectural features of the Type B sites were drawn. With this quality of information, it is reasonably certain that at least the foundations of all surviving ruins are known (Hall 1981).

The map of Type B sites in the Ntinini valley shows immediately that settlements were not

Clusters of contemporary Type B settlements in the upper valley of the Ntinini River. Boundaries are hypothetical reconstructions – the most logical use of the landscape.

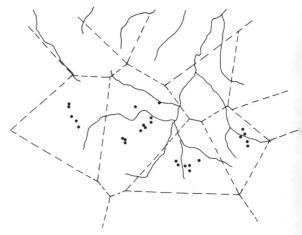

were linked to form the major secondary enclosure, while an additional primary and secondary enclosure was later added to the south-western edge of the settlement. An exploratory trench through the largest primary enclosure served to expose the foundation stones and to demonstrate, as in the case of the highveld, that there was no evidence that the occupants lived within the stone walls. This, coupled with the lowering of the ground level within the primary enclosures that resulted from the removal of livestock dung for fuel, again suggests that the Type B sites were built to house livestock rather than people (Hall and Maggs 1979).

Remnants of several former rubbish heaps lay within fifty metres of the Nqabeni walls, and these provided further clues to the nature of the settlement. A broken blade and a couple of other frag-

evenly distributed, for they were built in loose groups, mostly around the margins of the valley. These groups become far more clearly defined after a simple exercise in relative dating. The builders of stone enclosures on the Babanango plateau followed the same sensible practice as their counterparts on the southern highveld, for instead of laboriously choosing suitable building stones and carrying them to the site from stream beds or dolerite outcrops, stones were taken from nearby settlements that had been abandoned. As a result, the archaeologist can assume that the older walls are those that have been stripped down to their foundations, while the last-occupied sites are those that still seem largely intact. When the Ntinini Type B sites are sorted in this way, there is a strong case for arguing that there were four contemporary clusters of sites in the valley, probably dating to the eighteenth century (Hall 1981).

Although these clusters are far smaller than the large towns of the highveld, they do suggest a pattern of social and economic interaction beyond the level of the individual homestead. This in turn suggests that Basil Sansom's (1974) characterisation of the south-eastern settlement pattern as one of dispersed homesteads is too much of a simplification and that, rather than reading the present-day 'Zulu' architectural style back into the past, the archaeologist must acknowledge considerable evidence for change (Hall 1984d).

By making further assumptions, some tentative idea of economic conditions in the Ntinini valley in the eighteenth century is possible. Firstly, and on the basis of the opinions of local herdsmen, estimates of the numbers of animals penned in the primary enclosures in each cluster of sites have been made. These range between just over 100 and just under 300 mature animals. Secondly, a simple technique borrowed from geography has been used to work out how much grazing land may have been available to each settlement cluster. When these two sets of information are brought together, it is clear that the eighteenth-century farmers in the Ntinini valley could not have kept all their livestock close to their homes, and must have moved at least parts of their herds down into the major river valleys in the winter months. Even with such transhumance, it is probable that carrying capacities had been exceeded and grazing quality was deteriorating (Hall 1981).

As with the southern highveld, a correlation between archaeological evidence and oral tradition has been attempted for the Babanango plateau and adjacent areas, although in a different way. Here,

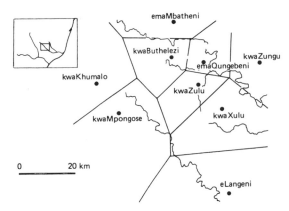

The capitals of eighteenth-century chiefdoms in the Mfolozi valley and across the Babanango plateau. Boundaries have been reconstructed by assuming the most logical use of the landscape. (Figure by Daniel Maggs.)

an early compilation of oral traditions (Bryant 1929) has been used to locate the capitals of chiefdoms at the end of the eighteenth century. Again using the methods of locational geography, the probable area of influence of each chiefdom has been worked out, and the boundaries deduced in this manner have been checked against recorded traditions of significant landmarks and territorial disputes. The results of this exercise suggest that the eastern boundary of the Type B sites correlates with the probable border between the eighteenth-century chiefdoms of kwaKhumalo and kwaButhelezi (Hall and Mack 1983).

The distribution of Type-B settlements recorded against the reconstructed 18th-century boundary between the kwaKhumalo and kwaButhelezi chiefdoms. Environmental factors cannot explain the coincidence, as both chiefdoms occupied the undulating Babanango plateau. More likely, different styles of domestic architecture were used to signify the political distinctions between the chiefdoms. (From Hall and Mack 1983.)

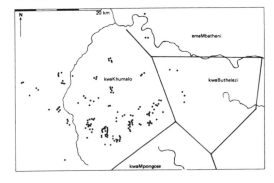

Khoikhoi: herders of the western lands

Although the people who lived on the highveld and the grassland watersheds of the south-east depended heavily on their domestic livestock they also grew crops: sorghum and, increasingly, maize, after its introduction by the Portuguese in the sixteenth or seventeenth centuries. Furthermore, although livestock were vital in the social and political networks that bound society together (Kuper 1982a; Hall 1985b), it is probable that the harvest provided most of the food consumed (Puzo 1978). Consequently, although the highveld farmers probably moved to outlying cattle posts to take advantage of seasonal grazing (Sansom 1974) and, as already argued in this chapter, the people who lived on watersheds such as the Babanango plateau moved down into the valleys in the winter months, the perennial tasks of agriculture kept the population tied to one area for some time.

But in the western lands it was not possible to cultivate crop plants such as sorghum and maize, either because annual rainfall was too low and unpredictable or because the rains came in the winter months, preventing propagation of the African cereal crops (Maggs 1980a). These areas came to be used by nomadic pastoralists – descendants of the Tshu-khwe-speaking people whose diffusion into southern Africa was traced in the last chapter, and who used their domesticated resources rather differently to the mixed farmers who lived to their east.

Although bones of domestic sheep, as well as pottery, which many archaeologists consider to be a sure indicator of pastoralism, have now been found in many dated contexts in western and south-western southern Africa (Deacon *et al.* 1978), the remains of actual settlements have been frustratingly difficult to find (Robertshaw 1978b). The sheep whose bones have been found in rock shelter deposits could often have been the remains of hunters' kills, although excavation of Boomplaas Cave, in the foothills of the southern Cape Swartberg, has shown accumulations of dung dated to about A.D. 250, suggesting that livestock were kept in the shelter when grazing in the nearby valley was optimal (Deacon *et al.* 1978).

Andrew Smith has pointed out that the itinerant character of nomadic pastoralism, with shepherds moving frequently in search of pasture and rarely returning to the same place, would militate against the accumulation of substantial archaeological deposits (Smith 1984c). But in some areas there were

specific resources which repeatedly attracted groups back to the same area, resulting in more substantial debris for the archaeologist to study.

One such area was the south-western coastland of St Helena Bay. Here, from the second century A.D., herders camped many times near the distinctive rock outcrop of Kasteelberg, collecting shellfish while their sheep and cattle grazed nearby (Smith 1983, 1985). Another was far to the northeast, where herders built distinctive stone settlements on the lower reaches of the Riet River, a source of perennial water, between the sixteenth and nineteenth centuries (Maggs 1971, 1976a; Humphreys 1973). Other than these few settlements, the archaeological evidence for nomadic pastoralism is indirect: the changing settlement patterns of gatherer-hunters, perhaps reflecting their response to immigrant herders, and the efflorescence of rock painting in the mountains which, it has been suggested, may have been related to the social stress that gatherer-hunters underwent in adjusting to the changes that followed the introduction of food-producing into their world (Manhire 1984; Manhire *et al.* 1984; Parkington 1984; Smith 1985).

Fortunately, historical sources are richer than the archaeological evidence. Indeed, from the late fifteenth century, voyagers from Europe began to make landings on the western and southern Cape coasts, recording some details of their encounters with pastoralist communities, whom they called by the now-abusive name 'Hottentots', but who called themselves Kwekwena or *Khoikhoi*, according to dialect (Elphick 1985).

Although earlier writers described the Khoikhoi in the same terms that they would employ for the agro-pastoralist societies who lived in the east and south-east, observing towns, tribes and kings, Richard Elphick has pointed out that, in reality, political and social affiliations were more fluid than these terms imply (Elphick 1985). Thus the 'village' was mobile and unstable in composition, and was based on the kinship relations between its members rather than on any ownership of territory. Similarly, the larger groups were in a state of 'endemic flux', with 'tribes' splitting and reforming as affiliations changed.

Despite the distinctive way of life of these western nomadic pastoralists, it would be a mistake to see the Khoikhoi and their predecessors over almost two thousand years as completely separated from either the gatherer-hunters with whom they shared the western lands or the agro-pastoralists who made their living to the east. Recent compara-

Kasteelberg. Early south-western Cape pastoralists built camps in the shelter of the rocky outcrop. (Photograph by courtesy of Andy Smith.)

Khoikhoin at the Cape (from Dapper 1668).

tive studies of nomadic pastoralists in many different parts of the world have shown that all such communities depend on at least occasional interactions with people practising different economies in order to obtain essential commodities (Monod 1975; Assad 1979; Goldschmidt 1979).

In Chapter 4 it was pointed out that, rather than a straightforward migration with the abrupt replacement of one way of life by another, the expanding frontier of food production represented a zone of interaction, in which gatherer-hunters were to develop a variety of economic interactions with pastoralists. As Monod (1975) has pointed out such relationships, whether based on subservience or clientage, could have provided the economic breadth necessary for pastoralism. But Elphick (1985) and Carmel Schrire (1980) have also argued that there was additional economic flexibility, as herders were able to turn to gathering-hunting, and gatherer-hunters could obtain livestock, according to changing fortune. 'Bushmen [gatherer-hunters] sometimes kept stock, and sometimes lost it, their subsistence depending on changing historical and environmental circumstances. They acted in a way that underscores the plasticity and opportunism of their socioeconomic behaviour . . . .' (Schrire 1980: 10) Smith, on the other hand, has argued that such fluidity would be improbable, as herding demands a different attitude to resources, planning for the future in a way that is not necessary for gatherer-hunters (Smith 1983).

Whatever the nature of the relationship between herders and gatherer-hunters, there is evidence for long-distance connections between nomadic pastoralists and sedentary agro-pastoralists to the east. In this regard there are historical records of Khoikhoi trading cattle in return for dagga (a narcotic similar to hemp), iron and copper goods along trade routes that extended both eastwards and northwards, tracing back the routes of initial pastoralist dispersal (Elphick 1985). These contacts are reflected in the archaeological record as well, with a copper bead and bone that may have been cut with an iron blade found in the dung floors at Boomplaas Cave (Deacon *et al.* 1978) and fragments of copper artefacts from graves and enclosures once used by pastoralists on the Riet River (Maggs 1971; Humphreys and Maggs 1970). Such connections are common in other pastoralist societies, and were probably essential if herders were to obtain important commodities (Monod 1975).

Thus in the interactions between nomadic pas-

toralists and sedentary agro-pastoralists in southern Africa, sustained it would seem for almost two thousand years, evidence can be found for Alexander's 'static frontier', across which long-term and mutually advantageous relationships developed (Alexander 1984). Rather than being separate, the highveld farmers and the nomadic pastoralists grazing their herds far to the west must be seen as part of a single, interlocked system of food-producing – a 'division of labour' more than two distinct societies (Assad 1979) and a relationship perhaps similar to that which developed in the Sahel after 500 B.C., when nomadic copper-using pastoralists traded with settled Tigidit villagers (Grebenart 1983).

6

The nature of society

Nature and society

In earlier chapters, the origins and dispersal of pastoralism and agro-pastoralism have been seen within the environments of Africa: the forests, woodlands and grasslands that provided opportunities for farmers and herders to establish new ways of life south of the Zambezi River. It has been suggested that there was a constant interplay between communities and their ecosystems which led to environmental changes as trees were felled to provide plots for cultivation and as grasslands were established in which livestock could graze. Through the centuries, farmers gradually succeeded in ensuring a more stable livelihood, moving from cereal cultivation supplemented by shellfish-collecting to the keeping of small stock and then increasingly to a reliance on cattle – an economic development which opened large new areas of the subcontinent to farming settlement.

It is clear that this relationship between farmer and environment was not one in which the structure of the landscape and the distribution and nature of resources preordained human behaviour – the 'environmental determinism' that has been much criticised in disciplines such as archaeology. Although the ecology of the subcontinent defined the possibilities open to farmers at any particular time, their ability to modify their surroundings and change the character of their economy was constantly changing the ecological parameters. Throughout their history, farmers in southern Africa have had a dynamic, mutually interactive relationship with their environment.

But it is also clear that not all behaviour can be understood in such ecological terms. The fact that environmental relationships are often relatively easy to deduce from settlement patterns or the results of archaeological excavation can disguise the truth that communities also interact with other communities. This web of social relationships binds people together and influences considerably their response in any situation.

Uncovering the nature of these social relations, where there are no documentary records, is a considerable challenge, largely because the evidence is either intangible (for example, a kinship connection) or not amenable to interpretation by 'common sense' (for example, an artefact used in a now-

The interpretation of rock art

The interpretation of rock art has been one of the most contentious areas in recent southern African prehistoric studies. David Lewis-Williams (1984a) has distinguished two schools of thought, each with differing philosophical and methodological approaches to the art. The first starts from the premise that the art 'speaks for itself', and assumes that most paintings were the product and embodiment of an aesthetic sense and depict everyday activities or historical and mythical events. The second approach contends that analysis must start with theory, and holds that the art should be seen in the context of San beliefs. This approach has led to the argument that the art was closely associated with the trance experiences of medicine men, central in San society.

The implications of these conflicting viewpoints are well illustrated by different readings of the same paintings – such as the well-known Bamboo Hollow scene at Giant's Castle in the Natal Drakensberg. Those who prefer a simple narrative explanation see this painting as the depiction of an everyday hunting expedition (Willcox 1956). Men holding spears are grouped around an animal, probably a cow. One man (2) has been knocked over by the quarry and lies prone on the ground.

Scene from Bamboo Hollow, Giant's Castle, in the Natal Drakensberg (from Lewis-Williams 1983).

Many other points of detail remain unexplained, but can probably be attributed to the personal whims of the artist.

Lewis-Williams (1983) reads this scene very differently. He interprets the panel as an attempt to control rain by leading a mythical animal over the parched landscape – a San belief recorded ethnographically. In this view, the 'trance-buck' to the upper right (1) represents a medicine man in trance, with arms in characteristic thrown-back position with a typically bent posture. The prone figure (2) is a man in trance, the lines depicting his spirit leaving his body. The figure above the rain animal (3) has his hand to his nose in depiction of 'snoring', which the San believed to be associated with the curing of sickness. The line of small crosses above the rain animal's back (4) are bees – a further manifestation of the trance experience. The panel as a whole is a complex depiction of the San's central religious experience.

unknown ritual). Such 'social archaeology' also demands an uneasy alliance with ethnography. On the one hand many would argue that past behaviour can only be understood by reference to the present. But on the other hand, reading the present into an imperfectly preserved past may deny the possibility of discovering change (Hall 1984a, 1984b).

Despite these problems, social archaeology is of considerable importance, for it represents an attempt to gain a far more rounded interpretation of the past. The platform for such an approach in southern Africa is David Lewis-Williams's analysis of gatherer-hunter rock art. Lewis-Williams has rejected earlier approaches, which have sought only to describe the paintings, or have interpreted them as 'art for the sake of art'. Instead, he has searched for the meaning of these complex and intricately executed panels within the historical

Hallucinatory forms in San rock art. A: a human figure with hoofs and eland head from the north-eastern Cape. B: an elephant surrounded by a sinuous line from the south-western Cape. C: an abstract hallucinatory image from the south-western Cape. D: a human figure with lines from its head which probably represent a departing spirit and a superimposed white figure figure. (From Lewis-Williams 1984b.)

ethnography of the southern San, concluding that the art was a part of the process of trance, central to gatherer-hunter social relations in southern Africa (Lewis-Williams 1980, 1981, 1984a).

Lewis-Williams's approach has been closely paralleled in recent research by Tom Huffman, who has argued that agro-pastoralist settlement arrangement formed part of the social relations between village residents, and therefore represents a 'cognitive system' which can be read from archaeological debris (Huffman 1982). More recently, both Lewis-Williams (1985) and Huffman (1985a) have argued that rock art and settlement design were part of the 'ideology' of gatherer-hunter and farmer society, and therefore inform on the nature of social relations between people.

The task in this chapter is to follow the initiative of Lewis-Williams's and Huffman's work and to widen consideration of southern African communities beyond the nature of their relationships with their environments.

Chiefdom, mode and power

One of the first tasks in providing a social dimension to early herder and agro-pastoralist communities in southern Africa is to find conceptual devices suited to the analysis of their economic and political organisation. One such idea is the *chiefdom* – a stage in political and social evolution which lies between the gatherer-hunter band and the more complex 'state', and which is defined by Robert Carneiro as 'an autonomous political unit comprising a number of villages or communities under the permanent control of a paramount chief' (Carneiro 1982: 45).

Carneiro recognises several different scales of chiefdom, ranging from the minimal unit, in which a few villages may be grouped around the residence of a dominant individual, to a far more evolved form with considerable contrast between the wealth and status of chiefs and of commoners. Thus the concept is sufficiently broad to encompass both the small, scattered communities settled in the woodlands during the early centuries of the first millennium and the clusters of stone-built settlements on the Babanango plateau and the southern highveld, described in Chapter 5.

One of the characteristics of the chiefdom is a tension between the forces of centralisation, which allow individuals to build up political and economic power, and competition for authority by rivals. Thus through time, chiefdoms are constantly fragmenting and reforming as factions gain power, build up strength and subsequently lose control to other groups. Ronald Cohen (1978) has aptly termed this tendency 'fission', and has suggested that it is definitive of the chiefdom as a social form.

The societies described in the last chapter fit the concept of the chiefdom, and its inherent instability, well. On the Babanango plateau both kwaKhumalo and kwaButhelezi were, in the eighteenth centuries, examples of a large number of unstable political units that were constantly splitting and reforming with changed fortunes (Bryant 1929). Indeed, it could be argued that the wide dispersal of the Type B architectural style across the high-lying watershed above the Thukela River is a consequence of the abaKhumalo diaspora described in the oral traditions (Hall and Mack 1983).

On the southern highveld places such as Ntsuanatsatsi, Makwareng and Matloang were towns rather than villages: large concentrations of settlement in which members of separate family units must have acknowledged some more general authority simply to make daily life feasible. But the wide dispersal of Type V architecture strongly suggests Cohen's fission in action, as people moved away from established centres, putting an effective check on the amount of power that any single chief could gain. Indeed, Maggs's (1976b) study of historical sources suggests that expansion into the Caledon valley was still taking place in the nineteenth century.

Similarly, the historically known Khoikhoi of the western subcontinent clearly had a form of social organisation which can be seen as an example of the chiefdom. Each polity had leaders who inherited their power from their fathers. These chiefdoms were often ranked, with some owing allegiance to more powerful groups, often located a considerable distance away. But chiefs only held power by consent of their councils of leading followers, and authority was lost and gained in the active arena of political alignment and realignment (Elphick 1985).

But, valuable as the concept of the chiefdom is in pointing attention to political and economic organisation, the price of such a general idea, that can be used with ease throughout southern Africa or in other parts of the world, is a degree of imprecision. Recently, historians and anthropologists have begun to look for new ways of analysing the social history of societies such as those which have been described in preceding chapters.

One refinement is the idea of the 'mode of production' – a theoretical concept which juxtaposes the actual process of making a living – the 'forces of production' – with the way in which resources are distributed through society – the 'relations of production' (Hindess and Hirst 1975; Meillassoux 1972). The particular combination of these two

A seventeenth-century impression of Khoikhoin at the Cape, with exotic palm trees added to the background for enhanced effect. The seated figure is a chief, said to be holding a staff of office. (From the 1686 French edition of O. Dapper.)

facets of behaviour serves to characterise specific societies, both in the past and in the present.

When applied in the study of early southern African farming communities, the concept of the mode of production highlights some interesting distinctions which are not apparent from the archaeological evidence alone, and which tend to be obscured in the generalised model of the chiefdom.

Thus it is probable that, although there were some differences between the forces of production employed by pioneer woodland farmers and their gatherer-hunter contemporaries, the relations of production were in both cases much the same. In neither case was there much opportunity for the accumulation of wealth, and bands and villages were probably bound together by balanced relations of reciprocity (Sahlins 1972; Hall 1985b).

In contrast, the dominance of livestock in the forces of production employed by second-millennium highveld farmers would have allowed the accumulation of wealth and thus *unequal* reciprocity between villages. Historians have seen this as symptomatic of a 'lineage mode of production' in which elders – the senior members of lineages – control the distribution of livestock between villages, thereby holding economic power over their juniors (Hedges 1978; Bonner 1981; Hall 1985b). Such would include the Kwena and Kgatla lineages, which have been tentatively identified with the Type N architectural tradition; the Taung lineage and its Type V settlements; and the Tswana Rolong whom oral traditions link to the distinctive Type Z architecture of the north-western Orange Free State (Maggs 1976a, 1976b).

Although this approach to the past also has the value of alerting the archaeologist to that role of the wider society, not necessarily represented in the results of archaeological survey and excavation, in determining human behaviour, there are some difficulties with the concept of the mode of production. In particular, lineages often have little role in the political sense and are more a 'map' that enables an individual to identify his or her relatives than a specific group of people with whom power resides (Hammond-Tooke 1984; Kuper 1982b). In addition, searching for sequences of modes of production, or indeed assuming an evolutionary sequence from band to chiefdom to state, may give a false directionality to history (Giddens 1981; Hall 1985b).

An alternative to finding either chiefdoms or modes of production in southern Africa's past is to think of the occupants of villages and towns as exercising *power* over both their environment and the other communities they encountered in living out their lives (Giddens 1984; Miller and Tilley 1984). Through much of the first millennium the degree of power that people could exercise in the south-eastern woodland environments was limited. Men and women had to invest considerable labour in clearing trees and brush to make a living from agriculture, and there was little opportunity for accumulating wealth. But with the settlement of the grasslands and the expansion of herds and flocks some people could become wealthy, using their accumulated resources to ensure the fealty of others and build up followings of people.

But how did people with authority actually exercise their power? This question has been addressed by Anthony Giddens (1984), who has argued that the ability to bring about advantageous action is dependent on the control over both 'allocative resources' (goods and other material phenomena) and 'authoritative resources' (command of people and their actions). This is a useful distinction in considering the wider nature of early farming society in southern Africa.

Power and commodities

Many writers have assumed that the small villages of first-millennium farmers in the south-eastern subcontinent were economically self-sufficient – islands in a generally hostile environment, provided for by their own plots and fields and the technological skills of their occupants. To a large extent, this is probably true. Timber and thatch for building would have been available throughout the savanna lands, as would sources of clay for making pots. Excavation of many of these early villages has shown evidence for iron-working on a limited scale, suggesting that each village had people skilled in producing metal implements from the small quantities of low-grade ore that were available in many areas. Thus, in general, contacts with other communities were probably either sporadic, such as the interaction with gatherer-hunter groups proposed by Tim Maggs for the Thukela basin (see Chapter 4), or took place in times of hardship (a system of connections that will be discussed later in this chapter).

Nevertheless, there is evidence for early economic specialisation, suggesting that at least some communities were making part of their living by bartering with other villages. Although this is based on fieldwork in only one area, to the east of the Drakensberg, it is quite possible that more detailed research will reveal similar regional pat-

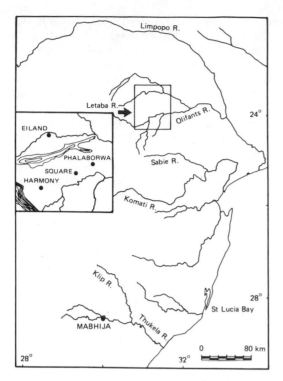

Sites with evidence for specialised economies. (Drawing by Tina Coombes.)

terns elsewhere in southern Africa.

The site of Eiland lies on the Mamazapi stream, a tributary of the Letaba River, and close to salt crusts that have formed as a result of seepage from nearby warm, saline springs. Low mounds of debris found at the site consist of layers of sand and ash, in which were large quantities of potsherds, fragments of stone bowls, some shells and animal bone. The earliest radiocarbon date for the site is late in the fourth century A.D., although people probably continued to visit through many centuries (Evers 1981).

A second site is on the banks of the Makhutswi River, a tributary of the Olifants, and has been called 'Harmony' by its excavator. Again, low mounds found here were made up of ash and sand layers, with broken stone bowls, animal bone and pottery, which suggest the site was used over many centuries (Evers 1979).

The association of both Harmony and Eiland with saline springs and deposits, added to the numerous stone bowls used, indicates that people were manufacturing salt. The process may have been similar to that described recently from the same area. Salt crust mixed with sand is filtered

through grass to produce a clean brine, which is then boiled down and formed into hardened cakes for easy transportation (Evers 1981). The soapstone bowls, which at Harmony were manufactured at the same site, were most likely used as evaporation pans (Evers 1979).

It is of course possible that salt cakes were made in this area only for local use. But on the other hand mineral springs offering the opportunity for salt manufacture are not evenly distributed through southern Africa, and in many areas salt must have been a scarce commodity. In addition, the harshly seasonal climate beneath the eastern escarpment is not best suited to subsistence agriculture, which suggests that a logical course of action for communities living there would be to redress inevitable scarcities in food supplies by setting up bartering with households in better-endowed areas.

For many villagers, availability of and control over allocative resources in the second millennium were probably much the same as they had been for

Salt and soapstone-bowl manufacture near Harmony in the eastern lowveld. Excavation of salt debris mounds has provided more detail of the technology. Some of the artefacts recovered are: (1) pottery spindlewhorl; (2) soapstone spindlewhorl; (3) soapstone 'strainer'; (4) fragment of bone spatula; and (5) bronze tube.

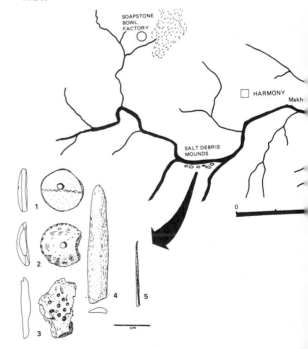

A recent mound of debris from salt-making near Sautini in the eastern Transvaal. (Photograph by Mike Evers.)

their ancestors during the earliest years of farming settlement. Many settlements in the savanna lands are similar in size to first-millennium villages and are located in similar environments, implying continuity in the way of life of their occupants (Hall 1981).

But for other communities – those who had been able to build up the sizes of their flocks and herds – opportunities for increased economic power were now greater. As was pointed out in Chapter 5, livestock could be accumulated, granting their owners an increased degree of protection from the vagaries of agricultural production. The importance of domestic animals is attested by the innumerable stone byres of the high grassland regions of southern Africa, by the place of livestock in the economies of communities that have been described ethnographically (Kuper 1982a), and, to the west, by the frequent raids that Khoikhoi carried out on their neighbours in order to increase their stock holdings (Elphick 1985). Apart from their social importance, which will be discussed later in this chapter, domestic animals provided hides for clothing, shields and shelter, bone for artefacts, and blood, milk and meat.

But settlement of the high southern African grasslands had additional economic implications, for it simultaneously made agro-pastoralists less independent in allocative resources and granted them an increased facility to barter for goods produced by specialists in other regions. For although the grasslands were rich in their potential for grazing, they lacked substantial deposits of iron ore and, what is more important, adequate supplies of timber for smelting (Maggs 1976a; Hall and Maggs 1979). Conversely livestock, with their high natural productivity and the ease with which they can be moved from area to area, provided an ideal resource for barter. Thus with the expansion of herding came structured economic specialisation and the development of trade networks.

One area where iron was produced on a substantial scale, presumably for barter into a wide hinterland, was likewise situated in the eastern lowveld. The modern town of Phalaborwa is the focus of industrial mining of copper and iron ore, and there is substantial archaeological evidence for a metalworking industry in the region dating back to the eighth century A.D. Deep shafts were cut into the volcanic hills, and copper ore was removed by cracking the rock with fire and working it with chisels and hammerstones. Iron ore was obtained from the magnetite pebbles readily available on the

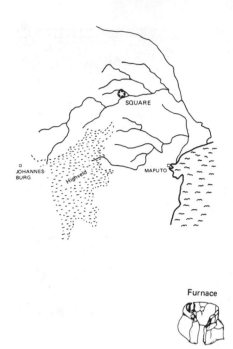

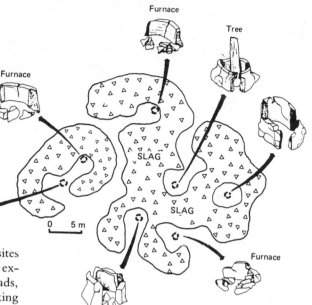

Square was a precolonial iron-working factory near Phalaborwa. The remains of clay furnace stacks, each with ports for tuyères, stand amidst the extensive slag heap. Iron could have been traded to the high grasslands of the highveld from sites such as these.

slopes of the hills. Several hundred smelting sites mark the places where copper and iron were extracted before being forged into wire, beads, bracelets, arrow and spear points, woodworking adzes and agricultural hoes (Van der Merwe and Scully 1971).

Interestingly, chemical analysis of slag – the main byproduct of the iron-smelting process – shows that iron ore was often moved some distance away from its source, perhaps to locations that were more convenient for obtaining wood to make charcoal. A detailed study of one smelting complex, about 25 kilometres to the south-east of Phalaborwa, has allowed some estimate of the input of labour and raw materials involved. In this case, a group of seven furnaces, each with thick clay walls and entrance slits, was surrounded by slag heaps of an estimated 180 tons. The equation which describes the process of reduction for magnetite indicates that this amount of slag would have been produced as waste to some 48 tons of iron, and that over 800 tons of charcoal, made from some 7 000 suitable trees, would have been required (Van der Merwe and Killick 1979).

The first villages in the Phalaborwa area were built on the flat land around the volcanic hills. Each comprised a dozen or so houses, and there is evidence for domestic animals and some wild species that were hunted. But it seems unlikely that agriculture was ever a prosperous process in this harsh landscape, 'a thoroughly unpleasant place to live'

(Van der Merwe and Scully 1971: 179). Nevertheless, oral traditions for the later centuries of settlement indicate that the local inhabitants were powerful and economically successful, and this must have been because they controlled the production of iron and copper goods essential to communities in other areas. Iron-working was probably a dry-season activity, given most attention when the crops had been harvested. Either people requiring iron implements came and worked for the smiths in payment, or else goods were exchanged in their finished form (Scully 1978).

A similar industrial centre, although not on such a substantial scale, flourished during the second millennium in the Mabhija area, some 20 kilometres down the Thukela River from the modern town of Colenso. Here there is evidence for the quarrying of iron ore on an extensive scale, as well as numerous smelting sites marked by scatters of slag and furnace fragments. Iron implements collected include chisel-like objects, a spear blade, and a fine awl (Maggs 1982).

Tim Maggs, who excavated some of the furnaces at Mabhija, has commented that this area would not have been particularly suited to herding

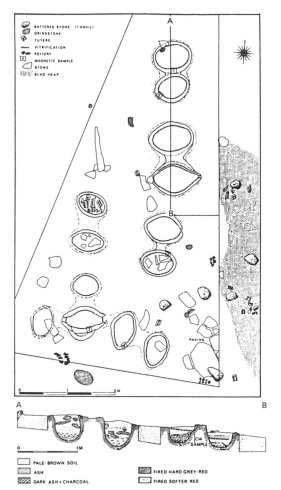

Plan of the main furnace group at Mabhija in the Thukela River basin, Natal. The furnaces were built to be operated in pairs, with the necessary temperature obtained by pumping air from bellows into the furnaces via clay tubes known as tuyères. The broken fragments of some of the tuyères were found in the furnace numbered 3 on the plan, while others had been abandoned on the rubbish heap to the east of the excavated area. Bottom: a section through two of the furnace pairs, following the line marked A–B on the plan. (From Maggs 1982.)

and crop cultivation, and certainly could not have supported a dense population. As with the Phalaborwa region, this deficiency in economic potential seems to have found compensation in the opportunity for barter. Indeed, Madaphu Gamede, an old man who knew the area and its traditions well, commented that iron articles were traded in return for sheep and sorghum, as well as for cattle and goats (Maggs 1982: 139). In this case

An old mine for iron-ore near Mabhija in the Thukela River valley. The mine probably supplied the smelters who worked nearby, and whose furnaces have been excavated by archaeologists from the Natal Museum. (Photograph by courtesy of Tim Maggs, Natal Museum.)

it is possible to work out the probable scope of the economic hinterland, for people who lived on the southern highveld had parallel traditions that told of exchanging cattle for iron goods with people in the Thukela basin (Maggs 1976a).

Power and people

Apart from control over salt, cattle, iron, timber and other commodities, power was exercised in southern African farming communities, as in societies in other parts of the world, through control over people: Giddens's (1984) 'authoritative resources'. Sets of mutual obligations provided security for ordinary farmers, offering the possibility of calling for support in the face of crop failure or stock loss. In addition, men or women from other communities were essential for the 'reproduction of society' (Meillassoux 1972) through marriage and the birth of children who would constitute the next generation to till the fields and herd the animals. For ambitious local leaders and chiefs, attracting larger followings through mar-

Symbols in action

Recent ethnographic studies have shown that material possessions do not simply mirror 'ethnic' identity but rather are active symbols which form part of the alliances and conflicts that shape societies. This has been well demonstrated by Ian Hodder, who carried out extensive fieldwork in the Baringo district of north-central Kenya (Hodder 1982).

Hodder's research was with three groups – the Turgen, Pokot and Njemps – which had clearly defined boundaries separating them one from the other. Each group was further identified by distinctive items of dress, particularly the ear decorations worn by the women. At this level, the Baringo ethnography conforms to traditional archaeological expectations that material 'culture' reflects socio-political entities.

But closer work showed that the situation was far more complex than this. Although group boundaries were unambiguous, individuals and families moved freely from one area to another, adopting the appropriate dress with the transition. Research showed that the dress code had a specific purpose, entitling the wearer to the protection of young male warriors – the *moran* – drawn from the appropriate group. Other material items had different specific associations and therefore did not have the same pattern of distribution. Thus spear decoration, for instance, was often similar on weapons used by *moran* from competing groups. Hodder has argued that spears are symbols of the tension between young warriors and the elders who control access to wives and cattle. Decorated calabashes, used by women to store milk, stress in their patterning associations by birth and marriage, and often specifically contradict boundaries marked by ear decoration, in what Hodder has termed a 'silent discourse'.

The implications of the Baringo study are that, although the style and decoration of material culture certainly have meaning, they cannot be read simply as reflections of 'culture', 'tribe' or 'ethnic group' without taking into account the specific contexts in which symbols are employed.

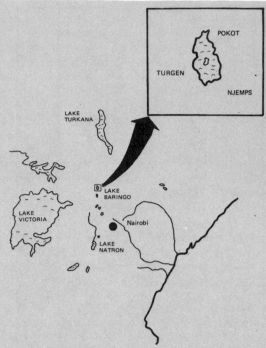

Lake Baringo and the distribution of the Pokot, Turgen and Njemps.

An Njemps woman wearing distinctive ear decoration. (Drawing by Tina Coombes, after Hodder 1982.)

riage, clientship or alliance provided opportunities for wealth and power beyond the immediate village.

At first sight, the exercise of power in this form would seem to lie beyond the archaeological gaze: such a category of relationships would appear to leave little in the ground. But recently, Ian Hodder and other ethno-archaeologists have shown how material culture is often vital in 'making real', or *signifying*, such connections. Writing of material culture, Hodder has pointed out that 'unlike much action and speech it has duration. It lasts, and so in a very direct way it channels and organizes perception and behaviour. . . . It is through material culture and its spatial organization in homes that individuals come to grasp meanings and relations in society. Material culture is itself, then, an important force in the regeneration of ideology and power. It has inherent properties which can lead to the naturalization of power relations and authority.' (Hodder 1984: 352)

What evidence is there that the earliest farmers employed such a system of material signification? In answering this question, a point of departure is provided by a consideration of gatherer-hunter society, both in the present and in the past. In her study of reciprocity in Kalahari !Kung San communities, Polly Wiessner (1982) points out that no San camp can be sure of adequate resources and that reciprocity between individuals is essential. Such alliances, known as *hxaro*, are signified by the delayed exchange of gifts. Within the camp, such relationships smooth income differences; between neighbouring camps they allow frequent visits and sharing, and between distant camps they allow sustained visits. '*Hxaro* paths wind through both camps and cores of these close relatives, thereby making them into nodes in the *hxaro* network, and travel through many camps over hundreds of kilometres' (Wiessner 1982: 70).

Similarly, and of more significance in understanding the southern African archaeological record, trance, rock art and the symbolic labour of San medicine men can also be interpreted in terms of power and resources. This connection has been recognised by David Lewis-Williams, who has identified the crucial role of the medicine man in the social process. 'Consumption is as important as production, and the San rules of distribution complement the exploitation of resources. Every man hunted, but the chance nature of hunting meant that not everyone was equally successful; the inequalities of production were counterbalanced by the sharing practices. The curer was therefore not merely healing the bodies of sick individuals or reducing private animosities; he was also keeping the social relations within the production process in good order and ensuring the essential distribution of the comparatively scarce resource of meat.' (Lewis-Williams 1982: 433)

Thus, through the trance dance, the medicine man performed 'symbolic labour' (Godelier 1975), which represented in mimetic form general co-operation within the camp. In addition, the medicine man's facility of 'out-of-body travel' when in trance established the rights in reciprocity between camps, which were essential to survival. Rock paintings, and in particular the meaning carried by key symbols, 'held in perpetuity what was otherwise an intermittent activity' (Lewis-Williams 1982: 438).

This reinterpretation of the *hxaro* network, and of the purpose of southern African rock art, suggests a new understanding of ceramic decoration, which, it was shown in earlier chapters, has yet to be satisfactorily explained. For, seen as carriers of symbols that signify power over people, ceramics have the potential to be particularly informative about connections between early households in southern Africa.

Such a role is evident in ethnographic studies carried out elsewhere in Africa. It is clear that, in many contexts, the manufacture of pottery is a 'symbolic process' (Thornton 1982) which is loaded with meaning beyond the functional act of creating a fired clay container. Similarly, the decoration of the pot is often not just a matter of applying design in the light of tradition (Welbourn 1984).

Archaeological evidence from first-millennium farming villages in southern Africa suggests an equivalent role for pottery in the past. The 'span' of similarly decorated ceramics (from 50 B.C. to A.D. 900 and from the Mozambican coast to western Transkei) is quite incompatible with any 'ethnic' or 'tribal' model of shared social system but it is consistent with a wide-ranging network of shared obligations similar in form to the *hxaro* of the Kalahari. By exchanging cereal products in vessels similarly decorated with potent symbols, householders would simultaneously signify and reaffirm their mutual connectedness. The conservativeness of the decorative codes – an accumulation of 'symbolic capital' in Bourdieu's (1977) term – reflects the high price of innovation. Faced with the daily uncertainty of agriculture in the southern African savannas it was vitally important that reciprocal obligations should be recognised unambiguously. Such a system of signification through ceramic design would be precisely analogous to, and to a large degree contemporary with, the system of signification through rock art.

Such a widespread system of material culture signification would only persist, of course, for as long as it served a useful purpose. This would be until such time as households began to build larger herds of cattle, thus becoming less dependent on a wide network of reciprocal obligations. This is indeed apparent in the archaeological record for, in A.D. 600, when swidden clearance could not have had a profound impact, ceramic decorative motifs were common across a wide area, indicating the need for a generally acknowledged system of signification. But by A.D. 900 localised variants in ceramic decoration are apparent in areas such as the eastern Transvaal (Evers 1981) and the Thukela basin (Maggs and Michael 1976), suggesting a degree of power accumulation and a need for distancing from the generalised system of signification to emphasise a new order of obligations. It is not surprising to find that such localised ceramic styles are accompanied by evidence for the greater importance of cattle (Maggs and Michael 1976).

It would be logical to expect that, once farmers in different parts of southern Africa had built up their herds of livestock, animals rather than ceramics would come to be used as the principal mode of signifying relationships between communities and power over people. Both ethnographic and archaeological evidence makes it abundantly clear that this was the case.

Adam Kuper has brought together a wide variety of sources to show how cattle in southern Africa are used in a system of hierarchical transactions 'in which ancestors, rulers and men enrich and fertilize their descendants, subjects and wives' (Kuper 1982a: 21). Of central importance are bridewealth payments which, Kuper reminds us, must not be seen as a consequence of cattle holding, but a system of transactions in which cattle are the signifier. 'Each bridewealth payment consequently formed part of a chain of transactions, not only between the immediate "wife-givers" and "wife-takers" (however they might be defined) but between debtors and creditors, related in a great many possible ways. . . . The system rested on a simple and ineluctable principle of reciprocity. Cattle were exchanged for wives, wives for cattle. This rule applied not only as between a man and his wife's family, but at every step between those who contributed to bridewealth payments, and those who exchanged bridewealth for wives.' (Kuper 1982a: 27,39)

Similarly, livestock were of central importance in the transactions in Khoikhoi society that bound people together in networks of mutual obligation. 'Cattle and sheep played an extremely important role in Khoikhoi society and, by extension, in Khoikhoi history. Possession of livestock was the main criterion by which Khoikhoi were distinguished from hunters, and rich Khoikhoi tribes from poor. Within each tribe, livestock was important in almost every realm of life: the eco-

nomic, aesthetic, political, and social.' (Elphick 1985: 57)

Unfortunately, there is insufficient historical or ethnographic evidence to determine to what extent the centrality of livestock as a Khoikhoi authoritative resource would have been evidenced in material culture. But Kuper has asked this question of the ethnography of agro-pastoralism in the east, with significant results. He has found that, despite apparent variability in the arrangement of houses and byres within villages, there is an underlying regularity which can be seen as a set of 'oppositions' in architectural arrangement. Thus the distinction between the right and the left side of the settlement symbolises the seniority of wives within the extended family, while kinsfolk and wives are ordered by the placement of their houses relative to the centre and sides of the village (Kuper 1980). In other words, the plan of a settlement is not simply a pragmatic or random arrangement of architectural features, but is rather a map of the relative status and interrelationships of members of the community.

Huffman has taken Kuper's insight further, arguing that archaeological site plans can be 'read' for indications of social relations. Huffman has called the cognitive system identified by Kuper the 'Southern Bantu Cattle Pattern' and has suggested that the minimum features required from the archaeological record to indicate the existence of the same set of social relations in the past are a central livestock byre with burials beneath it and houses arranged around the periphery – features known archaeologically from as early as the seventh century in the eastern Transvaal (Huffman 1982, 1986a). Although the concept of the Southern Bantu Cattle Pattern can be criticised, principally because of its ahistoric character (Hall 1986), Huffman has directed attention firmly to the problem of seeing livestock in southern Africa as authoritative, as well as allocative, resources.

Early southern African society

Thus although many problems of method and theory still remain, the results of recent research do give some indication of the nature of early farming society in southern Africa.

As with the ecological dimension which was explored in earlier chapters, the major contrast is between earlier farmers, with few livestock, and their successors, who had substantial holdings of domestic animals. Although economies in the earlier centuries of the first millennium were struc-

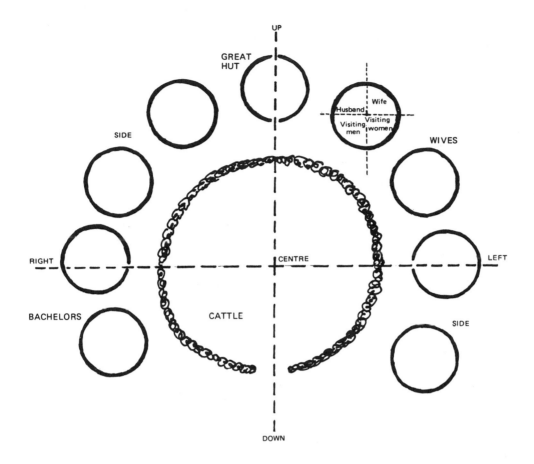

UP

GREAT
HUT

Wife

Husband

Visiting
men

Visiting
women

WIVES

SIDE

RIGHT

CENTRE

LEFT

BACHELORS

CATTLE

SIDE

DOWN

tured, by and large, for self-sufficiency, the uncertainty of farming necessitated wide-ranging networks of reciprocal obligation, probably signified by shared codes of ceramic decoration. Thus the normal expectation was probably of economic and social interaction within the village, while unpredicted exigencies were met by calling on wider-ranging connections.

But the acquisition by farmers of livestock on a substantial scale transformed these patterns of social relations. Although the village undoubtedly remained a basic production unit, herding allowed some people to gain power over others, thus widening the network of interaction to a regional rather than a domestic scale. At the same time settlement of the high grasslands made economic self-sufficiency impossible for many communities, and specialist groups, particularly of iron-workers, made much of their living by barter and trade beyond the local community. Not surprisingly, livestock gained considerable social significance and came to signify a large set of political and economic interactions.

The 'Bantu Cattle Pattern'. Adam Kuper (1980, 1982a) has argued that the architecture of farming settlements in southern Africa has symbolic dimensions, with oppositions such as left/right, up/down, and centre/side having social correlates, such as male/female, high status/low status, and cattle/wives. This interpretation has been extended to serve as a key to the interpretation of archaeological sites.

Toutswe, Mapungubwe and the East coast trade

The concept of the state

A common feature of Khoikhoi society and agro-pastoralist communities in the east and south-east of southern Africa was the limit to the power that any individual or group could gain. Although some settlements were more important than others – the camps of Khoikhoi leaders, larger settlements on the highveld grasslands, or the seats of Buthelezi and Khumalo chiefs, for instance – their status was fragile, for they and their occupants were always liable to be deposed in the constant flux of power.

But although such chiefdoms were often encountered during the early years of colonial penetration of southern Africa, this had not been the invariable social form in the subcontinent, as early ethnohistorians often assumed. Beginning before the twelfth century, close to the Limpopo River, there arose a series of polities in which power *was* retained, sometimes for several centuries, by lines of rulers living in major centres. Often the power of these important figures, who can be called kings, was given emphasis by rich, exotic possessions, by a large entourage of followers, or by impressive buildings – the first cities of southern Africa.

The ability of early kings to prevent fission, thus holding together their power-base, indicates a new political and economic order. This has by convention been called the *state*, although there is wide disagreement as to how and why the state developed. Some writers have argued that centralised control emerged by consensus of rulers and ruled – a 'social contract' originating in some need for strong government (Service 1980). Others have seen state origins in conflict rather than co-operation – a repressive mechanism which serves the interests of the ruling group (Fried 1967). Alternatively, it has been suggested that the state, as defined in other parts of the world, simply did not exist in Africa (Skalnik 1983).

As with the chiefdom, discussed in Chapter 6, the concept of the state is rather too broad to be of precise analytical value. Again, more precision is possible by regarding a particular society as the milieu for a mode of production, in which the manner whereby people make a living (the forces of production) is meshed with the social mechanisms by which goods are distributed through the society (the relations of production).

From this perspective it is clear that what is termed the state is a circumstance in which a proportion of the wealth of a society is systematically directed to, and retained by, a ruling group. Some historians in southern Africa have termed this a 'tributary mode of production' (Bonner 1981; Hedges 1978; Slater 1976) – an analytical device which has been profitably used in other parts of the world. Thus Eric Wolf, writing of Europe in 1400, found that the major agricultural areas of the continent 'were held by states based on the extraction of surpluses from the primary producers by political or military rulers. These states represent a mode of production in which the primary producer, whether cultivator or herdsman, is allowed access to the means of production, while tribute is exacted from him by political or military means.' (Wolf 1982: 79-80)

In what way was the position of kings and their followers different from that of chiefs, their families and associates? The essential point is the degree of permanence in the location of power. Although chiefship was often hereditary – as, for instance, with both the Khoikhoi (Elphick 1985) and the Buthelezi and Khumalo (Bryant 1929) – chiefs were essentially 'leaders among equals', ordinary men who usually kept herds and grew crops in the manner of those subordinate to them and who, if deposed, would revert to the status of their contemporaries.

In contrast, those at the apex of power in a society organised by the principles of the tributary mode of production constituted a distinct economic and political class. The very duration of their dominance must have led them to see their high status as permanent. In addition the ruling class in the tributary mode of production must control an effective means of coercion, whether ideological or military, in order to prevent the constant tendency towards fission that was such an effective constraint on the power of a chief.

In exploring the relations of production in a tributary mode of production and in piecing together the way in which a particular state was constituted, the historian again has the advantage of documentary sources which may reveal the structures of power, the distribution of wealth and the means of coercion at the disposal of the ruling class. But how can such social relations be discerned through archaeology alone? This problem has been addressed by Jonathan Haas (1982), who has suggested that class distinctions will be indicated in the archaeological record by differing patterns of artefact dispersal (suggesting variation in economic roles and the accumulation of wealth by particular segments of a society), different standards of residential architecture, stratification of settlements, and evidence for specialised military groups. To this can be added the expectation that a ruling class will signify its authority through material culture, as described for other modes of production in Chapter 6.

There is every reason to expect that the earliest states, and the location, economic characteristics and material signification of their ruling classes, can be found in the results of archaeological excavation in southern Africa. The more difficult problem of explaining *why* such transitions came about – why the chiefdom and lineage mode of production were superseded as a social form – is left to the end of this chapter, after some of the evidence has been reviewed.

Mapungubwe and the East coast

Just as settlement of the highveld grasslands was closely linked to the 'livestock revolution', so the Limpopo–Shashi basin only became economically viable when farmers had sufficient livestock to make a living. Much of the valley falls under the rain-shadow of the Soutpansberg to the south, and the mean annual rainfall is little more that 300 mm. Droughts are common and temperature ranges are extreme. Thus although crop plants were cultivated from the earliest years (charred grains of sorghum have been found at several sites: see Hanisch 1981), the true potential of the Limpopo basin lay in the grazing offered, particularly by the leaves and seeds of *Colophospermum mopane*, the tree which, by virtue of its density and prevalence, has given its name to the major vegetation type (Voigt and Plug 1981).

Because of the nature of the environment, it comes as no surprise that domestic stock were important to the occupants of the earliest settlements, and became increasingly more important. Thus at Pont Drift, the site of several extensive midden deposits near the south bank of the Limpopo, dated to between about A.D. 800 and 1100, one excavation showed that cattle and caprines (sheep/goats) together contributed almost 80 per cent of the meat brought into the settlement, and that by the end of the occupation, this had risen slightly to 83 per cent (Voigt 1980).

A similar pattern is evident at Schroda, a large site on a rocky plateau, also overlooking the Limpopo River and dated to the ninth century A.D.

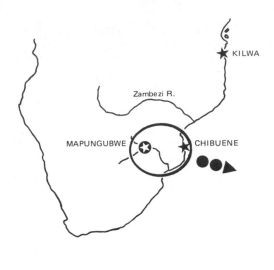

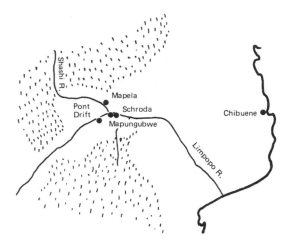

Early trade connections. Settlements in the Limpopo River valley and on the East African coast.

Schroda. Excavations in progress, with the Limpopo River in the background. (Photograph by Edwin Hanisch, with permission of the Director, National Cultural History and Open Air Museum.)

Although hunting, snaring and gathering were clearly important activities, domestic animals apparently contributed almost 90 per cent of the meat in the diet (Voigt 1981), not to mention other secondary products which are not evident from the archaeological record. Similarly, the massive rubbish tips or middens at K2 (so named by an early excavator because it reminded him of the settlement mounds, or *koms*, of North Africa), which accumulated in the tenth and eleventh centuries, attest to the overwhelming importance of domestic stock (Voigt 1983).

This was the setting in which the important centre of Mapungubwe was first occupied. Mapungubwe was built around a stark sandstone hill that rises abruptly from the surrounding valley. At the summit were richly adorned burials and the remnants of successive houses built over the rubble of their predecessors, while evidence of further extensive settlement extended in a broad apron beneath the 30-foot cliffs on the south-western side of the hill. Excavation of the deep, stratified deposits has shown that houses were built and rebuilt over many decades (Eloff and Meyer 1981).

Aerial photograph of Mapungubwe Hill. The remains of trenches from excavations can be clearly seen on the summit. Most of the town's population lived around the base of the hill. (Photograph by courtesy of the Archaeology Department, University of Pretoria.)

Radiocarbon dates indicate that the first buildings were constructed beneath the hill in the eleventh century and that the town had been extended over the summit of Mapungubwe by the early twelfth century (Hall and Vogel 1980).

As with states in other parts of the world (Johnson 1972), the town at Mapungubwe seems to have been at the top of a hierarchy of settlements. Contemporary and somewhat smaller sites with similar building layouts around the bases and over the summits of hills include Little Muck, about 10 kilometres from Mapungubwe (Huffman 1982), Mmamgwa Hill, which is 40 kilometres west of Mapungubwe (Tamplin 1977, cited in Huffman 1982) and Mapela, which is 85 kilometres to the north-west and close to the Shashi River, a major tributary of the Limpopo. Clearly, these were major centres, as Peter Garlake (1973a: 157) has observed: 'settlement at such sites was so intensive that at Mapela, for instance, in about the thirteenth or early fourteenth century, all the slopes of the 300 ft high hill were terraced with roughly piled stone walls to provide defences and levelled building sites. . . . '

Although domestic stock, and particularly cattle, continued to be of central importance in the economy of Mapungubwe (Voigt 1983), there was also a new commercial element of considerable significance: participation in a wider network of exchange, firstly with the coast, and indirectly with other states on the far sides of the Indian Ocean.

The earliest evidence for trade contacts along the East African coast comes from accounts of explorers and geographers. Often, these tales were recorded years later, after they had been passed down by word of mouth, distorted and exaggerated until they were 'meagre, often corrupt, often half-myth' (Chittick 1971). The first such account is the *Periplus of the Erythraean Sea*, a guide to the ports of Arabia, East Africa and India that was probably written in Alexandria in about A.D. 100. Here, we are told of 'the last mainland market-town of Azania, which is called Rhapta, a name derived from the small sewn boats. . . . Here there is much ivory and tortoise shell. Men of the greatest stature, who are pirates, inhabit the whole coast and at each place have set up chiefs. . . . ' Rhapta and other market towns were subordinate to a kingdom in Arabia, from where Arab captains sailed with 'hatchets, swords, awls, and many kinds of small glass vessels; and at some places wine and not a little wheat, not for trade but to gain the goodwill of the barbarians'. In return, merchants received ivory, rhinoceros horn, tortoise shell and coconut oil (Freeman-Grenville 1962). It is impossible to determine the location of Rhapta, although Neville Chittick believed that it may have been on the coast of modern Tanzania (Chittick 1971).

There are no further accounts for many years, but in the first part of the twelfth century al-Idrisi, who spent much of his life at the court of the king of Sicily, compiled a book of travels that was based on the experiences of other writers and informers. Al-Idrisi indicated that the Arabs knew of a number of landing points and collection places along the coast known as 'Sofala' (probably from the Arabic for 'shoal', reflecting the dangers of navigation). It is possible that exchanges of commodities took place near the estuary of the Zambezi and perhaps at locations further to the south (Trimingham 1975).

Although it is difficult to make precise connections, the archaeological evidence confirms the documentary sources. On the southern Tanzanian coast Kilwa, which was later to be a thriving Islamic city-state, was first occupied in the eighth or ninth centuries by a community that lived largely by fishing and gathering shellfish, although sorghum was also cultivated. Shell beads were ground in large quantities, and spindle whorls (flat circular discs with a central hole, usually made of clay, that were probably weights for the end of spindles and are therefore evidence for the manufacture of cloth) suggest that cotton was spun, both presumably for trade into the interior. Ivory was probably the major export, collected during occasional visits by trading ships in return for ceramics from the Persian Gulf (which have been found in the archaeological deposits at Kilwa) and other commodities (Chittick 1974).

A second early point of contact was at Chibuene, on the Mozambican coast between the mouths of the Zambezi and Limpopo, a recognised anchorage today, clearly important in the past as well and located close to the 'Jabasta' recorded by al-Idrisi (Trimingham 1975). As at early Kilwa, shellfish collecting was obviously important, while imported Persian ceramics and glass beads must have been obtained from visiting merchants (Sinclair 1982). A radiocarbon date indicates that Chibuene was occupied in the eighth century A.D., and must therefore have been contemporary with early Kilwa (Hall and Vogel 1980).

It seems likely that neither Kilwa nor Chibuene, or for that matter other contemporary trading stations along the coast, were outposts occupied permanently by Arab merchants. There is little evidence for the spread of Islam down the East African shores before the twelfth century, and it is more likely that the middlemen between the people of the interior and the itinerant Arab merchants were those known as the 'Zanj' – farming communities whose cultural connections were more with Africa than with Arabia (Trimingham 1975).

Although there may well have been several years between visits by Arab traders to their landing points on the coast in these early centuries, their persistence in making what must have been difficult and dangerous voyages attests to the value of the commodities that could be obtained from the southern African interior through the Zanj.

Similarly, the populace of Mapungubwe, and the people who lived in earlier settlements in the Limpopo basin, grasped the opportunity of obtaining exotic and rare goods.

By the ninth century glass beads and other goods from the coast had been received at Schroda: 'Trade was carried on with the coast, as is shown by the presence of trade beads and cowrie shells on the site. Other items that were traded included copper and iron, not necessarily in the form of finished products, but at least in metal form which could be heated and forged on site.' (Hanisch 1981)

Although the people of Schroda were principally agro-pastoralists, they also spent much of their time hunting. Apart from antelope such as grey duiker, klipspringer, steenbuck and impala, an unusual number of carnivores were caught, including smaller species such as mongoose, Cape wild cat and the bat-eared fox, as well as leopard. Elephant were also hunted, for the middens at Schroda contained slivers of ivory, discarded when tusks were cut up (Voigt 1981). It seems likely that ivory and animal skins were among the early exports from the Limpopo valley.

Archaeological evidence is again consistent with early documentary sources. Al-Mas'udi, for instance, who sailed the East African coast in about A.D. 915, noted that 'the land of Zanj' produced 'wild leopard skins', which were both worn by the people themselves or exported to Muslim countries, where they were used as saddles. Although al-Mas'udi's account is a collection of impressions, clearly drawn from many different parts of the coastline, his description of elephant hunting may well be concordant with practice in the Limpopo valley: 'There are many wild elephants but no tame ones. The Zanj do not use them for war or anything else, but only hunt and kill them. When they want to catch them, they throw down the leaves, bark and branches of a certain tree which grows in their country: then they wait in ambush until the elephants come to drink. The water burns them and makes them drunk. They fall down and cannot get up: their limbs will not articulate. The Zanj rush upon them armed with very long spears, and kill them for their ivory. It is from this country that come tusks weighing fifty pounds and more. . . .' (Freeman-Grenville 1962: 15)

By the late tenth century, when K2 began to become a centre of importance, there must have been an established flow of goods between coast and interior. Quantities of glass beads have been found in the middens, as well as fragments of ivory at virtually every level. Numerous similar beads

Beads

Glass beads were made in India before the sixth century B.C., and also at an early date in Persia. They were therefore an ideal commodity for trade when Arab merchants began to make use of the monsoon trade winds around the shores of the Indian Ocean.

Roger Summers (1986) has suggested that imported glass beads from archaeological sites in southern Africa should be divided into three series. The earliest beads – pale blue-green and yellow segments of blown canes of glass – are best known from Mapungubwe and other sites in the Limpopo valley. In some cases these beads were heated and reworked into large, locally made beads. Beads in the second series were more sophisticated, with the rough edges of the snapped canes reheated and smoothed. These had long been made in the numerous small Indian glassworks, and were imported into southern Africa once the Arab trade connections had been established. This class of bead continued to be traded successfully until the later nineteenth century, when the market was swamped by factory-made European beads. Summers's third series comprises ornate, decorated beads that were imported in the eighteenth and nineteenth centuries and are known from sites such as the Zulu royal capital, Mgungundlovu.

Archaeologists such as Gertrude Caton-Thompson and John Schofield had hoped to use beads to date sites, but the sustained popularity of the second series of imports, which were successfully traded for more than five hundred years, limited the success of the objective (Summers 1986). Interest in imported beads fell away as radiocarbon dates became available in southern Africa. Recently, however, interest in bead studies has revived, as it is possible that the distribution of imported beads will provide traces of the extent of early internal trade networks, which are themselves crucial in understanding the process of state formation in southern Africa.

came from excavations both on Mapungubwe Hill and in the thick debris from the town around its base – providing evidence for continuing trade through until the end of the twelfth century (Eloff and Meyer 1981).

But although the evidence for early trade between the coast and interior is exciting, there were other aspects to the Mapungubwe economy. For although pottery-making, iron-working and other crafts had clearly been at least part-time

Trapping elephants in southern Africa (from Kolb 1719).

Carved ivory from Mapungubwe. (Photograph by courtesy of Elizabeth Voigt and the Transvaal Museum.)

specialisations since the earliest farming settlement, and may have acquired the status of specialised industry at places such as Phalaborwa and Mabhija, it would seem that craftspeople were supported at Mapungubwe in a number of labour-intensive activities, and that considerable quantities of commodities were produced, presumably for redistribution within the Limpopo valley and its hinterland.

Firstly, by the time K2 was occupied not all the elephant tusks brought into the settlement were exported again to the coast, for there is evidence of a thriving local trade in worked ivory. A large part of a tusk was found among the ruins of a burnt house, as well as a solid tip in earlier excavations. By microscopic examination, Elizabeth Voigt has been able to show that the ivory was sawn through with a metal instrument and then trimmed to the required shape and thickness with a chisel. Finally, the ivory was polished with a fine material, perhaps wet leather. By far the most common ivory objects from K2 were bracelets, of differing width and with flat or bevelled edges. Some had perforations, perhaps for binding together the band after it had cracked or broken. The form of the bracelets is markedly consistent, suggesting that 'the working of ivory to produce armbands might have been a highly specialized craft which was limited to a small group of craftsmen' (Voigt 1983).

A second unusual feature of the collection of artefacts excavated from the deposits near Mapungubwe Hill is the number of bone tools. Although many of the specimens found in earlier years have now been lost, more than 600 examples, many of them finely worked, are known. Most of these were found either in the upper levels of the K2 middens, or in the deposits at the top of Mapungubwe Hill itself. It is probable that long-bones were first split, then shaped roughly by filing and chipping, and that the final tool was polished in the same way as the ivory bracelets. In 1937 a hoard of more than 100 rough bone tools was found in the K2 midden, perhaps unfinished blanks belonging to a particular craftsperson. Finished objects included sharp points, tools with a spatulate or rounded end, pieces with a split end that may have held an iron tip, and bone tubes, some of which were decorated with cut marks. As Elizabeth Voigt has noted, the sheer quantity of finely finished products is unique in southern Africa: 'It is difficult to visualize a group being able to utilise the amount of bone produced in what was probably a relatively short period of occupation. The evidence suggests that the bone tools were being made in sufficient quantities to produce a surplus, and that at Mapungubwe we have a group of skilled bone-working craftsmen who were

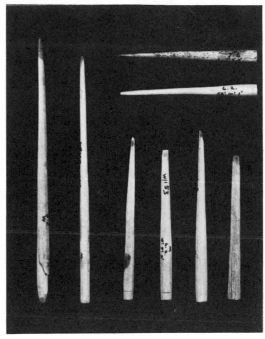

Bone points, excavated by Gardner from Mapungubwe. (Photograph by courtesy of Elizabeth Voigt and the Transvaal Museum.)

manufacturing well-finished tools for trade.' (Voigt 1983: 77)

Further evidence for craft specialisation is provided by spindle whorls. Apart from the earlier settlement at Kilwa, the spindle whorls from Mapungubwe are the earliest evidence for a weaving industry, suggesting that the cotton plants *Gossypium Herbaceum* and *Gossypium Arboreum* had

Textiles

Nineteenth-century cotton weaving (from Brown 1892).

Manufacturing textiles was just as complicated a task as working bone or ivory: 'The preparation of cotton for use was a highly labour-intensive process. The seeds had to be removed by hand or by rolling a wooden or metal bar over the picked cotton tufts. The cotton fibres were then teased out by being placed on the string of a light bow which was plucked continuously until the fibres were opened and spread out, ready for spinning.' (Davison and Harries 1980) Spinning was similarly a labour-intensive process. There are no early first-hand descriptions of the techniques used, but it would seem likely that these had changed little by the time the Portuguese began to describe southern Africa (Huffman 1971). Looms were probably of the low, fixed single-heddle type on which either narrow or wide cloth could be made (Davison and Harries 1980).

already been introduced from central Asia or India and were either cultivated or growing wild.

Thus although the archaeological evidence comes from only a few sites, which may not be fully representative of the Mapungubwe state as a whole, a definite outline is apparent. The foundation of the economy was the herds of cattle, as well as the trade networks that extended to the shores of the Indian Ocean. The fragments of ivory, glass beads and other objects, and the maddeningly incomplete testimony of early geographers and chroniclers, offer only the slightest of evidence for the complex relations that constituted the political economy of the state.

The differences in wealth and status that accompanied this economic system were reflected in patterns of settlement and the association of centres of power and importance with hills, as at Mapela, Mmamgwa and Mapungubwe itself. At Mapungubwe and its major satellite towns, livestock and the majority of the human population lived beneath the hill, the top of which seems to have been reserved for only a small part of the community. In addition, hilltops seem only to have gained significance in the Shashi–Limpopo basin after the economic structure of the state was

well established. It is worth looking at these changes in urban arrangements closely, both because they suggest patterns of relationship within the Mapungubwe state, and because they are relevant to later developments further to the north.

Although the evidence is suggestive rather than conclusive, it is possible that ninth-century Schroda was a settlement of some importance. The large extent of the middens and other debris of occupation may reflect a gradual shift from one part of the site to another as a small group of houses was built and rebuilt (Hanisch 1981) – a shift that seems to have happened at Broederstroom some three or four centuries earlier. On the other hand the large collection of clay figurines may indicate that Schroda was a religious centre as well as a centre for pioneering trade connections with the coast (Voigt 1984).

But certainly by the early eleventh century, K2 must have dominated the valley of the Limpopo. Although recent excavations have taken the form

Animal figurines from Schroda. (Photograph by courtesy of the Department of Archaeology, National Cultural History and Open Air Museum, Pretoria.)

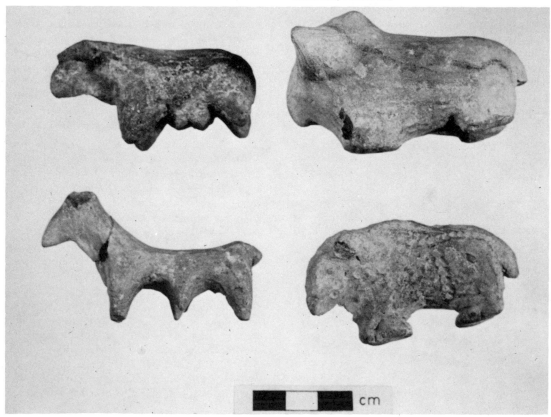

The deep sounding through the southern terrace, Mapungubwe. Excavations, with radiocarbon dates, obtained by the Archaeology Department of Pretoria University have shown that the deposits accumulated over a few decades. (Photograph by courtesy of Andrei Meyer, University of Pretoria.)

only of a deep test sounding through the midden deposits, and although there is little indication of the layout of K2 at any one point, the successive house floors and massive amounts of domestic rubbish attest to a thriving centre. Indeed, some measure of the intensity of activity at K2 is given by the fact that more than four metres of deposit separate layers which gave the same radiocarbon dates, suggesting that this all had accumulated in a single generation (Voigt 1983).

Although the size of the K2 middens is probably a direct index of the volume of day-by-day domestic events in the settlement, Tom Huffman has argued that it reflects political activity as well. In southern Africa today, and in the recent past, the cattle byre and an assembly area where men meet to hear argument and make decisions are both located at the centre of the settlement – part of the 'Southern Bantu Cattle Pattern' discussed in Chapter 6. Huffman suggests that the regional importance of K2 eventually rendered the central assembly area too small, necessitating the movement of the livestock enclosures out of the centre of the town (Huffman 1982).

Huffman has also argued that the centre of the Mapungubwe state shifted the short distance from K2 to Mapungubwe Hill at about A.D. 1075, when the small valley where the earlier town had been located became impossibly crowded. Keeping cattle outside the centre of the town must have had its advantages, for there is no evidence for the dung deposits that mark the location of byres at the base of the hill.

A further change in urban arrangement also took place at this time, as the leading families emphasised their status by having their houses

Part of the University of Pretoria's excavations on Mapungubwe Hill, showing sections through the deposits and the foundations of houses which had been built successively on top of one another. (Photograph by courtesy of the Department of Archaeology, University of Pretoria.)

built on the summit of the hill – a location 'that marked the beginning of an association between the majesty of hills and the majesty of kingship' (Huffman 1982: 143). It is possible that different parts of the summit may have been reserved for particular groups of the elite. The only grindstones to come from the hilltop come from one side, suggesting that this may have been the area used by the royal wives and their servants. The other end

of the hill was reached by an elaborate staircase from the court below, has stone walling and artefacts associated with men, and may have been reserved for 'the king and his entourage' (Huffman 1982).

Huffman argues that these changes in spatial arrangements were not *ad hoc* decisions of convenience, but are rather physical maps of the cosmology of the society, with the contrast between hill and town emphasising kingship; the separation of left and right areas on the hilltop exaggerating the distinction between men and women; and the whole orientation of the town associating the dichotomy between secular and sacred activities with cardinal directions (Huffman 1982).

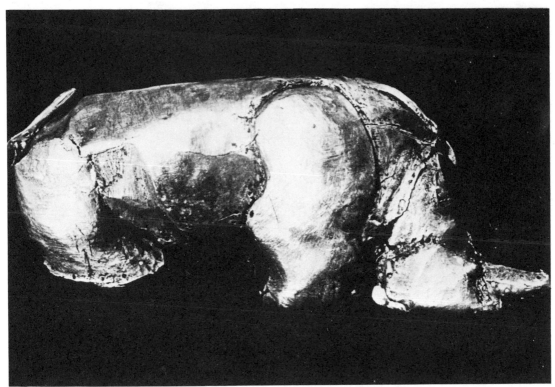

The gold rhinoceros from Mapungubwe: a model found in a grave on the hill. (Photograph by courtesy of the Archaeology Department, University of Pretoria.)

Toutswe: on the edge of a desert

Although Mapungubwe Hill and its complex of archaeological sites have been known and investigated for more than fifty years, this early state has often been considered in isolation from the general southern African social context. But the results of recent research suggest that the rise of Mapungubwe had effects over a wide hinterland and, in particular, above the upper headwaters of the Limpopo River system, on the margins of the Kalahari Desert. For many years it was assumed that these dry grasslands have only recently been settled by agro-pastoral communities. But in 1978 Jim Denbow of Botswana's National Museum began research that was to lead to the discovery of more than 250 archaeological sites as well as convincing evidence for herding and some form of political and economic stratification.

Eastern Botswana is an area of complex relief where the environment offers varied opportunities for human exploitation. But the major environmental factor is the unpredictability of the low seasonal rainfall, which makes agriculture a diffi- cult, high-risk venture. Nevertheless, much of the area is suited to pastoralism, since the grasses grow well in the summer wet season and may be managed to provide an adequate supply in the dry winter months as well (Cooke 1982).

Somewhere around A.D. 700 – perhaps at about the same time that the first permanent villages were built in the Lower Limpopo valley – farming communities making use of domestic livestock moved westwards towards the Kalahari margin. These communities have been called the 'Toutswe people' on the basis of pottery common to the sites of their villages, and were first described at the major centre of Toutswemogala. In Denbow's words, 'the movement of Toutswe peoples into Botswana marked the introduction of new ideas, technologies, and socio-economic systems to a country previously inhabited solely by Khoisan hunters and gatherers. Although these newcomers overlapped with Khoisan peoples in their use of wild resources, they also established new ecological relationships as land was cleared for fields of sorghum and millet and as domesticated stock were introduced to compete with indigenous fauna for grazing and water.' (Denbow 1982: 74)

Denbow had started work in the region around Toutswemogala, the only farming settlement previously to have been excavated (Lepionka 1978).

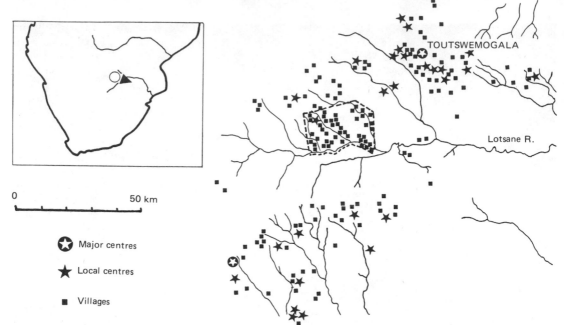

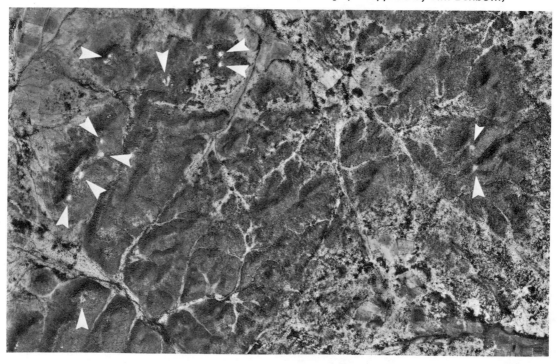

Toutswe Tradition sites in eastern Botswana. Settlements fall into three different size classes, suggesting a hierarchical system of control. The enclosed area was intensively surveyed, increasing the site density.

Aerial photograph of part of the Serowe–Palapye area of eastern Botswana, taken from about 10 000 metres. The white patches, marked by arrows on the photograph, are stands of buffalo grass (Cenchrus ciliaris). These clearly mark dung accumulations on former settlement sites, some of which have been abandoned for more than 1 000 years. (Photograph supplied by Jim Denbow.)

He soon discovered that, far from being an isolated example, Toutswemogala was one of many similar sites in eastern Botswana sharing a common ceramic tradition and thus apparently of the same period.

Denbow also found that the massive, vitrified deposits at Toutswemogala, which the earlier excavator had thought to be debris from iron-working, were in fact accumulations of animal dung that had caught fire sometime in the past and had thus been transformed to their present, durable condition. More than 80 per cent of the sites that Denbow found were marked by such middens, some of them still unfired. These deposits indicated the former position of livestock enclosures, and varied from 30 to 100 metres in diameter and from 15 to 150 centimetres in thickness – good evidence indeed for herding on a substantial scale and, in some cases, over a long period (Denbow 1984b). Moreover, these accumulations had so altered the soils on the sites that settlements were invariably marked by dense stands of buffalo grass (*Cenchrus ciliaris*), creating 'bald spots' evident on aerial photographs (Denbow 1979).

Although Denbow's large sample of sites shared a common ceramic tradition, some settlements were considerably larger than others and the places chosen for settlement varied considerably. In order to make sense of this variability, Denbow decided to divide his sites into three groups. The smallest had dung accumulations of between 1 000 and 5 000 square metres and were located in a variety of situations, sometimes on hilltops and sometimes on the surrounding plains. Denbow carried out trial excavations at three sites in this category – Maiphetwane, Serokolwane and Lechana – and found shallow deposits with little evidence for successive reoccupation. He has suggested that the livestock enclosure was surrounded by a ring of pole-and-plaster houses that were occupied for between ten and fifty years. Once abandoned, such villages were not re-used (Denbow 1984b).

The sites in Denbow's middle group have far larger accumulations of animal dung; on average middens are 10 000 square metres in area, ten times the size of the smaller settlements. An example of this category is the site of Taukome, some 30 kilometres west of Toutswemogala. There were houses around the central midden, while foundations indicate where grain bins once stood. But in contrast to the small settlements, Taukome appears to have been occupied over some three hundred years, as animal enclosures and houses were successively rebuilt. Taukome and other sites in

this group are located only on the tops of hills, and sometimes rough terracing and retaining walls have been built – perhaps, Denbow suggests, to extend the living areas available on these summits (Denbow 1982, 1984b).

Denbow's third category consists of the major centres in eastern Botswana: the three sites of Toutswemogala, Bosutswe and Shoshong. These are some 100 kilometres apart and are located on hilltops where good-sized summits are protected by sheer cliffs and steep sides. Midden accumulations are massive, between 80 000 and 100 000 square metres in area, again a tenfold increase in size against the next smallest class of site. So far, only Toutswemogala has been excavated, but the stratified series of house floors testifies to continued settlement over many years. Grain bin stands again serve as a reminder that, although domestic stock seem to have been of central importance, agricultural produce also had a role in the economy. Circular stone enclosures at Toutswemogala may, by analogy with recent practice, have been men's assembly areas – a glimpse beyond the broad outline of settlement pattern into the day-by-day functioning of this major centre (Denbow 1982, 1984b).

Although it is apparent that not all the Toutswe group of sites were occupied at the same time, Denbow feels that the clear size and status differences that serve to define his three categories of settlement do indicate a hierarchical system of political and economic organisation. The three largest sites must have been centres of regional importance, with the massive middens of livestock dung indicative of accumulated wealth beyond the immediate subsistence needs of the occupants. Following the same line of logic, the intermediate sites such as Taukome may have been lesser administrative centres, while the small sites were the cattle posts or transhumant camps used by the majority of the population. Settlement locations are consistent with this interpretation, for the positions of the larger sites suggest a concern with defence, while smaller settlements were placed to take best advantage of both clay soils and lighter, sandy-clay soils – presaging the preferences of modern-day farmers in the area (Denbow 1984b).

Although the boundaries of the political and economic spheres of Toutswemogala, Bosutswe and Shoshong can no longer be drawn, there are 15 intermediate-sized and 55 smaller settlements within a 30 kilometre radius of Toutswemogala, which gives some indication of the scale of its hinterland. As Denbow has concluded, 'the spatial distribution of sites in the Toutswe region strongly suggests that higher-order political systems, perhaps on a chiefdom or kingdom level, were developing along the edge of the Kalahari around A.D. 900' (Denbow 1984b: 34).

But why did this complex society develop? Denbow believes that the answer to this question is to be found in the dynamics of an expanding cattle-keeping economy. It is a common pattern for a new species introduced for the first time into a favourable environment to expand rapidly until the characteristic curve of exponential growth is arrested by pressure on available resources, which would have been grazing and water for cattle on the Kalahari margins. Such increases in herd sizes would result in problems of resource allocation and ownership for the human population, as well as in giving opportunity for wealth accumulation, leading in turn to a centralised and stratified system of political and economic organisation (Denbow 1984b).

But despite the logic of Denbow's ecological explanation, it seems more than coincidental that the emergence of Toutswemogola, Bosutswe and Shoshong as important regional centres should coincide with the rise of Mapungubwe to the east (Evers, personal communication). Furthermore, it can be asked why the constraints on power accumulation at particular settlements, which were to be such a prevalent factor in the political economy of the southern highveld in later centuries, did not apply on the Kalahari margins, leading to fission and the dispersal of less powerful chiefdoms southwards. It seems more probable that the rise of centres of power in a tributary mode of production was part of the process of state formation taking place lower in the Limpopo River system – a possibility that will be explored in greater detail later in this chapter.

Decline

Just as the Toutswe group of settlements rose to prominence at about the same time that Mapungubwe achieved high regional status, so political and economic power was to wane in tandem in both areas.

At least part of the problem on the Kalahari margins seems to have been environmental for, as Denbow (1982) has pointed out, the grasslands could easily have been over-utilised. From about A.D. 1250 there was a decline in the Toutswe economy, which may have been the result of overgrazing and the consequent diminishing returns

for livestock. After about A.D. 1300 there is no evidence for continued settlement in eastern Botswana by the people responsible for the Toutswe group of sites, and it seems likely that there was substantial migration out of the area, presumably to other lands which could still support domestic stock on a large scale. The magnitude of this transition can be gauged by the fact that there are four times as many sites attributed to the six centuries of the Toutswe Tradition as to the six hundred years that followed (Denbow 1982).

The decline of Mapungubwe may have been a little earlier, for at some time in the twelfth century the town was abandoned and not reoccupied. As with the Kalahari margins, there seems to have been an actual decline in population, for there is little evidence for further farming settlement on any scale in the Shashi–Limpopo basin for some two centuries.

Again, environmental factors may have been involved. Voigt (1984: 392) has suggested that 'increasing pressure from the Iron Age cattle population would lead to serious deterioration of the mopane veld. If the damaged veld were then subjected to the kind of periodic droughts that still devastate southern Africa the veld would be extremely vulnerable. If the dry and dying veld were swept by fire it would be unusable for many years by cattle herders.'

But an additional, and perhaps more decisive, cause of Mapungubwe's decline may have been a shift in the character of long-distance trading relationships. In the later deposits at both the foot and the summit of Mapungubwe Hill, there is less evidence of ivory, while burials at the top of the hill, which were robbed before systematic excavations began, contained gold beads and gold-plated grave-goods (Eloff and Meyer 1981). Although alluvial gold may have been obtained locally (Huffman 1982), it seems more likely that a shift in demand from the coastal entrepreneurs allowed people to the north to seize control of the power and prestige associated with trade in exotic goods (Voigt 1984) – developments that will be described in the next chapter.

The origin of the state

But why did Mapungubwe, Little Muck, Mmamgwa Hill, Toutswemogala, Bosutswe and Shoshong develop as major centres of power between the tenth and the twelfth centuries? Archaeologists have suggested two types of explanation for this problem, although neither of them is in itself satisfactory.

The first, already mentioned with regard to the Toutswe sites, is ecological: the idea that the state developed because of high economic productivity, particularly in cattle. But although it is certainly true that the rulers of Mapungubwe and Toutswe controlled substantial herds of livestock, it is difficult to see how this form of economic security alone could have enabled them to prevent dissident subjects from moving away rather than submitting to centralised authority. Certainly, the Kalahari Desert would have provided one barrier to such fission but there was no reason why putative chiefs could not have moved northwards onto the Zimbabwe plateau, or southwards into the southern highveld.

A second explanation centres on trade; the suggestion that Mapungubwe rose to prominence because the Limpopo basin was the first area in the interior of southern Africa to be integrated into the Indian Ocean trade network (Huffman 1982). Again, there is clear empirical support for this suggestion, for there is substantial evidence for commerce at Mapungubwe itself and at the settlements that immediately preceded it. But again the suggestion of trade in itself as a causal factor is not completely satisfactory. As shown in Chapter 6, simple forms of barter and exchange had probably been part of the economic life of farmers in southern Africa for centuries before the Limpopo valley was settled, while in later years complex trade networks in commodities such as iron were to develop, likewise without the development of states.

The reason why both the simple cattle-wealth and the trade hypotheses can at best be only partial is that they stress the role of the forces of production without taking into account the relations of production. When the possible nature of the economic and political relationships between people in Mapungubwe is taken into account, then the reasons for state formation become clearer.

An important pointer to the changing nature of the relations of production lies in the different character of the major commodities to change hands in the social fabric of early chiefdoms and states in southern Africa. In the last chapter it was shown how cattle transactions in chiefdoms were more than utilitarian, signifying a comprehensive set of social relationships. But livestock are a 'democratic' resource, for herds can be built up by anyone who can gain control of breeding stock; while given favourable circumstances existing herds will continue to multiply, bringing their

owners more wealth and the chance of expanding their 'power-in-people' by extending networks of affinity and clientship. Hence chiefs must rule by consent rather than by coercion.

But the commodities which were assiduously sought by the occupants of Schroda and K2 had very little in common with livestock as a source of wealth. Although personal ornaments could be made from shell and bone, and weaving was soon to become an important craft, the glass beads and exotic cotton cloth imported from the coast were not a 'renewable resource' like cattle, for their value was in their rarity rather than in their potential for increase. This suggests that those in power in the early settlements in the Limpopo basin were seeking a form of wealth that was qualitatively different from livestock, and would provide them with a means of breaking out of the chiefly cycle of fusion and fission.

But how could wealth in beads and cloth, goods with no inherent value of their own, be transformed into real power over people? As with all token currencies, this must have been achieved through the mutual agreement of those with an interest in establishing a new basis for power. Lesser chiefs were also subject to the loss of power through fission of their followings, and it would be in their interest to pay tribute to the new rulers at Mapungubwe in order to secure their positions. In return, their high status would be signified by ownership and display of the rare and valuable trade goods from the Indian Ocean.

But in any system where tribute is paid, some group must be exploited, for their labour must be used to produce the economic surplus that moves upwards through the society, ultimately to support the ruling class. It is, of course, *not* in the interests of such a lower, producing class to acknowledge new tokens of wealth, for to do so would be to acquiesce in additional labour without reward. Thus any state system must have some form of coercion through which rulers ensure that their subjects acknowledge their right to levy tribute. It is therefore probable that the rulers of Mapungubwe and of other states that were to follow in southern Africa commanded military power, even though the evidence for this is, at present, unknown in the archaeological record.

For all these reasons the relations of production in the Mapungubwe state would have created a pattern in which cattle, military service and other forms of tribute would have flowed inwards to the major centres of power, while beads, cloth and other valued signifiers of high status would have moved outwards to regional centres and to local chiefs who acknowledged the suzerainty of the Mapungubwe kings. In turn these networks would have generated economic flow beyond the boundaries of the actual state, for it would have been in the interest of minor tributaries of Mapungubwe to obtain livestock from beyond their borders in order to satisfy their political obligations without calling on their own reserves.

This suggests an explanation for the economic development of the Kalahari margins from the tenth century onwards. In many ways, the economy of the Toutswe population must have been analogous to that of pastoralists elsewhere, dependent on symbiosis with settled communities (Monod 1975). Although the Toutswe herders undoubtedly grew crop plants such as sorghum, their fields would have been subject to periodic droughts and their economic strength manifestly lay in their livestock. By trading surplus cattle to the Mapungubwe state, those in power at Toutswemogala and other major centres could ensure a flow of agricultural produce and other essential resources that were difficult to produce in the dry grasslands.

The Toutswe communities were clearly regarded as outsiders by the people of Mapungubwe, for they were denied access to the foreign trade goods that were the vital tokens of power. Yet the livestock that they could supply may well have been crucial to the network of social relations within Mapungubwe, and ecological collapse on the margins of the Kalahari may have been a major contributory factor in the decline of the Limpopo basin state. These and other questions must await the results of future research, but in the meantime it is abundantly clear that Mapungubwe was the hub of major political and economic developments in early southern Africa.

8

From desert to ocean: the Zimbabwe achievement

Capital and state

Although Mapungubwe Hill is known for the exquisitely worked gold objects that came from the graves on its summit, the metal is comparatively rare and probably only associated with the final years of the town's prosperity. Earlier exports seem to have been dominated by ivory, which was at the centre of a thriving economy. But from the twelfth century circumstances began to change. A dynasty of sultans was established at Kilwa, transforming the city into a prosperous Islamic port, and seeking out sources of gold in encounters with middlemen to the south.

This trade brought wealth to the rulers of a new state centred, between the eleventh and sixteenth centuries, on the impressively walled city of Great Zimbabwe. This has long been known as one of the most important sites in southern Africa either, as described in Chapter 2, because of the mistaken belief that its architecture was proof of an ancient 'civilisation' in the subcontinent, or because the city was correctly seen as the seat of powerful and influential rulers who were to have a lasting effect over a wide area. Its buildings and occupation, and the different interpretations these have attracted, will be discussed in detail in Chapter 9.

But, as Paul Sinclair has recently noted, Great Zimbabwe is the biggest and best known of a large set of sites that include regional centres and the villages of peasant farmers – the different levels of a hierarchy that would be expected in a stratified state system (Sinclair 1984). That few of these subordinate towns and villages have been excavated does not obviate the need to consider the wider nature of Mapungubwe's successor to power in southern Africa.

As with Mapungubwe, the name by which the rulers of Great Zimbabwe knew their domain has been lost. But although this territory was extensive, and certainly included lands between the eastern Kalahari and the Indian Ocean, the heartland was the high plateau between the Zambezi and the Limpopo rivers. It thus seems appropriate to call the state *Zimbabwe* (Beach 1980).

Madzimbahwe: regional centres in the wider state

Although Denbow's work in eastern Botswana

has suggested a threefold system of settlement stratification, the existence of lesser centres in central Mapungubwe can only be inferred at present. But the situation in early Zimbabwe is clearer, for at a number of towns stone walls of distinctive design were built, sometimes with characteristic patterns of decoration. These constructions are known as *madzimbahwe* (singular, *dzimbahwe*), the Shona term for the residence of a chief (Hannan 1974).

More than fifty *madzimbahwe* are known, mostly towards the boundaries of the high Zimbabwe plateau overlooking the lowlands of the Limpopo and Sabi rivers to the south and east and the Zambezi valley to the north. Peter Garlake has suggested that each site belongs to one of about ten different territories, and that their position close to the escarpment edge reflects a need to move cattle seasonally between the lowlands and the higher grasslands (Garlake 1978). This would be quite consistent with the standing of the *madzimbahwe* as regional centres, for each would have its own economic hinterland while at the same time acknowledging subservience to the capital.

But there are two interesting exceptions to this evenly nested patterning of regions within the

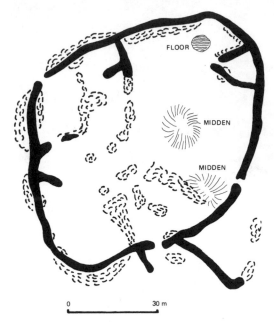

Plan of the dzimbahwe *of Manyikeni.*

The distribution of major madzimbahwe. *The stippled area is the Zimbabwe plateau, standing more than a thousand metres above sea level. Outlying settlements were on the eastern margins of the Kalahari and close to the Indian Ocean shoreline, but the overall distribution suggests a correlation between sites and the edge of the high plateau, leading some writers to suggest that the control of seasonally variable livestock grazing was of particular importance.*

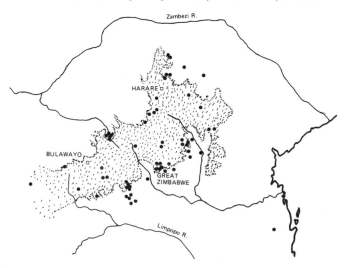

state. The first is Manyikeni, a *dzimbahwe* built more that 400 kilometres east of the edge of the Zimbabwe plateau, and only a short distance from the Indian Ocean (Garlake 1976). The second is Toranju, close to the Mosetse River in Botswana's Makgadikgadi Pans and 100 kilometres west of other known *madzimbahwe* (Denbow 1985). It is improbable that either Manyikeni or Toranju existed in isolation, and future work will show either that there were a great many other regional centres within the little-explored intermediate regions, or that these outlying centres had a more specialised economic and political relationship with the central state.

Usually elevated on hilltops, and often consisting of stretches of walling connecting boulders and other natural features to form an enclosed space, many of the *madzimbahwe* were small and had only a few wood-and-plaster houses within them. Nenga and PaMuuya, for example, are both on the south-eastern margins of the escarpment where the Lundi River cuts down towards its confluence with the Sabi. Walls have been built to join up natural outcrops at Nenga to form an enclosure which could only have been occupied by a single family, while PaMuuya is slightly larger, with two enclosures (Huffman 1978b). Harleigh Farm is further north, and close to the Inyanga Hills. Again, the walls had been built on a granite hill, this time with a main enclosure subdivided by additional stone work (Robins and Whitty 1966).

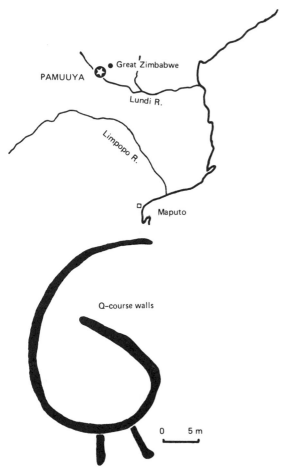

PaMuuya, a small *dzimbahwe with Q-course walls close to the Lundi River.*

The carefully built stone walls clearly served to set those who lived in the *dzimbahwe* apart from the majority of the population and occasionally there are other indications of high status. Copper, beads and some ivory were found at Harleigh Farm, and at Tsindi, a little way to the north-west, the plaster work of a house within a large complex of stone walling had been decorated with ornate designs (Rudd 1968, 1984). At Chumnungwa, near the southern edge of the Zimbabwe plateau, early adventurers unearthed seven burials with gold gravegoods at a large *dzimbahwe* with decorated stone walling (Garlake 1973a).

It is probable that all the walled hills were once surrounded by the wood-and-plaster houses of the ordinary populace, and this interpretation has been supported by archaeological work at several sites. At the outlying site of Manyikeni, the walled enclosures are surrounded by a large area across which is scattered the debris of ordinary town life,

including plaster floors, areas where iron was worked, and concentrations of broken pottery (Morais and Sinclair 1980). In addition, excavation of middens both inside the stone walling at Manyikeni and in the town beyond have provided evidence enabling a comparison of diets to be made, showing that while the elite were able to eat more beef than any other meat, the poorer part of the population made do mostly with mutton (Barker 1978).

Far to the north-west, at Ruanga, is evidence of a similar separation. The upper part of this town is walled to form a *dzimbahwe* of four enclosures that could have contained no more than eight houses. In this area were found gold, copper and iron ornaments as well as imported glass beads. But below the walls, in the lower part of Ruanga, were far less substantial houses made of plaster and wood, with metal utensils of practical value, but little evidence of wealth (Garlake 1973b).

But much, and perhaps the majority, of the population of early Zimbabwe lived away from the *madzimbahwe*, in small villages that fell within the political and economic domain of the regional centres or of the capital itself. As these sites lack stonework they have been little studied by archaeologists – a circumstance that Paul Sinclair has sought to correct by excavations at Chivowa Hill and Montevideo Ranch, sites that lie within 50 kilometres of Great Zimbabwe (Sinclair 1984).

The village at Chivowa Hill was occupied in the eleventh century, soon after the rise of the Zimbabwe state. Excavation has revealed a well-preserved house floor and a possible grain bin, other buildings, and evidence for the artificial levelling of the land surface on which the village had been built. In contrast, Montevideo Ranch is known from its midden deposits rather than its buildings, although there are the fragmentary remains of two houses as well as five burials. This village seems to have been occupied throughout the span of the Zimbabwe state (Sinclair 1984).

There must have been hundreds of villages like Montevideo Ranch and Chivowa Hill scattered throughout the lands of early Zimbabwe, and it will be the achievement of future research to reveal this aspect of the state. In the meantime, it is only possible to examine this formative phase in southern Africa's history through the remains of the towns of the ruling class.

Power and authority in early Zimbabwe

As with Mapungubwe and other states, the ultimate sanction of power in early Zimbabwe must have been force: the possibility of coercion that encouraged peasant communities to acknowledge the authority of regional administrators at their *madzimbahwe*, and that led this local nobility, in turn, to respect the dominance of Great Zimbabwe. Although it is not possible on presently available evidence to know whether the organisation of Zimbabwe was similar to European feudalism with a weak central authority and powerful regional rulers, or to Asiatic 'despotism' with power concentrated in the hands of a strong central authority (Wolf 1982), the very persistence of Great Zimbabwe and the rural *madzimbahwe* as places of importance indicates that the ruling class held the means to prevent the desertion of their subjects and the fission of their realm.

But if force was the ultimate sanction, there were nevertheless more direct ways in which the rulers of Zimbabwe underlined their authority and worked for the cooperation of their subjects. Archaeologically the most obvious of these was the monumental architecture of the capital and the *madzimbahwe* – a classic example of the signification of power described by Anthony Giddens (1984). For despite earlier opinion, still sometimes repeated, the walls were clearly not built for defence and would have been of little value for that purpose (Garlake 1973a). They were rather a statement of the power of the ruling class, a very visible reminder that the nobility could control labour on a large scale. Tom Huffman (1982) has suggested that this symbolism was accentuated by the hilltop locations of the *madzimbahwe*, continuing the physical emphasis on authority first established south of the Limpopo at Mapungubwe.

There were undoubtedly other symbols of royal power at Great Zimbabwe and other *madzimbahwe*, many of which have been lost with time. But artefacts which probably did fill such a role are the distinctive stone monoliths known from a number of sites including Chipukuswi, built on a bare granite hill on the southern edge of the plateau (Houser 1975), and Musimbira to the east (Monro and Spies 1975). Huffman has argued that the monoliths were symbols of authority, the 'horns of the ruler', 'implying that the king was metaphorically like a bull, defending his people with his spear as a bull defends its herd with its horns'. Similar wooden monoliths have the same

meaning today for the Venda, who live to the south of the Limpopo River (Huffman 1986b). The most ornate and developed examples of the symbol were the carved soapstone birds from Great Zimbabwe itself, to be described in the next chapter.

Other forms of control may have involved manipulation of people's cosmological perceptions, their ideas about the nature of the world and their own place within it. Such 'ideology' is a part of all social systems and, in those with class structures, serves to preserve the status quo between different groups.

A central figure in recent Shona cosmological interpretation has been the *svikiro*, or spirit medium, who is seen as the living representative of an important ancestor (Garbett 1966, 1977). Although, as David Beach (1980) has argued, the role of religion has probably been considerably exaggerated in the historical interpretation of Zimbabwe, there is nevertheless some archaeological evidence for the association of spiritual control with buildings at Great Zimbabwe (which will be discussed in Chapter 9) and with other *madzimbahwe*. An example is Tsindi, a *dzimbahwe* built near the northern edge of the Zimbabwe plateau. Here, in the third phase of settlement, which postdates the mid-sixteenth century and therefore falls late in the time-span of the Zimbabwe state, three houses were built which were clearly not conventional dwellings. One has been interpreted as a *banya*, or religious house used by a spirit medium, the second as a venue for sacrifices, and the third as the possible dwelling of the spirit me-

The Shona spirit medium

Research among Shona in the Zambezi valley has shown the important role the *svikiro* (spirit medium) plays in the political administration of society – solving succession disputes by conferring 'spiritual legitimacy' on the favoured candidate and mediating between the ancestors and their living descendants to ensure good rains and harvests. Because of the respect in which *masvikiro* are held, they could bolster the authority of the nobility whom they had been instrumental in installing in power, for 'to fail to obey the order of a medium is to run the risk of being killed by a lion or struck down by lightning. . . . Every time the crop fails, the rains are late, lightning strikes, or a lion attacks a man, this provides proof that the spirit guardians are still actively concerned with the behaviour of men upon earth.' (Garbett 1966: 151)

dium. It has been suggested that the incorporation of a large cave within the walling of the *dzimbahwe* was deliberate, as such a rock shelter would be a focal point in any religious ceremony (Rudd 1984).

Peter Garlake has offered a similar interpretation of the remains of the houses within the *dzimbahwe* of Nhunguza, one of the northernmost centres of the early Zimbabwe state. Of the five structures excavated within the stone enclosure, three were probably for sleeping, one was an ordinary living area, and the last was a complex building subdivided into three internal sections. In Garlake's own words, 'the Main Hut appears unsuited for any domestic role and cannot be paralleled. A consideration of the visible remains suggests that it was designed to fill a ceremonial or communal role: one can envisage a comparatively large group of people assembling in the eastern half of the hut: they would have had restricted or indirect communication with the occupier of the seat in the small adjoining room. In turn, only he and the few people with him in this room could see or handle the objects standing in almost complete seclusion on the platform in the final room: these may well have been tribal relics.' (Garlake 1973b: 115)

But ideological and military control may not be consistently successful within a state, and, as Haas (1982) has emphasised, there may often be archaeological evidence for rebellion against the ruling class. Although the evidence is slight, it does seem possible that those in authority at regional centres in Zimbabwe had their buildings sacked on more than one occasion. At Manyikeni, buildings alongside an entrance to the enclosure were destroyed and rebuilt on at least two occasions, and although this could have been accidental, it may also be an indication of revolt (Garlake 1976). Similarly, buildings around the entrance to the Harleigh Farm *dzimbahwe* collapsed and were rebuilt (Robins and Whitty 1966) and houses in Tsindi 'suffered violent destruction; walls were razed to an even height and fragments of structures scattered. There was no evidence to suggest that they disintegrated through weathering.' (Rudd 1968: 48) At Musimbira a large house had collapsed in the fifteenth century, apparently crushing to death a young member of the nobility whose skeleton, still adorned with a copper bracelet and a gold bangle, was found amongst the rubble (Monro and Spies 1975).

The internal economy of the Zimbabwe state

Thus the framework of the Zimbabwe state was a set of regional centres from which members of the nobility signified their authority over the mass of the population by lavish public architecture, symbols of status and ideological control. But both the basis and the object of such political power was control over the economy – the network of transactions that linked peasant villages, *madzimbahwe* and the capital and, beyond this, the state itself with the wider commercial world.

In ordering discussion of this aspect of early Zimbabwe, Marshall Sahlins's (1972) model of political economy as a set of widening co-membership spheres is helpful. In their most simple form, these would comprise concentric circles, with the household at the centre and wider forms of association, such as the village, the administrative region and the state, beyond. Sahlins suggests that each sphere has its own characteristic set of relationships.

As has already been pointed out, little is known of lower-class village life in early Zimbabwe – the 'peasant economy' that forms one of the inner circles in Sahlins's model. Sinclair (1984: 52) has suggested that villages such as Montevideo were 'relatively self-sufficient peasant communities engaged in a variety of production activities'. He has pointed out that the faunal assemblages from both Chivowa Hill and Montevideo Ranch consist mostly of adult cattle, 'characteristic of the husbandry of breeding herds in the rural peasant communities', in contrast to the predominantly juvenile animals slaughtered at Great Zimbabwe (Brain 1974), which may have been 'the result of appropriation from the rural peasant communities' and 'a form of conspicuous consumption' (Sinclair 1984: 51).

But it is likely that future research will show the apparent self-sufficiency of peasant villages within states such as Zimbabwe to be illusory. It has been argued in earlier chapters that farming communities can rarely, if ever, be self-sufficient, and this would apply as much for a lower class within Zimbabwe as for member villages of a chiefdom. In addition, peasant villages were the source of the surplus production that was the economic foundation of the nobility in the *madzimbahwe*, and it can be predicted that there were frequently used economic channels between peasant farmers and their superiors, along which both tribute and gifts in return for fealty moved. Indeed, it is notable that glass beads were found at both Montevideo Ranch and Chivowa Hill, indicating that at least some of their occupants had access to a major form of wealth in the state.

A wider co-membership sphere must have bound together town and countryside. As with any urban centre, the size of the population of Great Zimbabwe must have prevented its citizens from obtaining their means for survival by agriculture immediately outside the town, and grain was probably brought in from those parts of the state within a few days' walk of the capital. In the smaller regional towns, in contrast, necessary produce could probably be grown locally and by the townspeople themselves.

As in Toutswe and Mapungubwe, cattle were of paramount importance in early Zimbabwe. Their role in the food supply, for both meat and milk, must have been central, and it is clear that towns were sited carefully in order to control a balanced spread of grazing land (Garlake 1978). In addition, it is probable that livestock had an important social role, signifying relationships in the manner described by Kuper (1982a) in his analysis of the ethnographic record. If this was indeed the case, then cattle would have been important in economic ties between villages and regional centres – a third, and wider, economic sphere.

But political and economic relations were not only established through the medium of cattle, for the evidence of craft specialisation, slight though it is, indicates that other commodities were available to be given and received. Peter Garlake has argued that the finely finished, graphite-burnished pottery found at the *madzimbahwe* was the product of a court craft (Garlake 1982b), presumably made for use by the elite, but perhaps also for redistribution. Similarly, the weaving industry established earlier at Mapungubwe continued, and spindle whorls are known from many regional centres, and in their hundreds from Great Zimbabwe. Copper and gold ornaments were worn to signify status and wealth, and must therefore have been valued gifts, exchanged to insure alliances between members of the ruling class (Garlake 1973a).

A further commodity, which may have been of considerable economic importance and which had been traded since the earliest years of farming settlement in southern Africa, was salt. Denbow (1985) has suggested that the Mosetse River *madzimbahwe* of Toranju, as well as other settlements recently located in this part of the Makgadikgadi Pans, may have been placed to control the processing of salt and its trade to Zimbabwe

– activities that are still carried out by local gatherer-hunter communities today.

Thus the internal economy of the Zimbabwe state must have involved agro-pastoral production beyond the needs of the ordinary village community, generating an economic surplus which formed the basis of the transactions that constituted the political economy. But apart from grain, livestock, trade beads, salt, ceramics and other commodities which are no longer archaeologically visible, the population of Zimbabwe mined and traded gold. This mineral seems to have had little use value within the state, but was central to the wider trade networks that will be discussed later in this chapter.

Earlier writers suggested that the techniques of gold mining used in early Zimbabwe must have been introduced from beyond the continent and that large quantities of the metal were mined and exported before the colonial period (Summers 1969); but more recently, Ian Phimister has argued that methods of extraction were primitive, severely restricting productivity (Phimister 1976).

Phimister has suggested that mining was a marginal activity, carried out in the winter months between harvesting and planting. Most of the gold exported from the Zimbabwe plateau was either panned from alluvial deposits or mined from the narrow quartz reefs that push up, usually vertically, through the granites. Ore, probably bearing less than an ounce per ton, was extracted from large open pits which were dug in pursuit of the reefs, or else from narrow shafts. At the surface, the quartz was heated, crushed and washed (Summers 1969; Phimister 1976) – an extremely labour-intensive process that was only viable when work was not required in the fields. As Phimister (1976: 7) has written, 'gold mining operations . . . were undertaken in a capricious geological environment which imposed its own severe limitations on the volume of gold which could be produced.'

The ultimate destination of most gold from the Zimbabwe plateau was the Muslim world via the East coast trade. But nothing is known of the manner by which the metal was collected from rural villages and traded for cloth, beads and other imports. Phimister (1976) suggested that there may have been little central control of mining and that village heads may have traded directly with Muslim middlemen, but this seems unlikely. The network of regional *madzimbahwe* and the size and obvious pre-eminence of Great Zimbabwe indicate a structured and sustained political economy in which the acquisition of wealth by the nobility

was assured. This in turn suggests strong control over the distribution of gold, which was after all the main basis for the wealth of the state. Therefore, even though gold mining was clearly an industry at the disposal of many peasant villagers, it would seem probable that the metal was a major part in the tribute payable to the nobility.

Mining reef gold on the Zimbabwe plateau. (Drawing by Tina Coombes, after Summers 1969.)

The Zimbabwe state and the wider world

Although the political and economic sphere of activity for most of the population of early Zimbabwe must have been within the state, important contacts were also maintained with other societies, both beyond the network of *madzimbahwe* in southern Africa and, through intermediary traders, with many other parts of the medieval world. Sahlins (1972) perceives relations such as these as the periphery of spheres of interaction – a twilight area where the rules of conduct are far less clear and the tendency is more to chicanery than balanced reciprocity, and where interactions may be infrequent and often subject to fortune.

It is probable that societies both to the north and to the south of the Zimbabwe plateau contributed to the wealth of the state, but only from the Zambezi valley is there firm evidence for such a connection. Above the river, on a ridge called Ingombe Ilede (which means 'where the cow sleeps'), a cemetery and an extensive and dense scatter of broken pottery mark the position of a settlement which was probably occupied intermittently from the seventh century, but which clearly thrived in the fifteenth century, when the power of the Zimbabwe state to the south was firmly established (Phillipson and Fagan 1969).

At the centre of the cemetery eleven people had been buried, most of them richly adorned with jewellery, including necklaces of gold beads, copper-wire bangles, and girdles made from glass beads. Some of the bodies had been wrapped in cotton shrouds for burial and had grave-goods

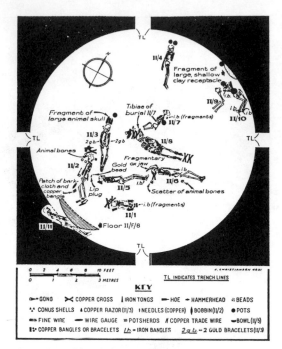

Burials at Ingombe Ilede, discovered during the construction of a water tank. (From Fagan 1969.)

Ingombe Ilede and Great Zimbabwe. (Drawing by Tina Coombes.)

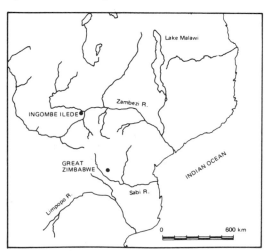

placed at their heads and feet. Some sixty metres to the south was a second burial area, where 31 corpses, many of them of younger people, had been more casually interred (Fagan 1969). Unfortunately, the relationship between the two parts of the cemetery is not entirely clear. The adorned and unadorned burials could be contemporary, which would be strongly suggestive of a socially stratified society, or the southern part of the site could be part of an earlier occupation.

It is clear that the fifteenth-century community at Ingombe Ilede was trading with the East African coast, if only indirectly. Indeed, from this site has come the earliest definite evidence of the importation into Africa of completed textiles: fragments of a fine cloth, used as a shroud, that probably originated in India (Bushnell 1969). But it is also interesting that far fewer glass beads were found at Ingombe Ilede than at, for instance, Mapungubwe, where the total volume of external trade was probably far lower. From this it has reasonably been inferred that trade from the middle Zambezi area in the fifteenth century was orientated more to the Zimbabwe state in the south than to the coast to the east (Garlake 1973a).

The special interest of the Ingombe Ilede community was trade in distinctive copper ingots, per-

A copper ingot, excavated from the site of Ingombe Ilede. Copper in this form was traded extensively in southern Africa. (Drawing by Tina Coombes.)

haps smelted from ore obtained from the surrounding hinterland. Such ingots were found in graves in the central cemetery at Ingombe Ilede, as well as at several *madzimbahwe*, including Chumnungwa, one of the southernmost regional centres in early Zimbabwe. In addition, large quantities of copper wire have been discovered both at Ingombe Ilede and at *madzimbahwe*.

In return, the Zambezi community may have obtained iron goods. Ceremonial flange-welded gongs, hoes, axes and bangles were among the grave-goods at Ingombe Ilede, but there is little evidence for iron-smelting (Fagan 1969). The vast hoard of trade goods found at Great Zimbabwe included a large amount of iron wire, in R. N.

Hall's words, 'two hundred-weight of hoes, axes and chisels' and a welded gong similar to that from the Zambezi valley cemetery. Garlake (1973a) has suggested that this ironwork had been assembled in preparation for trade with the north.

In trading with the coast, the Zimbabwe state continued a practice that had been initiated, however tentatively, some three centuries earlier in the Limpopo River valley. But there are indications that the volume of trade had increased significantly by the time that Great Zimbabwe was established as a centre of major importance. With the ironwork at the capital were numerous objects that had been amassed, and these were presumably awaiting redistribution at the time when the town was finally abandoned. This hoard included many thousand Indian glass beads, thirteenth-century glazed Chinese celadon dishes, glazed stoneware from the Far East, a fourteenth-century Persian faience bowl, and probably other trade items, such as silks and fine cotton cloth, that have since perished by decay (Garlake 1982b). As this collection was abandoned at the very end of Great Zimbabwe's time as a capital, it must reflect only a small part of the total volume of trade goods entering the town in any one generation.

In return, the rulers of Zimbabwe undoubtedly sent the goods that had become known as the produce of Africa in the Middle Ages: animal skins, ivory, rhinoceros horn and other exotica. In addition, they were able to supply the gold that insured that south-central Africa received the special attention of the coastal entrepreneurs, something of whose activities are known from both archaeological and documentary sources.

In the later part of the twelfth century the existing community at Kilwa, who in common with other coastal middlemen in settlements to the north and south had probably lived a precarious existence waiting for occasional landfalls by Arabian trading vessels, were incorporated into a new city-state. This was governed by a Muslim dynasty, the Shirazi, who were probably aristocratic refugees from further north on the African coast (Chittick 1965). Under their rule, and that of the sultans who followed them, Kilwa developed as a typical Islamic city. At its centre was the Great Mosque and the stone residences of those close to the court, built from blocks of coral cut from reefs at low tide, while around the perimeter were the less substantial houses of the poorer classes (Chittick 1974). The size of the population clearly fluctuated with the changing fortunes of the town, but probably varied between 4 000 and 12 000

The Great Mosque at Kilwa. (Photograph by courtesy of the British Institute in Eastern Africa.)

people (Chittick 1971).

The prosperity of Kilwa rested on trade or, more specifically, on the ability of its merchants to speculate successfully on the differences between the cost of goods brought in from other parts of the Islamic world for transport to the interior and the prices obtained for the commodities sent by the Zimbabwe state and other societies at the extreme edge of the commercial network.

By the early fourteenth century, Kilwa had enjoyed a considerable increase in such prosperity, with sufficient wealth to extend the Great Mosque and to build the massive palace of Husini Kubwa, which stands a little distance from the centre of the town and includes in its design many storerooms for goods in transit through this commercial centre. As Neville Chittick has suggested, 'it is probable that the increased wealth of Kilwa was a result of her securing for herself a virtual monopoly of the gold trade, and establishing trading ports under her control at Sofala and at other points north of that place' (Chittick 1974: 239-40). In addition, Chinese ceramics were imported into Kilwa in large quantities at this time – surely the source of the celadon found in the enclosure at

Great Zimbabwe. Indeed, identification of the connection between these two great centres has been sealed by the discovery at Great Zimbabwe of a coin that was in all probability minted by al-Hasan bin Sulaiman, sultan of Kilwa between about A.D. 1320 and 1333 (Huffman 1972).

Beyond Kilwa was a vast network of Islamic cities and towns, linked together by sea routes and caravans. Around the Indian Ocean, 'the great navigational currents from the Hadramawt to Indonesia, and from the Deccan to Zanzibar or the northern cape of Madagascar, which put the great rhythm of the monsoons to profit long before Islam, ensured a perpetual flux entirely favourable to cultural interchange. The movement grew by degrees; the Muslim colonies established in the ports of south India sent out their own swarms; and the Indian merchants spread the new religion in this manner throughout the Malay world; meanwhile, the Arabs dominated the east coast of Africa down to Mozambique. . . .' (Holt, Lambton and Lewis 1970: 452)

Merchants first raised capital from the wealthy in the cities of Iraq or Persia, for 'all men of substance, from the caliph or sultan downwards, invested part of the income that they drew from their landed properties in trade of this kind, to increase their wealth' (Holt, Lambton and Lewis 1970: 525). Ships were then sailed first to Uman on the

Husuni Kubwa, Kilwa. (Photograph by courtesy of the British Institute in Eastern Africa.)

Arabian coast, then to the Yemen and on to East Africa, or eastwards to India, Malaysia or China. The goods with which they returned were largely acquired at the merchants' home ports by the aristocracy, although some were sent by caravan and sea to other parts of the Islamic world and beyond.

Arab captains also carried merchants from other countries on their vessels, and the East African ports were occasionally visited by traders from

The zaruk *and* badan, *used extensively in the Persian Gulf in Arabic coastal trade. (From Landstrom 1961.)*

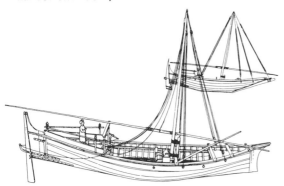

further afield. Indian vessels, particularly from Cambay, made their way along the coast (Chittick 1975), while in 1414 the African coastal city of Malindi sent ambassadors to the court of the Chinese Emperor, bearing with them as a gift a giraffe. Within ten years, the courtesy had been returned by the Chinese Muslim admiral Cheng Ho, who sailed with a large fleet of ships to trade in the Indian Ocean (Davidson 1959).

All this journeying was expensive, but the persistent availability of capital to merchants, and the obvious wealth of Kilwa and other coastal cities, indicate that the return was normally greater than the investment. Fernand Braudel observes that this success was due not so much to the pure volume of the trade, or to the acquisition of goods that were crucial in the technology and everyday economy of the Arab world, but to the fact that long–distance trade was the source of all rapidly accumulated wealth (Braudel 1973).

There was, however, a further consideration in Kilwa's favour, that made trade with this far outpost of the Islamic world particularly attractive. In a complex economy, a balance between imports and exports could rarely be achieved by direct exchange alone, and payment in coin, made from metals that could acquire a relatively stable value by virtue of their scarcity, often had to be made. Thus gold was particularly important both for the practical function of the economy and for the ability that it granted to dominate markets: 'If medieval Islam towered way above the Old Continent, from the Atlantic to the Pacific for centuries on end, it was because no state (Byzantium apart) could compete with its gold and silver money, *dinars* and *dirhems*. They were the instruments of its power.' (Braudel 1973: 329)

But the trading relationship between Islam and the Zimbabwe state was not one in which a primitive economy and naive rulers were exploited by more sophisticated merchants, for when the system is viewed from the African end a certain symmetry is apparent. Just as Indian glass beads were mass-produced at little cost, and shiploads of porcelain were exported by order of the Ming dynasty in place of ordinary coinage, so gold was probably acquired by the rulers in their *madzimbahwe* as tribute, mined as a marginal activity in the interstices of the annual agro-pastoral cycle. Thus Kilwa and Great Zimbabwe emerge as partners in a mutually beneficial relationship, both exchanging trinkets of little value in their own economies for exotica that were important because of their rarity.

Zimbabwe and Mapungubwe

The persistence of Great Zimbabwe as a centre of major importance through several centuries is testimony to the economic and political strength of the realm of which it was capital. Indeed, if longevity is an appropriate criterion for measurement, it could be argued that early Zimbabwe has thus far been the most successful of all the states in southern Africa, both before and after colonial settlement.

But what was the basis for this florescence of power on the Zimbabwe plateau, and why was Mapungubwe eclipsed after the twelfth century? Certainly the ecological crisis that was described in Chapter 7 would have weakened Mapungubwe by reducing livestock productivity, a crucial branch of the economy. But linked with this factor were shifts in the international patterns of trade, which enabled communities on the Zimbabwe plateau to capture vital markets from Mapungubwe.

The basis of Mapungubwe's trading power had been the ability of its rulers to supply Indian Ocean merchants with ivory, animal skins and other exotic commodities. But merchants must also have been demanding gold, for the price of the metal reached a peak in the Muslim world between the ninth and the twelfth centuries (Phimister 1976).

The nobility at Mapungubwe were certainly able to acquire gold, as their own grave-goods attest, but their supply must have come from tributary communities on the northern edge of the state, for there were no goldfields within the Limpopo basin. Thus there must have been a continual economic and political tension between the centre and the periphery of Mapungubwe, as rulers sought to maintain control over tributaries who were aware of their potential economic power. Decline in livestock productivity, particularly on the dry Kalahari margins where Toutswe clients had been able to produce a substantial surplus, may have been the decisive factor, preventing Mapungubwe from paying for the commodity that was vital to satisfy the demands of the coastal traders.

Once established, the Zimbabwe state would have benefited immediately from the high gold price. The nobility would have taken over well-established trade networks, and Muslim merchants would have sent in large quantities of trade goods, as the large storehouses that were built at Kilwa indicate. Ironically, the price of gold was soon to drop, largely because of a massive increase in supply from West Africa to the Muslim world (Phimister 1976). But by this stage the infrastructure of the state, including the capital and the regional *madzimbahwe*, were already well established, and the rulers of Zimbabwe probably gave emphasis to other economic activities that could consolidate their power, particularly the cattle husbandry that was to be of central importance in the centuries that followed.

9

Great Zimbabwe

A place of significance

Great Zimbabwe was one of the first archaeological sites in southern Africa to attract widespread attention, and the town has continued to act as a focus of interest over the century that has followed its first description by explorers from Europe.

Carl Mauch, who found the site ruined and overgrown in September 1871, believed that the stonework, incorporating Lebanese cedarwood, was built at the instruction of the Queen of Sheba (Burke 1969), while later writers advanced the cause of Arabians and Egyptians (Bent 1892; Wilmot 1896; Hall and Neal 1904). As explained in Chapter 2, these interpretations were closely connected to the world view of the time, which sought evidence for stages of barbarism and civilisation and a moral justification for the colonial settlement of Africa. There is a strong strand of continuity between this nineteenth-century viewpoint and more recent apologists of colonialism, who have looked for anything but an African initiative in the architecture of the site (Gayre 1973; Hromnik 1981; Mallows 1984).

But, fortunately, Great Zimbabwe has also attracted professional attention and interpretation, starting with MacIver's excavations in 1905 (MacIver 1906) and Caton-Thompson's major contribution (Caton-Thompson 1931), and continuing with important investigations by Roger Summers, Keith Robinson and Anthony Whitty in 1958 (Robinson, Summers and Whitty 1961) – a painstakingly conducted and reported field programme that was to provide the basis for subsequent interpretations by Garlake (1973a, 1982b) and Huffman (1986b). As a result, the chronology of Great Zimbabwe and its place within the wider Zimbabwe state described in Chapter 8, as well as the probable functions of many of the major buildings, are now apparent. Despite the titles of popular accounts, Great Zimbabwe is not a 'mystery'.

Stratigraphy and chronology

The town of Great Zimbabwe consists of three parts: the buildings on and around the hill of bare granite which rises above the north side of a central court; the structures to the south of the court; and the surrounding town where the common people lived. Although it is clear that these parts com-

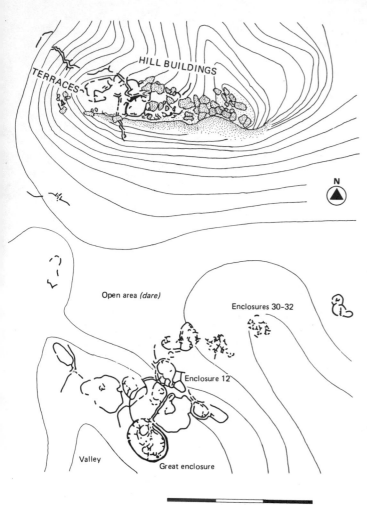

N

Plan of the central town, Great Zimbabwe.

prised an integrated whole, it is convenient to describe the chronological and stratigraphical evidence from each area in turn.

The hill ruins, once known as the 'acropolis', consist of lengths of stone walling over and between large granite boulders, forming a set of enclosures, in some of which were substantial accumulations of occupation debris. Beneath the western walls on the hill summit an extensive and elaborate series of terraces falls away to the valley beneath.

Early excavations by Hall (1905) and by the Southern Rhodesian Public Works Department in 1915 (Robinson 1961b) made it clear that the elaborate walls on the hill had sheltered plaster-and-timber houses which had been built and rebuilt over a sustained period, leading to the accumulation in some areas of substantial archaeological deposits. But this early work was unsystematic

and poorly documented, and it was not until later researchers began far more careful fieldwork that interpretation of the sequence became possible.

Gertrude Caton-Thompson doubted the value of excavating on the hill, and was subsequently to be relieved that she had not 'lavished precious time on the deceptive delights of an Acropolis enclosure dig' (Caton-Thompson 1931: 69). She did, however, excavate in three parts of the hill's western terraces, finding evidence for successively built houses and fragments of stone walls. But it was left to Keith Robinson, working within the Western Enclosure at the top of the hill in 1958, to establish the first systematic sequence.

Robinson was constrained by the earlier removal of the central core of the Western Enclosure deposits, and he was forced to place his trenches where intact material seemed to have survived. However, he was able to identify four periods of occupation, arguing that these applied to the whole Western Enclosure and probably the entire hill ruins.

Period 1, the first settlement of the hill by a farming community, has been dated to early in the first millennium and was unconnected with later occupation and building (Huffman and Vogel 1986). The earliest evidence for Great Zimbabwe as a town comes with Robinson's Period 2, when buildings were constructed with close-set saplings covered by plaster, and small quantities of glass beads were obtained by trade. There was, however, no building in stone at this time (Robinson 1961b).

But in the next phase of occupation – Robinson's Period 3 – far more substantial plaster houses were built in addition to the earlier wattle-and-daub dwellings, and construction began of the massive south wall of the Western Enclosure. Large quantities of glass beads were received in trade during this 'period of energy, organization and improved craftsmanship' (Robinson 1961b: 187). Finally, during Period 4, the walling was extended, and crafts and trade continued to flourish.

While Robinson was directing work on the hill, Roger Summers was excavating in the Great Enclosure: the largest of the stone buildings that form the southern part of the town. Once known, with romantic imagination, as the 'temple', this structure is bounded by Great Zimbabwe's most substantial and elaborate walling and contains a number of smaller enclosures and other architectural features, including the impressive conical tower. Although earlier workers, and particularly R. N. Hall (1905), had removed large amounts of

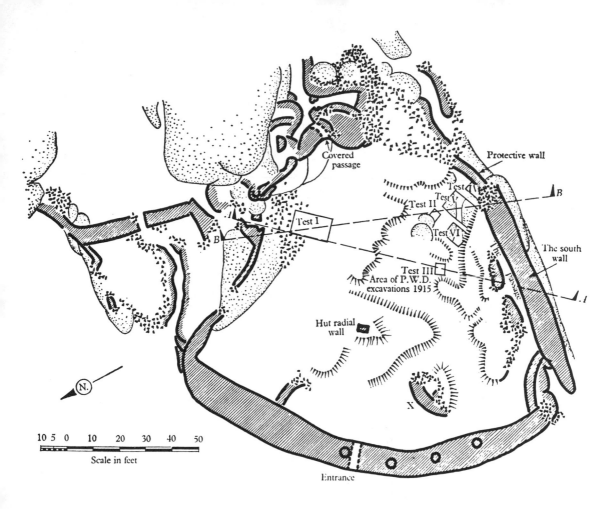

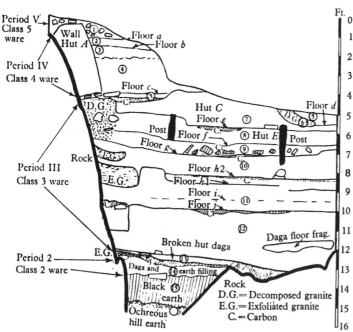

Top plan labels:
Covered passage

Protective wall

Test IV
Test II   Test V
Test VI

The south wall

Test I

Test III
Area of P.W.D. excavations 1915

Hut radial wall

B

A

X

N.

10 5 0   10   20   30   40   50
Scale in feet

Entrance

Section labels:
Period V
Class 5 ware

Ft.
0

Wall Hut A
Floor a
Floor b
1

2

3

Period IV
Class 4 ware

Floor c
4

D.G.

Hut C
Floor e   Floor d
D.G.
5

Post   Floor f   Hut E
Floor g   Post
6

Rock   E.G.

Period III
Class 3 ware

E.G.

Floor h2
7

Floor h1
8

Floor i
9

Floor j
10

11

Daga floor frag.
12

Broken hut daga
13

Period 2
Class 2 ware

E.G.

Daga and earth filling
Rock
14

Black earth

D.G.=Decomposed granite
E.G.=Exfoliated granite
C.=Carbon
15

Ochreous hill earth
16

Keith Robinson's excavations in the Western Enclosure on the hill, Great Zimbabwe. Top: plan of the enclosure, showing the positions of the excavated trenches. Bottom: section through 'Test 1' excavation, with the debris and remains of a succession of houses against the rock face. (From Robinson 1961b.)

105

The Great Enclosure at Great Zimbabwe, seen from the summit of the hill. (Photograph by the author.)

deposit, little was known of the sequence and chronology of the Great Enclosure before Summers's work.

Summers decided that the best approach was to place a network of trenches to cut all major walls in the hope that some sequence of layers would become evident which would help to unravel the history of the building. Fortunately, excavation revealed a series of distinctively coloured and textured clays that had been used in building work, and these could be matched up from trench to trench, allowing different stages of construction to be identified (Summers 1961). As Summers was to point out, his excavations in the Great Enclosure allowed the relative order in which the walls were built to be calculated from archaeological consid-

erations alone. But his interpretation was considerably strengthened by the collaboration of an architect, Anthony Whitty, who studied building styles of the Great Enclosure and worked out a construction sequence. This tied in with the results of Summers's excavations and could be extrapolated to other stone buildings in the town.

On the basis of their technique of construction, Whitty identified seven classes of walling in the Great Enclosure, of which the most important for the purposes of this discussion were Class P, Class Q, Class R and Class PQ (Whitty 1961). Class P walling was built with irregularly shaped and sized blocks laid roughly horizontal but with many inconsistencies in the coursing. In contrast, Class Q walls were far more regular, with approximately rectangular blocks laid in relatively even courses and some evidence of dressing by the masons. Class R walls were again rougher in their construction, with some blocks that could have been used

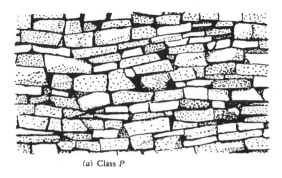

(a) Class P

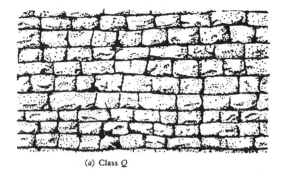

(a) Class Q

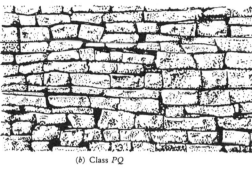

(b) Class PQ

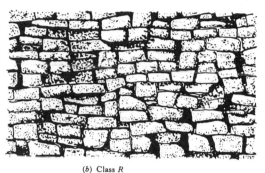

(b) Class R

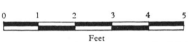

Feet

Different classes of walling at Great Zimbabwe (from Whitty 1961).

in either P or Q coursing interspersed with irregular lumps of stone; while Class PQ seemed to be intermediate between Classes P and Q, with some of the features of both styles (Whitty 1961).

Whitty also noted that particular sets of architectural features tended to be associated with the major classes of walling. Thus, for example, entrances through Class P walls tended to be squared and to lack flanking buttresses, while Class Q entrances were formed with two rounded wall ends and the foundations carried through to form a threshold and, sometimes, recessed steps. Flanking buttresses were common. Class R entrances were either rounded or indeterminate in their form. Platforms and conical towers – distinctive features that accompanied Class Q walls – were not associated with Class P or Class R structures, while drains had been built into the bases of Class P and Q walls but not into Class R walls (Whitty 1961).

Whitty's problem was to arrange the walling classes in their correct order. A method lay in another aspect of the Zimbabwe architecture, 'the fact that where two walls intersect they are invariably constructed with a vertical join at the point of junction, so that, taking the batter of the walls into account, one wall in fact leans against the other. The wall which thus leans must have been built

later in time than the one against which it abuts.' (Whitty 1961: 294)

By studying the 28 wall intersections in the Great Enclosure, Whitty deduced that Class P and Class PQ were earlier than Class Q and that both Classes PQ and Q were probably earlier than Class R. Furthermore, when the walls of the town as a whole were considered, it was found that Class P walls predominated on the hill, Class Q in the Great Enclosure and other southern buildings, and Class R in the outlying and peripheral buildings of the central town. This, then, suggested a building sequence for the town as a whole, with earlier stone work on the hill and later buildings in the south town. Whitty noted, however, that the status of Class R walling remained somewhat ambiguous and could have been either a later addition to existing structures or else a 'simpler, if less elegant, building method, employed when needed at any time during the building period, to fulfil some relatively less significant function such as forming cattle enclosures and boundary walls' (Whitty 1961: 304).

Whitty's architectural study provided a relative chronology, linking the results of excavations on the hill and in the Great Enclosure and thus extending Robinson's proposed periods to the town as a whole. But dating Great Zimbabwe in calendar

Abutting walls, forming part of the structures on the hill at Great Zimbabwe. By noting the different styles of stonework, and considering which wall must have been constructed first, Anthony Whitty was able to work out a building sequence for Great Zimbabwe. (Photograph by the author.)

years had had an inauspicious start, for Caton-Thompson's pioneering analysis of the imported goods had continued to be contested, while the first radiocarbon dates, obtained from samples of wooden lintels over a drain in the Great Enclosure, gave readings in the fifth and sixth centuries A.D. (Summers 1955). However, a second radiocarbon series obtained from Robinson's trenches on the hill were consistent with the other chronological evidence, and Robinson, Summers and Whitty felt justified in setting the rogue readings to one side: a decision which has been subsequently vindicated by the re-dating of the wooden lintels (Huffman and Vogel 1979).

During Period 2 (the first use of the site for a settlement of major importance), the first houses

An entrance into the Great Enclosure, Great Zimbabwe. The wall courses have been continued to create steps. Originally the door was lintelled (above the level of the photograph), although it was incorrectly reconstructed earlier this century as an open gap in the walling. (Photograph by the author.)

were built on the hill, and trading connections were established with the East African coast. In Period 3, which the excavators believed lasted from about A.D. 1085 to 1450, the first stone walls were built on the hill, and the town was extended down into the valley, including the construction of the first Class P walling of the Great Enclosure. The highest level of technical skill in stone work, however, only came in the following Period 4. This, it was argued, spanned the years between about A.D. 1450 and the early nineteenth century, a period which saw the building of the Class Q walls and a massive expansion in trade and prosperity for the town. Finally, an additional Period 5 was evidence for the later deterioration of the town and was perhaps the phase during which most of the Class R walls were built (Robinson, Summers and Whitty 1961).

But although the 1958 expedition was the turning point in understanding Great Zimbabwe, Robinson, Summers and Whitty's interpretation of the chronology of the town was to undergo modification following further archaeological research.

In the first place, Peter Garlake argued that there was no evidence for a substantial occupation of the town after the mid-fifteenth century. The most common imported ceramics at Great Zimbabwe were Chinese celadon, all made during the Ming dynasty (A.D. 1368–1644) or earlier. Similarly, the Persian bowls and Islamic glass found at the site have been dated to the thirteenth and fourteenth centuries (Garlake 1968), and other archaeological and historical evidence (discussed in Chapter 10) indicates that the Portuguese, who arrived on the East coast of Africa early in the sixteenth century, traded with capitals other than Great Zimbabwe.

Secondly, a new series of radiocarbon dates from the hill, the Great Enclosure and from an outlying part of the central town has shown that Great Zimbabwe was built over a shorter time than Robinson, Whitty and Summers believed. The first solid plaster houses in the Western Enclosure on the hill are now dated to about A.D. 1130 while the south wall (the earliest stone work on the hill) could not have been constructed before the early thirteenth century. Thus, rather than spanning 400 years, Period 3 is now dated to the twelfth and early thirteenth centuries (Huffman and Vogel 1986).

New dates for Period 4 buildings, when Great Zimbabwe was at the centre of a thriving trade network and when the most impressive stone walls were built, are consistent with the shorter Period 3 chronology. Dates from the Great Enclosure place the earliest of its Class P walls in the mid-thirteenth century and suggest that Class Q walls came into use after the mid-fourteenth century, indicating that Great Zimbabwe was a major capital and trading centre for little more than a century (Huffman and Vogel 1986).

One further result of the new dates was to resolve the status of Class R walling, which had been taken as part of Period 5, following the decline of Great Zimbabwe (Robinson, Summers and Whitty 1961). Radiocarbon determinations from the Nemanwa ruin, a Class R building on the periphery of the central town, showed that it was built early in the fifteenth century and was therefore contemporary with the Class Q walling of Period 4. In Huffman and Vogel's (1986) words,

'R-walling was an integral part of Period 4, rather than a later, decadent phase', suggesting that Robinson, Summers and Whitty's Period 5 now has little interpretative value.

Thus, in summary, it is now clear that Great Zimbabwe was built later, and abandoned earlier, than archaeologists had once believed; that at least some of the Class R walls were contemporary with Class Q structures, as Anthony Whitty had tentatively suggested; and that 'the entire rise, florescence and decline of this capital occured within 200 years' (Huffman and Vogel 1986).

The buildings explained

But what was the purpose of the elaborate architecture of central Great Zimbabwe, obviously built at considerable cost in human labour? Firstly, it is clear that, as with other *madzimbahwe*, the walls of central Great Zimbabwe were not integral parts of buildings, but rather served to shelter some areas from public view and to emphasise status and authority. 'The walls of Great Zimbabwe were built primarily to display the power of the state. They symbolize, in permanent and obvious fashion, the achievements of the ruling class. They are therefore essentially a political statement.' (Garlake 1982b)

The relationship between the walls and the houses of the central town is best illustrated by excavations carried out in the southern town by Gertrude Caton-Thompson in 1929. Here, in Enclosures 30, 31 and 32 (the numbering follows

The 'Maund Ruins' at Great Zimbabwe, excavated by Gertrude Caton-Thompson. Each of the circular areas was the location of a clay-and-thatch house.

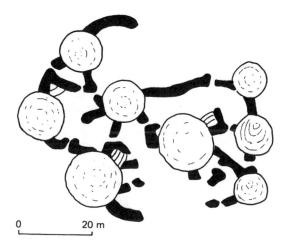

0   20 m

Garlake, 1982b; Enclosures 30-2 were formerly called the 'Maund Ruins'), 29 stretches of stone walls were built up against 10 houses to form a coherent structure of dwellings surrounded by small, stone-walled courtyards, each entered through doorways in the walls (Caton-Thompson 1931). Although no other part of the site has been examined in the same systematic detail, it is clear that the same architectural concept runs through other buildings at Great Zimbabwe.

The significance of Great Zimbabwe as a centre of power is further indicated by the size of its *dare*, or central court: the large, open space, devoid of occupation debris, located between the hill and the southern part of the central town, where the leaders of the nation 'handled disputes between people in different chiefdoms, national policy and other matters of national concern' (Huffman 1986b).

But there has been some disagreement about the functions that the buildings surrounding the *dare* served. Peter Garlake sees the buildings in Enclosures 31, 32 and 33, as well as the other smaller structures south of the great court, as the houses of the ruling class in general. But Tom Huffman has a more specific interpretation, arguing that the numerous grooved slots in these buildings were female symbols and that these were the residencies of the royal wives (Huffman 1981). Peter Garlake suggests that Enclosure 12, which also lies to the south of the court and is part of the building that used to be called the Renders Ruin, was the royal

One of the stone platforms that form part of the 'Maund Ruins', excavated by Gertrude Caton-Thompson (from Caton-Thompson 1931).

treasury, so identified by the rich hoard of imported goods found there in 1902. But Huffman feels that such a cache would be in the keeping of the king's first wife, for 'according to Shona custom, the only person with the right to take care of a man's possessions is his first wife, and so it follows that the king's first wife must have lived in this enclosure' (Huffman 1986b).

Huffman and Garlake also disagree about the place where the ruler himself lived. Huffman is convinced that the Western Enclosure on the hill, which was a major living area with thick-walled plaster houses that were built and rebuilt over a long period, was the residence and audience chamber of the king. In contrast, the secluded Eastern Enclosure, at the other end of the hill, may have been a religious centre. Here were found most of the carved soapstone birds which have become a national emblem of modern Zimbabwe. Huffman points out that, in Shona religion, the spirits of former kings intercede with God on behalf of the nation, often through birds, which carry messages between heaven and earth. Therefore it is likely that the bird theme was 'a metaphor for the mediating role of royal ancestors, especially while procuring rain' (Huffman 1981: 141) and that each of the soapstone birds commemorates a different king (Summers 1963).

Garlake agrees that the lack of domestic debris in the Eastern Enclosure, as well as the many vestiges of architectural symbolism, suggests a spiritual role, and also that the king may have lived on the hill in Great Zimbabwe's earlier years. But Garlake sees the Great Enclosure, in the southern central town, as the king's residence through the later

CEMENT FLOOR

The Zimbabwe birds

A total of eight birds were found at Great Zimbabwe, each carved from soft, grey-green soapstone, about 30 cm long and perched on top of soapstone pillars a metre or so in length. The birds fall into two stylistic groups. Three birds have wings wrapped around vertical bodies and short, fan-shaped tails, while in contrast five birds, their wings folded over the backs of sloped bodies, have bent legs and horizontal heads. All are birds of prey, resembling eagles, but with toed human limbs and, in one case, lips instead of a beak.

The symbolism and probable function of the Zimbabwe birds can be understood in terms of Shona beliefs. Birds, and particularly eagles, were seen as messengers to and from ancestral spirits and between men and God. Propitiation of the ancestors was important to ensure well-being, and the role of the ancestor spirit depended on the importance of the earthly person in whom the spirit had once resided. Consequently, the ancestral spirits of past kings were of vital importance in major issues affecting the nation – rain and the well-being of the state in general. It is thus probable that the carved birds from Great Zimbabwe were metaphors for the spirits of departed kings.

This interpretation is supported by the locations where the birds were found. One was in the Western Enclosure on the summit of the hill, and may have been used by the ruling king in private ceremonies. Six were in the Eastern Enclosure, where they were probably mounted on low terraces and used in formal ceremonies of national propitiation. The eighth bird was in a building in the valley, and may have formed part of women's worship (Huffman 1985b).

Detail of one of the carved stone monoliths from Great Zimbabwe, showing the bird-like figure which may have represented the spirit of an earlier king. (Photograph by courtesy of the South African Museum, Cape Town.)

periods of occupation, with the towering outer wall built to emphasise status. Once the king had moved down to his new residence the buildings on the hill became the domain of those who could control the spirit world, for 'king and medium are independent and autonomous. They maintain entirely separate establishments. Each however depends on the goodwill and co-operation of the other. And it is not unusual for their courts to be close together. All told, it seems reasonable to

The only monolith at Great Zimbabwe still standing in its original position (in one of the valley ruins). Peter Garlake has argued that many of the slots built into the walls of Great Zimbabwe originally held monoliths as well, and that these were symbols of ancestors. (Photograph by the author.)

suppose that, in the later years, the Great Enclosure was the ruler's residence and the Hill was the seat of a senior spirit medium.' (Garlake 1982b: 28)

Tom Huffman interprets the Great Enclosure very differently. Taking as his analogy the Venda *domba* initiation school for girls, he suggests that women who lived in the southern part of the town used the different buildings within the Great Enclosure during their instruction of the daughters of ruling families. 'Among the Venda, every three or four years all girls of marriageable age are supposed to go to the chief's (or headman's) settlement for about twelve months. For part of this time they serve as a labour force, working, for example, in the leader's fields, and the remainder of the time they attend the school. Some aspects of the school are public, such as the "python dance", and take place in the court. Some aspects are secret, such as esoteric formulae and lessons about proper moral behaviour, sex and etiquette. These lessons

The Great Enclosure at Great Zimbabwe. Tom Huffman has extended Adam Kuper's symbolic model to the early Zimbabwe state, arguing for oppositions between male/female and sacred/secular parts of the building. This has led to the suggestion that there were separate male and female entrances, each reinforced with distinct sets of symbols such as monoliths and vertical grooves, leading to a sacred area where oppositions were repeated through the symbols of the conical tower (male) and the smaller tower next to it (female). Huffman has suggested that the Great Enclosure was an initiation centre for girls.

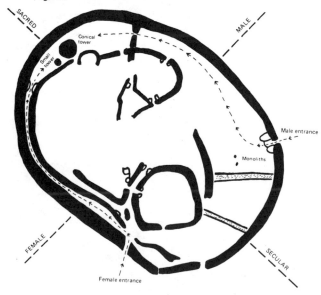

are taught in a special enclosure inside the royal wives' area by masters of ceremony through physical exercise, riddles, proverbs, songs and shows that use various figurines as props.' (Huffman 1984) Following this idea through to the architecture of the Great Enclosure, Huffman interprets different features as symbolic aids to the process of instruction, with the giant conical tower representing the senior male status, the smaller tower expressing the role of the senior women, and the double chevron design and the bands of dark stone in the walling of the Great Enclosure symbolising male virility and female fertility.

Huffman also develops further Adam Kuper's (1980) concepts of spatial symbolism, which have been discussed in Chapter 6. He suggests that the Great Enclosure was clearly divided into male and female sectors, with monoliths used to indicate the men's entrance, and vertical grooves marking the approach to the parallel passage that was used by women to approach the secluded area of ritual instruction beneath the highest walling in the building.

Indeed, Huffman extends this opposition to other buildings in the central town, arguing that a stairway, elaborately decorated with male symbols, was used by men to move between the central court and the king's audience chamber on the hill above, while an inconspicuous stairway, marked by different designs including the distinctive vertical grooves and built on the far side of the hill from the court, was used by women. In contrast, Peter Garlake feels that the buildings on the hill were probably entered from a completely different direction, along an approach that has since been destroyed, and into the religious sanctuary of the Eastern Enclosure. 'The pillars and platforms of the Eastern Enclosure make it, in essence, an extremely dramatic vestibule to the whole hill complex. [It is possible that] the Hill ruin was usually entered from the east, using a path that is no longer traceable but which is rumoured to have existed along the cliff top running towards the east. It is possible that the Eastern Enclosure was the dramatic public introduction to a westward progression of spaces which had its climax in the Western Enclosure.' (Garlake 1982b: 45)

Therefore Huffman would see the town plan of

The Conical Tower, built inside the Great Enclosure at Great Zimbabwe. It has been suggested that this was a symbol used during female initiation ceremonies. (Photograph by the author.)

114

Great Zimbabwe as a symbolic design, with the structured oppositions of male versus female reflected in the positioning of the king's residence on the hill to the north and the girls' education centre in the Great Enclosure on the south side, with the wives' residences clustered around. Garlake's vision is more prosaic, with the king secluded behind the high walls of the Great Enclosure, his courtiers living close around, and the spirit mediums providing a channel between heaven and earth from the hill, slightly removed to the north.

Understanding the third part of Great Zimbabwe – the surrounding houses of the lower class – is even more difficult. Limited excavations have shown that there was a marked contrast in living conditions, for 'while the elite lived in spacious conditions, the common people were cramped into high density housing units outside the stone enclosures' (Huffman 1977). Often one living and two sleeping houses were grouped tightly together, suggesting that this was a basic domestic unit. Estimates of the overall population of the town have varied from a total of 1 000–2 500 (Garlake 1973a: 195) to between 11 000–30 000 (Huffman 1986b), although it should be remembered that almost all archaeological estimates of the number of people who lived in a settlement tend to be extremely tenuous. Only future archaeological research will provide insight into the relationships between town centre and periphery, and between rulers and the people, who comprised the majority of the population.

Great Zimbabwe in its wider context

It is difficult to weigh the relative merits of Tom Huffman's and Peter Garlake's differing interpretations of Great Zimbabwe from the archaeological and architectural evidence of that site alone, for decisive questions, such as whether the king lived in the Great Enclosure, may now be unanswerable in consequence of the damage done to the deposits by early treasure-seekers. But when the town is considered in its wider context other evidence becomes relevant, and the development and function of the central town of Great Zimbabwe becomes intricately bound up with the question of the orgins of the Zimbabwe state itself.

It was argued in Chapter 6 that power, particularly in a centralised state, must often be *signified* in some material manner, and both Garlake and Huffman agree that the massive walls of central Great Zimbabwe would have served such a pur-

pose. But Huffman's interpretation of the town plan takes this concept further by suggesting that the rulers who designed Great Zimbabwe were reproducing quite explicitly the symbols of power that had earlier been employed at Mapungubwe. Thus the hill had become a metaphor for royal authority, as opposed to the lower situation of buildings occupied by the king's inferiors, and the physical separation of male and female areas had come to represent the different roles of men and women within the structure of the society. Huffman also argues that the same set of symbols continued to dominate the design of later capitals on the Zimbabwe plateau (these are discussed in Chapter 10) and are still evident today (Huffman 1986b). For these reasons, Huffman would argue that it is inconceivable that Great Zimbabwe could have been an exception to this 'cognitive system'; the exercise of power and symbols of authority were inexorably bound together.

Such an interpretation implies that Great Zimbabwe was designed as a whole with, for example, the Great Enclosure sited carefully in relation to the buildings on the hill. As long as the eleventh-to-fifteenth-century chronology adopted by Garlake (1973a) and others was acceptable such an interpretation was unlikely, for it would have demanded that the town plan was conceived generations before it was executed. But the new interpretation of the radiocarbon dates proposed by Huffman and Vogel (1986) indicates that, although the buildings on the hill were constructed before those in the valley and the Great Enclosure went through several phases of construction, as shown by Summers and Whitty (1961), these stages probably followed close upon one another.

Thus on balance it is probable that the architecture of Great Zimbabwe, along with the design of the regional *madzimbahwe* found throughout the domain of the Zimbabwe state, continued the metaphors of power which had earlier been established in Mapungubwe.

10

Kings and conquistadores, merchants and markets

New states

One of the achievements of the rulers of the Zimbabwe state was to establish sustained and, on balance, stable commercial relations with Islamic communities on the Indian Ocean coast, allowing both Great Zimbabwe and Kilwa to prosper as centres of major importance. But dramatic changes came with the opening years of the sixteenth century. In 1500 the first Portuguese fleet dropped anchor off Kilwa, and two years later the Sultan was made a tributary of the King of Portugal. In 1505 the city was sacked, and a fortress was built to house the first Portuguese garrison on the south-east African coast (Axelson 1973).

But although the Portuguese were fired with legends of Prester John and the lost gold of Africa, and although they initiated many of the tales and rumours that are still woven into a shroud of mythology, they were too late to trade with the Zimbabwe state. By the end of the fifteenth century Great Zimbabwe had ceased to be a centre of national importance (Huffman and Vogel 1986), and political power had passed to new states on the northern and south-western margins of the high plateau.

It has been suggested that the capital had become too large for its immediate environment and that firewood, grazing and other essential resources

The Dutch and Portuguese compete for control of the south-east African trade in a sea battle off the garrison of Mozambique. (From a seventeenth century Dutch illustration, reproduced by Axelson 1960.)

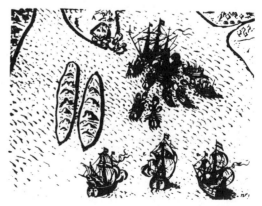

were depleted (Brain 1974). But this is not an adequate explanation for the collapse of the state as a whole. It would seem more likely that the network of regional centres had become too wide, and the power of the central authority too thinly spread, to prevent from developing those tendencies towards fission which are endemic to state organisations and which had probably caused the collapse of Mapungubwe's power several centuries earlier. An additional factor may have been the exhaustion of gold deposits within early Zimbabwe's economic area, weakening the access of the ruling group to the wealth that was probably crucial for their political power (Phimister 1976).

But although neither the geographical extent nor the longevity of early Zimbabwe was to be matched, a succession of powerful rulers came to control large parts of southern Africa for several centuries. These kings, and their economic relations with the wider world, form the subject of this chapter.

Mutapa and Torwa

A few years after they had established garrisons on the coast, the Portuguese began to collect information about the interior in an effort to locate the source of the gold and ivory that they were trying to obtain by trade. They found that the north and east of the Zimbabwe plateau, as well as a large part of the Zambezi lowlands, were controlled by a group of leading families known collectively as the Karanga and dominated by the Mutapa dynasty, from which was derived the title of the ruler, the Monomotapa. Although the Portuguese could find out little about the interior, and their surviving records are often inaccurate, contradictory and exaggerated, David Beach has been able to piece together an outline of the Mutapa state, correlating early accounts with other sources of information (Beach 1980).

It must be presumed that early in the fifteenth century the Karanga nobles were subject to the Zimbabwe state. Beach has suggested that their gradual expansion northwards may have been motivated by a need for more grazing lands and by the economic possibilities offered by the northern goldfields, and the Mutapa ruler must certainly have had economic power to support his secession from Great Zimbabwe and control over his new territory. There is insufficient information to identify precisely when this break took place, but very soon after the Portuguese built their first fortress at Sofala in 1505, messengers arrived from the

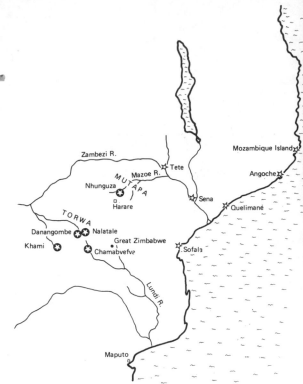

East Africa: Portuguese expansion, and the Torwa and Mutapa states.

The Portuguese base at Sofala in 1636 (reproduced in Axelson 1960).

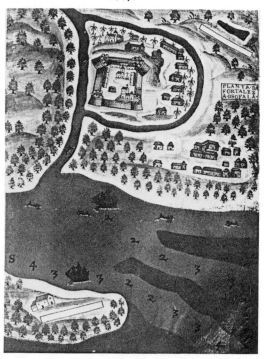

118

Monomotapa seeking to open up trade.

Beach has argued that the Monomotapa's anxiety to entice Portuguese merchants indicates that the far shorter route from the Mutapa heartland and along the Zambezi River to the Muslim markets at Angoche was blocked by a hostile intermediary. This scenario would be quite consistent with the interpretation of the Mutapa state as a relatively new economic power that was still in the process of trying to establish its economic hinterland. For their part, the Portuguese were of course delighted to secure the connection, and by 1541 a permanent Portuguese community had been established within the boundaries of Mutapa, linked to the political structure (Beach 1980).

Earlier interpreters of the Portuguese records describe the Monomotapa as the ruler of a vast empire, but Beach has made a strong case for the existence of a far more limited political sphere of influence. Beyond his area of supremacy, the Monomotapa may have been able to collect tribute from neighbouring groups, but the extent of his influence probably varied with changing economic and political circumstances.

Beach has suggested that some of the northern *madzimbahwe* may have been centres of Karanga power and that the large house at Nhunguza, with its three, specialised rooms excavated by Peter Garlake (1973b) and described in Chapter 8, may have been built to house the throne of a Mutapa, but there is no confirmation of this connection. The capital of the sixteenth-century Mutapa state has not been precisely located, but was probably on the plateau and in the upper valley of the Ruya River. Portuguese chronicles put the population of the capital at between two and three thousand people, and although this must be taken as only the roughest of estimates, the town seems definitely to have been smaller than Great Zimbabwe (Beach 1980).

An archaeological understanding of the Mutapa state has yet to be developed, but there is every indication that the overall structure of economy and settlement pattern was similar to the earlier Zimbabwe state. The majority of the population must have been dependent on the cultivation of crops and on domestic livestock. The facility of moving stock from the high plateau to the lowlands with the changing seasons, which Peter Garlake has identified as a major determinant of settlement location in earlier centuries (Garlake 1978), must also have been important for the subjects of the Monomotapa. Dominant lineages, courtiers and the Monomotapa himself would also have had wealth in cattle, as well as the ability to obtain prestige goods by trade and taxation, and to distribute these to establish and maintain political power.

The Monomotapa was not the only major political figure in sixteenth-century south-eastern Africa, for at much the same time as the Karanga dynasties were building up their control of the northern plateau, a second group was establishing a power-base north of the Limpopo River valley on the southern margin of the Zimbabwe plateau. The Portuguese seem to have had little, if any, direct contact with this state, and the chronicles record only rumour and conjecture. But the archaeological evidence is far more substantial, for the location and architecture of the capital towns are well known, allowing some aspects of the organisation of this society to be inferred.

This southern state, which seems to have been known as Torwa, clearly had as its capital the town which now stands in ruins on the banks of the Khami River, from which it derives its name (Beach 1980). Khami was built in the fifteenth century, immediately after the demise of Great Zimbabwe, and flourished until the late seventeenth century when, after a change of ruling dynasty that will be discussed in the next chapter, the capital was moved to Danangombe, which is also known as Dhlodhlo.

The distinctive architecture of Khami, Danangombe and other major centres, which consists of combinations of house platforms and low, free-standing walls, often intricately decorated with chequered and herringbone patterns, allows the probable extent of the Torwa state to be mapped. More than twenty settlements are tightly clustered in the south-western part of the Zimbabwe plateau, to the west of the Lundi River (Garlake 1970).

Keith Robinson mapped and excavated the ruins at Khami over a number of years, starting in 1947. As at Great Zimbabwe, a central group of buildings, incorporating stone walls in their architecture, mark the court and the residences of the more important members of the society while in less substantial peripheral buildings lived the ordinary people. At the hub of the town of Khami was the aptly numbered No. 1 ruin, also known as the 'Hill Ruin', which has three platforms, built one above the other in an imposing tiered structure above cliffs that fall away to the Khami River.

As a result of Robinson's careful fieldwork, a good deal is known about the construction and design of the Hill Ruin. The platforms were con-

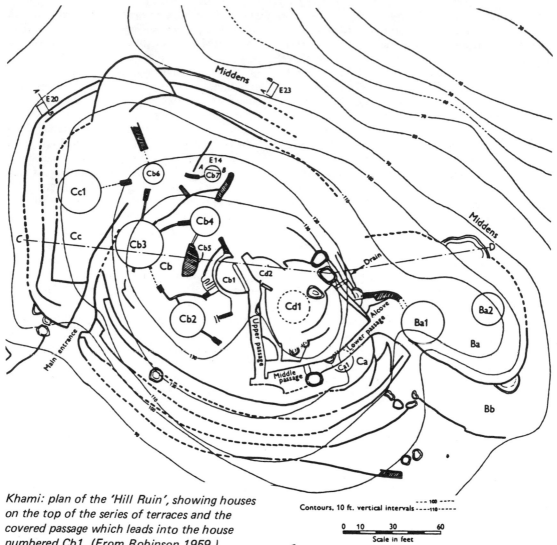

Khami: plan of the 'Hill Ruin', showing houses on the top of the series of terraces and the covered passage which leads into the house numbered Cb1. (From Robinson 1959.)

Contours, 10 ft. vertical intervals ---- 100 ---- ---- 110 ----

0   10   30   60
Scale in feet

Retaining wall   Independent wall   Collapsed wall

structed from rubble, capped with a thick layer of plaster and surrounded by retaining walls that were often ornately decorated. The highest platform was a living area, with at least seven separate house sites. The buildings were circular, mostly roofed with thatch and between 9 and 4 metres in diameter. The houses had been burnt down, and most of them were empty at their abandonment, although beneath a layer of ash on the floor of the smallest building were fragments of imported porcelain vessels, rough pottery and part of a clay figurine (Robinson 1959).

The entrances to the Hill Ruin form a set of striking architectural features. The main entrance consisted of a stairway on the north-west side of the building, rising some 12 metres beneath

heavily decorated walls – certainly an impressive approach to the buildings on the summit. There may possibly have been a second, minor entrance from the direction of the river to the north-east, while a third, 'private' passage went from the middle platform to the summit. This had been roofed with plaster and led through a secluded chamber to a semi-circular, plaster-roofed building. Unlike the other houses, the passage terminus still had a number of valuable objects amongst the rubble from its destruction. These included glass beads, bronze spearheads, iron goods and two lions carefully carved in ivory. Robinson has argued that the bold declaration of prestige and status of the other buildings high on their platform and the grand, decorated main entrance contrast markedly with the discreet roofed passage, secluded chamber and low flat-roofed terminus, suggesting the residence of the ruler and the location of important regalia (Robinson 1959).

The other buildings comprising Khami's central town are arranged in a rough arc with the river running behind. Three buildings still stand near the Hill Ruin to form the northern part of the crescent. Ruin No. 2 is a platform about 6 metres high and 24 metres in diameter with the remains of three houses still visible on the summit. Ruin No. 3 is a well-decorated, free-standing wall and Ruin No. 4, which is just to the south of the Hill Ruin, is a plaster house with stone walling.

At the centre of the crescent, and almost 300 metres south of the Hill Ruin, is a platform on which are the remains of two houses (Ruin No. 5). There are two free-standing enclosures alongside the platform.

Three buildings survive of the southern part of the town centre. Two of these (Ruins No. 6 and 7) repeat the now-familiar combination of a platform with a few houses. The third, Ruin No. 8 which is also known as the 'passage ruin', is more substantial, and has two platforms, some 3 metres high and with a passage entrance between them. The foundations of a single house survive on one platform, and free-standing walls form enclosures at the back of the building (Robinson 1959).

Recently, Tom Huffman has suggested that the town plan of central Khami was built to the same principles as Great Zimbabwe. Thus he sees the open area at the centre of the arc of buildings as the assembly area where cases were heard and political decisions made, and the Hill Ruin as the residence of the king, with the covered passage and underground chamber 'the conceptual transformation of a cave and the equivalent of the Eastern Enclosure on the Acropolis [of Great Zimbabwe]' (Huffman 1981). In this interpretation, the 'passage ruin' mirrors the Great Enclosure at Great Zimbabwe as an initiation centre for girls, with the other southern buildings constituting the residences of the royal wives (Huffman 1984).

If, as Huffman (1986b) has suggested, the architecture of Khami continues the metaphors of power used at both Mapungubwe and Great Zimbabwe, then this interpretation of the capital of the Torwa state is appropriate. Nevertheless, one important consideration militates against an unreserved acceptance of the proposal: it has not been proved that the central town of Khami was built as a single exercise, and the sequence of construction of the different buildings is not known. Indeed,

Robinson's excavations at the Hill Ruin suggest a complex history of construction, modification and reconstruction, with the form of the building changing considerably through time. 'As we see it today, Khami is the end-product of many rebuildings, wall being added to wall so that there is sometimes a succession of layers all standing vertically and capable of being peeled off one by one. In other places, platform has been piled on platform, sometimes stepped back terrace-wise and sometimes built so that older work was completely obliterated by the later platform.' (Summers 1971) Thus excavation of the middle platform of the Hill Ruin showed that the first building was a floor lying over an ashy midden. Later, the original platform had been heightened and enlarged, changing the form of the building (Robinson 1959).

Little is known of the lower-status housing that surrounded the central buildings of Khami. Robinson commented on 'hut remains', sometimes associated with short courses of walling extending about a kilometre to the north and west of the Hill Ruin, and excavated one of these (which he called Site 10), finding a round floor a little over 3 metres in diameter, which had a central pole supporting a thatched roof. The walls had been built of upright poles placed close together and plastered – a design quite unlike the houses of the central town and, Robinson thought, 'probably typical of the dwellings of the humbler members of the tribe or clan' (Robinson 1959: 99). Huffman has suggested that the overall population of Khami may have been 7 000 (Thorp 1984) – larger than the Portuguese estimates of the size of the Mutapa capital, but smaller than estimates of the population of Great Zimbabwe.

Danangombe was a smaller town than Khami, but its architecture shows that the same distinctive principles lay behind its construction. The main building consists of two large tiered platforms, the higher with a retaining wall up to 6 metres high, separated by a passage. Walling is profusely decorated in styles familiar from Khami (Summers 1971). Excavations early this century exposed the foundations of houses on the plaster-capped platforms and other buildings which may have been grain stores (MacIver 1906). During a later expedition, Gertrude Caton-Thompson found clear evidence that this main building had been altered and reconstructed several times, with new plaster floors on the platforms and the debris of past occupations mixed with the rubble fill (Caton-Thompson 1931).

Chevron, herringbone, check and panelled herrringbone decoration on the walling of Nalatale. (Drawing by Tina Coombes.)

Behind the platforms of the main building are rough walls that enclose a very large open area with no evidence of houses or other structures. This has generally been assumed to be an enclosure for livestock (Summers 1971), but Huffman has argued that this is yet another female-orientated complex, with the residences of the royal wives and an initiation centre for the young girls of the court (Huffman 1984).

Other parts of the town of Danangombe have generally escaped description, although it is clear that the main building was similarly the centre of an extensive residential complex. Gertrude Caton-Thompson pointed out that there was evidence for occupation for a radius of almost one kilometre from the main building and that 'weathered midden heaps and crumbling hut emplacements are noticeable, and every animal burrow has thrown up bones, beads and pottery' (Caton-Thompson 1931: 166). Unfortunately no archaeologist has subsequently taken up this lead and the larger settlement has remained unexplored.

Other towns with buildings similar to those of Khami and Danangombe were presumably regional administrative centres, performing for the Torwa state much the same function as the smaller *madzimbahwe* in the Zimbabwe state (Garlake 1970). For example Nalatale, with particularly richly decorated walling and the remains of a large, plaster-built house, was built 25 kilometres east of Danangombe on a large granite dome (Summers 1971). Further east again, and near the Lundi River and the probable boundary of the Torwa state, the small town of Chamabvefva consisted of a central, stone-walled building containing at most four houses and a few dwellings outside on the hilltop (Huffman 1979b).

Although the Portuguese made little contact with the Torwa state, both the general patterns of political economy in south-eastern Africa at this time, and the limited archaeological evidence, suggest that trade was important. Early treasure-hunters removed considerable quantities of worked gold from Danangombe, Khami and other contemporary sites, and later systematic excavations have led to the discovery of a variety of imported goods derived from a range of exotic sources. The Torwa ruling lineages may have traded with Islamic merchants, who continued to make a living through the sixteenth century despite Portuguese sea-power and blockades of Muslim ports. Thus the Portuguese explorer Antonio Fernandes, who travelled extensively in the interior during a series of expeditions starting in approximately 1511, found an extensive network of trade-routes and markets which were prospering despite Portuguese control of Sofala and Kilwa (Axelson 1973). Alternatively, Torwa may have been an anonymous partner in the Portuguese trade through the offices of intermediary groups.

The conquistadores

Although the rulers of Torwa and Mutapa may have seen the Portuguese and Islamic settlements on the coast as interchangeable economic partners, there were contrasts in both motive and style of operation that were to prove increasingly important as the commercial penetration of south-eastern Africa gained momentum in the decades that followed Portuguese settlement.

As described in earlier chapters, Islamic merchants expanded their activities steadily down the East African coastline over several centuries, building city-states that were politically independent and economically linked to a complex network of import and export from and to the wider Islamic world. Although, as Fernandes found, merchants did penetrate the interior, the coastal towns were heavily dependent on intermediary traders, some of them Islamicised, who visited the interior states with goods to trade. Portuguese claims that there were many thousands of 'Moors' in the interior early in the sixteenth century are undoubtedly exaggerations (Beach 1980).

In contrast, a different imperative lay behind Portuguese imperial expansion. Medieval Portugal was a small impoverished country which, in common with other European states, was economically restricted by the commercial dominance of the Islamic world. Because of this unfavourable balance of trade there was a great shortage of precious metals in the West. It has been estimated that the value of foreign gold coinage increased more than a hundredfold against Portuguese currency between 1383 and 1416 (Axelson 1973) – about the same period that the Islamic world was receiving a steady supply of gold from Zimbabwe.

In addition, Islam controlled the lucrative trade with the East, particularly the spices which were in great demand in Europe. As Fernand Braudel has explained, 'the medieval west . . . was carnivorous. We might assume that the badly preserved and not always tender meat cried out for the seasoning of strong peppers and spicy sauces, which disguised its poor quality. . . . ' (Braudel 1981) Spices were a particularly favoured commodity for merchants trying to maximise the return on their capital outlay, because small quantities fetched high prices and the costs of transportation were easily absorbed. Thus the search for the sources of Muslim gold, coupled with the possibility of gaining direct access to the spice-producing countries of the East, were more than sufficient stimulus for Portugal's imperial adventure.

In 1415, Portuguese forces captured the North African town of Ceuta, and in the following decades fleets sailed regularly from Lisbon to establish trading connections down the West African coast. A major advance came in 1487, when Bartolomeu Dias opened a sea-route to the Indian Ocean. In the same year Pero da Covilha left Portugal with instructions to discover all he could about navigation and commerce in the Indian Ocean. Passing as a Muslim, Covilha travelled

A Portuguese caravel (from Landstrom 1961).

southwards down the East African coast and visited both Kilwa and Sofala, reporting back to Portugal via messengers from Cairo. With information from Dias and Covilha to guide him, Vasco da Gama rounded the Cape of Good Hope and arrived off the East African coast in 1498, raiding Muslim trading vessels and sailing on to pioneer the final leg of the route to India (Axelson 1973).

But although the scope of this Portuguese expansion was impressive, its substance was extremely thin. Territories were held by small groups of men, completely dependent on the superiority of firearms over spears and the regular visits of fleets from Portugal and India to maintain supplies of trading goods and new recruits for the garrisons. In south-east Africa, control of trading depots such as Sofala was given to members of the nobility and gentry as a political favour for three years or so. Remuneration was considered nominal, and the main aim was to gain maximum profit through trade in the limited time available (Axelson 1973).

Given this milieu, few Portuguese commanders had much concern for the longer-term political and economic stability of south-east Africa, in contrast with their Islamic equivalents, who had far more to gain from stable, dependable trade connections. In addition, it was often in Portuguese interests to penetrate the interior, both to avoid losing profit to middlemen along the trade-routes and also to cut off sources of trade goods from their Islamic competitors.

In 1531 the Portuguese established a market on the Zambezi at Sena, and a few years later a similar trading point at Tete, higher up the same river. In

Portuguese mercantile expansion provided this new symbol in San rock art: the 'Heidedal Galleon', near Porterville in the western Cape. (Drawing by Royden Yates.)

1544 a garrison was positioned at Quelimane to superintend the estuary of the Zambezi (Alpers 1975). But ambitions often exceeded means, for it was one thing to attempt to control trade at points of embarkation along the coast and the Zambezi, and quite a different proposition to attempt to mount expeditions into the interior, with its alien climate and hostile population. Thus more grandiose initiatives, such as the attempt to conquer the interior for the Portuguese Crown between 1569 and 1575, were less successful (Axelson 1973).

Although the major aim of the Portuguese had been to secure a major supply of gold, they were never particularly successful in achieving this. From the earliest years of the fortress at Sofala, gold was only brought to the coast irregularly and in small quantities, probably because of disputes between middlemen. In addition, gold had now been discovered in the Americas, which led to a consequent decline in the value of the metal and decrease in the volume of trade goods that Portuguese traders could offer (Phimister 1976).

As a result, ivory soon became the principal commodity available for export, although in this respect as well the Portuguese did not achieve the successes that they anticipated. During the seventeenth century much of the ivory from the interior of south-central Africa was carried by Yao middlemen north to Kilwa, which was by this time again in Muslim hands. Early in the eighteenth century political disputes disrupted the northern markets, and the Yao began to favour Mozambique Island. But at much the same time Indian merchants, principally Hindu, came to dominate East African trade. Unlike the impoverished Portuguese traders and officials, who had come to Africa largely without resources in order to build up their wealth, the Hindu merchants had a strong financial base and a virtual monopoly over the source of cloth, essential in trading enterprises. The risks involved in investment in south-east Africa were well worth the reward, for high-quality African ivory was in constant demand for the manufacture in India of marriage bangles (Alpers 1975).

Thus although the Portuguese railed at the Indian traders, and periodically introduced measures to restrict or outlaw their commercial activities, capital from India proved essential to prevent the complete collapse of the Portuguese economy in eastern Africa. Deprived of much of the profits from the ivory trade, and with the export market in slaves still undeveloped, Portuguese officials had to content themselves with income from taxes. These were very heavy. In the years before 1787, for instance, some classes of trade bead were taxed at 20 per cent on initial import, and then a further 40 per cent if they were transferred to the markets on the Zambezi (Alpers 1975). Such an imposition naturally encouraged all traders, whether Muslim, Hindu or Portuguese, to bypass official points of collection and the over-extended Portuguese military forces and to engage directly in trade entirely on their own account.

Thus the surprising thing about the Portuguese empire, as C. R. Boxer has pointed out (Boxer 1961), is not so much its extent and the rapidity with which it was established, but the fact that it survived at all. By the middle of the eighteenth century widely spaced, under-supplied and fever-ridden garrisons were still attempting to monopolise trade along a vast stretch of often hostile coastline.

States in formation: the Zulu and Xhosa cases

A constant thread that runs through the archaeology and history of the Mapungubwe, Zimbabwe, Mutapa and Torwa states, and through settlement in southern Africa by Islamic and Portuguese communities, is the trade imperative.

'An ivory carrier' (from Baines 1864).

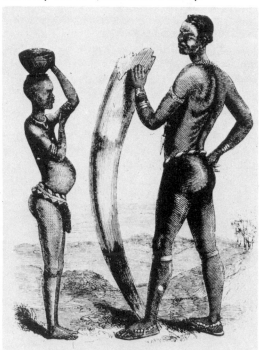

124

Thus although early African states had complex internal economies in which foreign trade only directly touched the lives of a small segment of the population, their rulers were more often than not anxious to secure trade connections with the coast and, on several occasions, seem to have lost power when access to markets was severed.

In Chapter 7 it was suggested that, although foreign trade should not be seen as the primary cause of state formation, the possession of commodities given value by their rarity was essential if an emergent ruling class was to signify its power and authority. In other words, possession of an exclusive form of wealth (a condition that livestock could not easily fulfil) was a corollary of class formation and therefore of the tributary mode of production.

Although potentially useful, it has only been possible to apply this model tentatively in exploring the early states of southern Africa, for despite advances in the theory of social archaeology, relations of production remain difficult to discern in the material remains of past settlements. But by the eighteenth century political and economic developments were taking place in the south-east coastlands that reveal the impact of Portuguese and other traders on agro-pastoral chiefdoms. Because archaeological information is here supplemented by documentary sources and oral traditions, the question of the relative importance of foreign trade and internal economic change in state formation can again be addressed.

Both the Zulu and the Xhosa have for many years been recalled in histories of southern Africa for their warlike tendencies, and for the resistance they offered to colonial expansion in the subcontinent. But recent revaluations of their past and of the structure of their society (Guy 1982; Peires 1981) have uncovered a different picture, revealing political and economic structures that did not merely serve to place large armies in the field.

Nevertheless, there is still disagreement as to whether these polities can be called 'states', for although their leaders were often successful at preventing fission, thus building up substantial followings and the facility to defy the considerable power of colonial governments, it is difficult to discern distinct classes of rulers. Indeed, it is this indeterminate condition that makes the Zulu and Xhosa polities particularly valuable in seeking to understand state formation in southern Africa, for while the tributary mode of production may not have been fully fledged, it was certainly in the making.

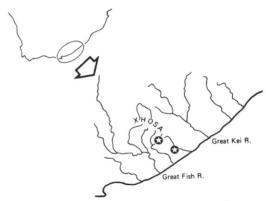

The Xhosa domain in the early nineteenth century, and the paramount's capitals.

The Xhosa royal line can be traced back to Tshawe, who was paramount over one of several major political groups that were competing for power in the years before 1675. The amaTshawe steadily expanded their power-base by incorporating other groups, including Khoikhoi pastoralists such as the Gona Dama and the Hoengiqua. In Jeff Peires's words, 'the limits of Xhosadom were not ethnic or geographic, but political: all persons or groups who accepted the rule of the Tshawe thereby became Xhosa' (Peires 1981). But despite the ascendancy of Tshawe's line, the Xhosa paramouncy remained a loose structure, with considerable authority retained by the heads of different family lines.

The Zulu kingdom was also based on the incorporation of a widening sphere of communities,

The heartland of the emerging Zulu kingdom.

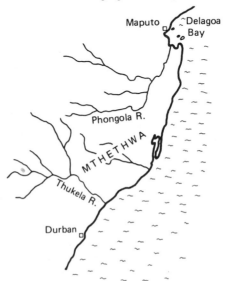

125

often in a tributary relationship with the core of the nation, although the course of events was somewhat different from that experienced by the Xhosa. By the later eighteenth century a number of powerful chiefdoms had developed in the area between the Thukela and Phongolo rivers, including the Mthethwa under Dingiswayo. This 'confederacy' was the basis from which Dingiswayo's successor in power, Shaka, built up the powerful kingdom that was to dominate south-eastern Africa in the first half of the nineteenth century (Marks 1967).

What then was the spur for the process of expansion and incorporation which was characteristic of both the Xhosa paramouncy and the Zulu kingdom? One school of thought has stressed the dominance of internal economic processes. Writers who have favoured such explanations have seen the crucial forces as catastrophic – population pressure (Omer-Cooper 1966), soil erosion (Marks 1967), or the natural propensity for cattle herds to increase in size, thereby leading to overgrazing (Guy 1978).

Others have emphasised the role of trade in permitting and promoting the accumulation of wealth, and therefore power, in the hands of ruling groups. This possibility has been examined both through the records of early traders who developed connections with the kingdoms (Smith 1969, 1970), and from an African perspective, in terms of the political and economic structures that could have served to translate trade items into a source of power (Hedges 1978).

It is difficult to evaluate these competing hypotheses from the documentary sources alone, as the records are mostly silent about the crucial couple of centuries that embodied the formative phase of each kingdom. But the archaeological evidence does narrow the possibilities and provide some indication as to which of the two models is likely to be the more appropriate. For the alternative causal factors of trade and internal forces both presuppose suitable economic conditions: either sufficient political power to control trade-routes in the first place, or else conditions of environmental deterioration that were the spur of expansion and conquest (Hall 1980).

In fact, there is little evidence for environmental deterioration within the area that was to come under the control of the Zulu kings. In the coastal area and the river valleys, settlement patterns suggest that there was adequate agricultural land until the present century, while in the upland areas abandoned villages were probably used as gardens

for agricultural products (Hall 1981). Thus although soil erosion may have been a factor of occasional local importance, it is improbable that a decline in agricultural productivity lay behind the formation of the Zulu kingdom. Insufficient research has been carried out in the Xhosa area to discern whether or not the same conclusion is reasonable in this case, but as the overall environmental structure and range of pre-paramouncy settlement patterns are the same, it would seem fair to lay aside the factor of soil erosion in this area as well (McKenzie 1984).

Similarly, archaeological research has lent little support to the idea that there were inadequate grazing resources in the crucial years when state institutions began to be forged. The coastal plain and river valleys within the Zulu kingdom were probably self-contained pastoral systems which complemented each other under varying climatic circumstances, and there is no evidence for any substantial build-up of animal numbers (Hall 1981). In contrast, settlement densities in the higher lands seem to have been greater, and estimates suggest that, by the late eighteenth century, livestock numbers were close to, or indeed greater than, the maximum density that could be supported by available grasslands. But the patterns of political and economic fission show that agro-pastoral communities from the affected areas moved to other, available grassland areas, which suggests that there was no general ecological crisis (Hall and Mack 1983).

To the south, as Bruce McKenzie has argued, the overgrazing that is so prevalent today is a recent phenomenon, and in the years prior to the emergence of the Xhosa paramouncy cattle numbers were well within ecological limits. 'Early Iron Age people had little effect on the landscape. Woody vegetation would have been cleared for cultivation and livestock numbers would have been low. From the beginning of the Late Iron Age up to the twentieth century, livestock became more important, increased areas of woodland . . . were cleared for cultivation, livestock condition was good and soil erosion was not a major problem.' (McKenzie 1984) Although current archaeological research will provide a test of this proposition (Granger, Hall, McKenzie and Feely 1985), there seems little possibility that ecological crisis will be invoked as the major cause of Xhosa state formation.

This lack of evidence for a crisis strengthens the case for a review of the evidence for trade contacts in these southern areas. The major point of contact

'Two of King Panda's dancing girls' (from Angas 1849).

during the period of concern here was Delagoa Bay, which Portuguese traders from Mozambique began to visit after 1544. It became a major trading centre after 1750: 'Between the mid-sixteenth century and the early nineteenth century the Delagoa Bay area was transformed from an isolated region, far removed from the mainstream of East and Central African commerce, into one of the most important commercial centres on the East African coast' (Smith 1970: 265). Merchants stayed at the bay for six months at a stretch, working from a temporary camp on an off-shore island and visiting the various chiefdoms in the immediate hinterland. During the seventeenth century, English vessels occasionally visited, while Dutch and French traders also participated at various times in the years that followed (Smith 1970).

Although a variety of commodities were obtained from Delagoa Bay, ivory seems usually to have been the principal export. The failure of traders to obtain gold, tin or copper in the six-

teenth or seventeenth centuries is instructive, suggesting that the trade network that fanned out from Delagoa was separate from the economic catchment area of Sofala, Angoche and Mozambique Island, all of which were in some form of contact with Torwa, Mutapa and the states that followed them (Smith 1970). A further indication that the Delagoa Bay trade was dependent on lands to the south was the success of the chiefdoms on the southern shores of the bay in securing ivory: 'almost all Europeans who commented on the subject agreed that those chiefdoms on the southern side of the bay, that is, those whose immediate hinterland led towards northern Natal, were the best places to trade' (Smith 1969).

Comments made by shipwrecked Portuguese as they made their way northwards towards the East coast garrisons are consistent with the pattern. In the mid-sixteenth century, people were observed carrying ivory for trade with Nyaka, the chiefdom on the southern shores of the bay. Others were wearing beads and possessed brasswork that probably came from English traders. Dingiswayo was concerned to control and monopolise such commerce as soon as the Mthethwa had built up political and economic power, sending ivory and cattle to the bay and making all trade a royal prerogative (Smith 1969).

Evidence for the role of trade in the formative years of the Xhosa paramouncy is more tenuous, and Jeff Peires prefers to leave the question of the origins of this polity open (Peires 1981). Nevertheless, the dominant lineages of the Xhosa paramouncy succeeded in drawing most of their neighbours into reciprocal relationships, and were energetic in seeking trade contacts with European settlers from the Cape from the early eighteenth century. Copper, cattle, iron and beads were obtained at the frontier and redistributed back towards the centre, with escalating prices ensuring profits for the middlemen involved (Peires 1981). It is also possible that the Xhosa participated in the Delagoa trade from an early date, for on one occasion early in the nineteenth century Ronga traders from the Delagoa hinterland were observed at the capital of a Xhosa chief (Smith 1969).

But how did the intervention of trade begin to transform economic and political institutions? It is probable that, before Dingiswayo and Tshawe began to form the network of alliances that were to comprise the basis of their confederacies, the dominant social form was the chiefdom, in which relations were established through livestock transactions and political groupings were frequently formed and reformed. But, it has been argued, the goods obtained by trade and given prestige by their rarity broke the established order by allowing some people to circumvent the power of the lineage elders, attract a following, and dominate and exact tribute over a wide area (Bonner 1982).

This process alone may be sufficient to account for the Xhosa paramouncy with its comparatively loose structure, but to the north another factor came into play early in the nineteenth century. For whereas trade connections between the Xhosa paramouncy and the Cape Colony were expanding at this time, the Mthethwa were experiencing a decrease in supplies from Delagoa Bay (Bonner 1981), in the aftermath of the destruction of the Portuguese fort by a French fleet in 1796 and the virtual cessation of the ivory trade (Smith 1970). This problem was accentuated by a crippling drought and consequent famine (Hall 1976), and Dingiswayo's Mthethwa must have perceived all too clearly the need for drastic action if the flow of prestige goods, on which their political power rested, was to be maintained. Their response was to mould the system of age regiments, or *amabutho*, into the powerful army which was used to such effect by Shaka (Bonner 1981) – the coercive element essential in any state system.

For all these reasons the examples of the Zulu kingdom and the Xhosa paramouncy reinforce the suggestion that control over an expensive, and exclusive, form of wealth was essential if ambitious chiefs were to break away from the checks and balances surrounding their power that were intrinsic when the commodity used to signify political and economic relationships was livestock. But these putative states also show that the particular form and trajectory of political and economic change varied from case to case. Thus whereas the readiness of colonial settlers to trade across the eastern Cape frontier may have sustained the loose Xhosa confederacy, the declining supply of essential trade items to the Zulu kingdom seems to have had the opposite effect. It can be anticipated that, were more detail known of the Mapungubwe, Zimbabwe, Mutapa and Torwa states, a similar degree of variation in the details of economic and political processes would be evident.

'Utimuni, nephew of Chaka' (from Angas 1849).

11

Warriors, adventurers and slaves

Three centuries of turmoil

According to a widely accepted version of southern African history, Shaka's kingship of the Zulu state introduced an era of widespread conflict in southern Africa. Having transformed military techniques, the king first subdued those smaller chiefdoms around him and then disrupted formerly peaceful societies southwards towards the frontier with the white settlers at the Cape, inland to the highveld, and northwards into the area that is today Mozambique. Other leaders either moved away with their armies to avoid the Zulu maelstrom, or else seceded from Shaka's kingdom with their followers, founding conquest states far to the north. In this way the *difaqane* – 'the scattering' – brought a dramatic and sudden ending to centuries of essentially stable society in southern Africa (Omer-Cooper 1966).

But in wider perspective, this reading of the past now seems to be an oversimplification. The concept of a single *difaqane* is suspect (Cobbing 1983), and, although there can be no doubting their existence, Shaka's military conquests seem rather to have been one manifestation of new political and economic forces that had begun to make themselves felt before the Zulu state was born, and involved many other leaders and their followers.

Indeed, when the three centuries between the first penetration of the southern African interior by Portuguese traders and the beginning of industrial development around the new goldfields of the southern highveld are considered overall, a recurrent theme becomes apparent. For in general this was a period of widespread turmoil in which leaders gained power rapidly and often lost it equally quickly, and in which the practice of slavery became widely established across the subcontinent.

Prazeros and slaves

The begining of this new tendency – the age of what Paul Lovejoy (1983) has aptly termed the 'war lord' – can be traced back to Portuguese expansion inland along the valley of the Zambezi River in the first half of the sixteenth century. By 1530, a number of renegades, or *sertanejos*, had moved away from the coast. Some of these 'were illiterate criminals, some were noblemen, but all were reacting against the discipline of fortress life and against the constraints of the royal monopoly of commerce' (Newitt 1973).

By participating in trade as middlemen, at first under the patronage of established political leaders, but increasingly with the support of their own followers, the renegades soon became a factor of consequence. 'The story of the fairs in the seventeenth century is a story whose meaning is quite clear. Renegades and traders pioneered commercial contacts in the interior. Wherever they were successful permanent settlements were established under the surveillance of the local chief. A captain would be appointed and a church constructed as the centre of a mission. The men who had come as traders were then superseded by fortune-hunters anxious to exploit the gold mines themselves or to dabble in African politics with their lucrative by-products in land concessions, slaves and loot. The conflict of the various interest groups either led to the total expulsion of the Portuguese or to the collapse of the local African state and the dislocation of society. Thereafter the Portuguese might mine gold for themselves, but the supply always fell below that obtained in the days of peaceful trading. The trade frontier then moved further into the interior and the process began again.' (Newitt 1973: 46-7)

The politically skilful and fortunate renegades became extremely powerful and were soon able to form alliances with the rulers of states on the Zimbabwe plateau in return for further concessions. A significant connection of this kind was forged in 1606, when the Mutapa state enlisted the aid of Diogo Simoes Madeira, one of the most powerful traders in the Sena area, who was able to raise an army of more than 4 000 mercenaries and gain wide-ranging political and economic rights as the price of his assistance. Ever watchful for an opportunity to regularise a situation to its advantage, the Portuguese Crown soon granted powerful figures like Madeira land titles, or *prazos*, long leases that had become popular in medieval Portugal (Newitt 1973). Thus by royal decree *sertanejos* became *prazeros*, renegades became land-holders and loyal subjects of the King of Portugal, and the first of the war lords were established in south-east Africa.

It is a mistake to see the seventeenth-century *prazeros* as the vanguard of Portuguese colonial settlement in south-east Africa, for the men and women who held power over their massive Zambezian estates at this time were in every respect 'transfrontiersmen' – people who had crossed the frontier of their own cultural area, often taking up a new way of life (Isaacman and Isaacman 1975). Thus *prazeros* rarely removed established chiefs, but rather imposed a new set of political institutions above the old, receiving tribute and taxes that had been passed up the political hierarchy, retaining profits and redistributing

Massangano, sketched immediately after its destruction in 1888 (from De Castilho 1891).

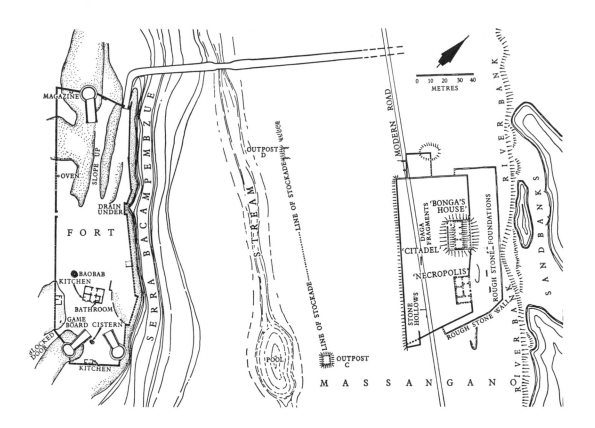

Plan of the prazo at Massangano. At the junction of the Luenha and Zambezi rivers, about 40 km below Tete, this fortified residence may have been first built by Manuel Paes de Pinho before 1667. (From Newitt and Garlake 1967.)

goods and favours down the hierarchy again to secure support. Despite considerable pressure from the Portuguese authorities, very few *prazeros* attempted to develop any form of commercial agriculture on their estates, rather depending on tried methods of trading and serving as middlemen linking the Indian Ocean coastline with the African interior. In this way *prazeros* obtained gold and ivory from their estates at depressed prices and sent them to the coast, from where cloths, beads and other trade goods were obtained and bartered at inflated prices on the *prazos* and beyond (Isaacman 1972).

Profits from this trade could be as high as 300 per cent, and the *prazeros* enjoyed a comfortable standard of living, which 'most observers characterized as vulgarly opulent and decadent. *Prazeros* compensated for the hardships of living in the interior by surrounding themselves with all the goods necessary to satisfy their material and sen-

sual needs. Their homes were often furnished in the latest styles; their tables were loaded with exotic fruits and meats; and the *prazero* smoked the best cigars and drank the finest wines . . . [while] . . . the women led an equally frivolous existence, passing their days beautifying themselves and being entertained by their male slaves.' (Isaacman 1972: 58) But for all their affluence, the *prazeros* were soon influenced by local beliefs and customs, including witchcraft and the use of diviners. Many *prazeros* began to use the symbols of African chiefship in their dress, while plaster-and-thatch houses were more common within the fortified stockades from which they controlled their territories (Newitt and Garlake 1967). Thus although the *prazos* had formal status in Portuguese law, they were in practice groups of chiefdoms (run by the same structures of authority as had existed before the Portuguese arrived) which served as sources of revenue and trade markets for the *prazero* and his immediate family.

The *prazo* system was essentially parasitic, drawing profit from the population within the *prazero*'s control and holding the subjects of the estate to a closed market in imported commodities, perpetuating inflated prices. Obviously, such

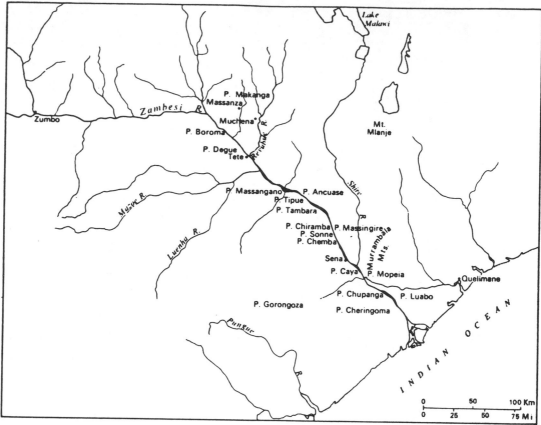

The major prazos *on the Zambezi River, 1750–1900. (From Isaacman 1972.)*

a system could not survive without considerable military force as backing, and for this the *prazeros* were dependent on large armies of slaves, the *achikunda*. These could consist of many thousands of men and were divided into regiments deployed at strategic positions through the *prazo*. The *prazero*'s army ensured that tribute was collected from the estate's population, provided protection on trading expeditions into the interior, guarded the *prazo* from hostile neighbours, and allowed the *prazero* to expand his holdings and involve himself in the political intrigues of the region. Nevertheless, the *achikunda* were an unpredictable force, and although some *prazero* families held power through several generations, others lost their estates when their armies revolted or formed alliances with other war lords (Isaacman 1972).

The dependency of the *prazeros* on their slave armies had implications beyond the Zambezi valley, for in one form or another slavery was to be an important element in the power of many other rulers and leaders in the subcontinent for several centuries to come. As Paul Lovejoy has pointed out, the institution of slavery was far wider in scope than the form that provided labour for plantations on the East African coast, the Mascarene Islands and in the Americas (Lovejoy 1983). Apart from the *prazo* armies that have already been mentioned, slaves were employed in domestic service by Portuguese and Arab traders and extensively within African societies in order to enlarge lineages. The definitive characteristic was not how slaves were employed but the manner in which they were obtained, for 'the traumata of capture, transportation and sale severed slaves from the social fabric of their original communities [with the result that] slaves were outsiders, with no ties except to their master and through him to his kinship and communal groups' (Cooper 1977).

Once obtained, slaves could be used to create economic and political power, and here lay both the attraction of the institution and the means whereby war lords were able to build up their strength. For power lay in the people who provided labour and other resources for their leaders – support that had previously been gained from kin groups and through marriage, with the consequent payment of bridewealth and commitment to reciprocal sets of obligations. Slavery gave a leader the opportunity to build up a following rapidly and without the expense of marriage settlements, the sanction of relatives or continuing commitment to assist other groups (Kopytoff and Miers 1977).

It is probably futile to search for the origins of African slavery. Indeed, it is likely that abrogations of reciprocal relationships between communities occurred at different times and in different places, leading to the enlargement of followings by means of force (Kopytoff and Miers 1977). In addition, Islamic communities on the East coast had created a steady demand for slaves, both for export and for service in the city-states such as Kilwa (Lovejoy 1983).

But it is certain, for a number of reasons, that slavery became more widespread after the Portuguese penetration of the interior of south-east Africa and that its incidence gathered momentum through the centuries that followed. Firstly, the very nature of Portuguese settlement demanded slaves, for there were inadequate immigrants to maintain settlements and very few women. In addition, and in contrast to the tendency in indigenous African communities, the Portuguese kept their slaves in a marginal position. Thus where the interior states integrated slaves and their offspring into their kin groups, often after only a single generation, the Portuguese used up their labour supply and then had to obtain replacements (Lovejoy 1983). This was particularly the case on the prazos, where the unstable political climate caused a high rate of loss from the achikunda, whether from defection or loss in battle. Prazeros were constantly obtaining new slaves from the Yao to the north of the Zambezi, from other prazos, or from raids and warfare (Isaacman 1972). As a result there was a constant frontier zone of turbulence in which traders and war lords sought to obtain the slaves they needed, in turn encouraging more opportunists to seek fortune with the aid of rapidly constructed followings (Lovejoy 1983).

Responses: Mutapa and the Rozvi

Slavery gained its own dynamic from the struggle to control trade between the wider world and the African interior, for slaves provided a means for leaders to circumvent the political and economic structures of the established states and gain rapid power and profit. One of the first casualties of this new era was Mutapa, which was compromised by its call for military assistance from the prazeros early in the seventeenth century and never again achieved the same extent of power that the Monomotapas had enjoyed during the first century of their contact with the Portuguese. But although earlier historians saw these misfortunes as the end of Mutapa power, David Beach has shown convincingly that the state adapted rapidly to the new conditions, employing similar methods to those of the war lords who threatened their borders (Beach 1980).

By 1607 the Mutapa state was in decline, and the Monomotapa could no longer control Portuguese settlement. That part of the state which included the high plateau was lost, and the capital was moved to the hostile environment of the Zambezi lowlands. In 1629 a treaty made the Monomotapa a vassal of the King of Portugal, additional Portuguese settlement was permitted within Mutapa, and the prazeros built fortified settlements across the country, diverting economic and political power away from the royal dynasty.

The low point of this decline was reached in 1663, when the prazeros deposed the ruling Monomotapa in favour of their own nominee. But in the years that followed, the state was steadily reconstructed from within its much-diminished boundaries. This was probably made possible by the prazeros themselves, who had so damaged the economic infrastructure of Mutapa that returns from trade and mining had greatly declined. The ruling dynasties began to re-establish their power, and in 1693, with the aid of allies, the Monomotapa was able to drive out many of the traders.

The territorial integrity of the state was maintained through the eighteenth and nineteenth century, partly with the backing of a small standing army which could be enlarged if the necessity arose, but also by employing slaves after the fashion of military leaders in other parts of the subcontinent. In this way, members of the powerful dynasties were supported by groups of slaves, of which the women were incorporated into domestic life and the men became warriors, or vanyai. The vanyai were grouped into companies, each one hundred strong, carrying out ordinary economic activities, but also serving as a fighting force. 'The emergence of the vanyai appears to be the main reason for the continued existence and surprising resilience of the Mutapa state. They provided the military muscle to repel Portuguese attacks and extend the Mutapa's influence. . . . They also supplied [the] subrulers of the Mutapa dynasty with the force with which to claim the Mutapa title, and by trading or, very often, robbing traders, they bought in extra wealth to their subrulers.' (Beach 1980: 150)

A second consequence of the general confusion in Zambezia that followed the rise of the *prazero* war lords was the fall of the rulers of the Torwa state to the south. The origins of the Rozvi are still obscure, but Beach has shown that they were most likely a lineage that moved out from the umbrella of Mutapa as conflicts with the Portuguese escalated. By 1696 at the latest, and after a brief conquest, the Rozvi had taken over control of Torwa and its capital, which was by this time probably Danangombe. The details of the Rozvi economy are not known, but it is probable that the ruling dynasty used military force to ensure a flow of tribute from neighbouring communities, while the Changamire (as the leader of the Rozvi was known) was undoubtedly involved, as were other leaders at the time, in raids to gain wealth in cattle and other commodities (Beach 1980).

Responses: the Zambezi Tonga

Of course, not all communities in the Zambezi valley and its hinterland were successful in adapting to the new political order, and many became victims of the war lords. One such case were the Tonga communities who lived in the Ruenga valley and on the adjacent Inyanga plateau in the seventeenth and eighteenth centuries, before losing the area to Manyika regiments.

The very extent of the stone ruins of the Inyanga area, which cover some 8 000 square kilometres and include substantial fortified settlements, villages built of stone and many thousands of kilometres of hillside terracing, has suggested to some interpreters that this must represent the architecture of a flourishing and powerful community. But, ironically, it is the very poverty of the area, combined with continual threats against the occupants, that necessitated such intensity of labour.

Although there are patches of alluvial soils in the lower-lying areas, the predominant granites of the Inyanga region have weathered into poor soils, which provide little potential for either agriculture or livestock grazing (Summers 1958). Terraces, which are often built along the slopes of the dolerite hills with their somewhat better soils, allowed the best possibilities for cultivation while reducing the risk of rapid erosion. As Roger Summers has pointed out, the soils contained by the terraces were probably not manured and would have rapidly diminished in fertility when cultivated, demanding the further extension of the contoured hillslopes (Summers 1958). Thus this form of agriculture was probably far from cost efficient, as very considerable amounts of labour must have been invested as the price of a fairly modest return.

The designs of the stone buildings fall into a number of categories, with some types being confined either to the upland or to the river valley parts

TERRACES   FORTS   ENCLOSURES   FURNACES   EXCAVATED SITES

Terracing and settlement in the Inyanga area. (Drawing by Royden Yates.)

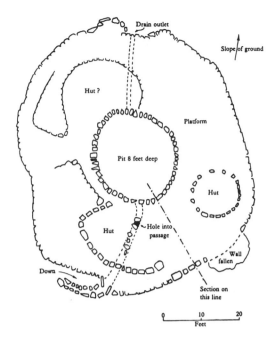

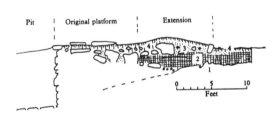

Fortified Tonga village in the eastern highlands of Zimbabwe, excavated and mapped in 1951 by Roger Summers. Houses were built on platforms around a sunken livestock enclosure which was entered through a passage that could be blocked from above, and that had a stone floor and a drain down the slope of the ground. (From Summers 1958.)

of the regions. Nevertheless, there are some consistent themes which can be regarded as responses to common problems. At the centre of most villages were enclosures for livestock, in the design of which particular attention was paid to the problems of defence. In some cases the livestock byre was a stone building around which were clustered platforms for houses, with a perimeter wall and lintelled doorway surrounding the whole settlement. In other examples, such as the sites along the banks of the Nyangombe River which Keith Robinson and Roger Summers studied in detail, a wide

rubble-filled platform was built up against the retaining wall of the livestock enclosure, creating an underground passage that formed the entrance to the byre. Houses were built on the platform, and an outer enclosure, with a well-built doorway, gave added protection.

This architectural form was developed even further in the higher parts of the Inyanga area, where circular cuttings were excavated from the hillsides and again surrounded by stone-built platforms on which houses were built. These central byres were up to 3 metres deep, paved with stone slabs and again entered by means of a passageway beneath the house platform. The passages were less than a metre wide and little more than a metre high, suggesting that they were used for small stock rather than cattle (Summers 1958). This is another indication of the poverty of the Inyanga communities, who must have gone to extraordinary lengths to protect a class of animal that was undoubtedly considered inferior by the leaders of the Mutapa and Torwa states to the north-west and south-west.

Livestock were clearly not the only economic resource at risk, for Summers and Robinson found the ruins of fortified granaries in the Nyangombe River area. These had been built on the summit of hills and were heavily protected by walling and a set of lintelled doors. There were no midden deposits or house sites inside these enclosures, which instead shielded numerous stone-walled platforms on which were the remains of grain bins and potsherds (Summers 1958).

Although there is no overriding regularity in settlement pattern, these village enclosures often form loose groups of up to twenty, built around rather different structures that have aptly been called 'forts'. A good example is Nyangwe, high in the upland part of the Inyanga area. The building consists of a central complex of six enclosures, with lower terrace walls on the slope beneath. Entrances were by lintelled doorways through the walls, which were also broken by numerous loopholes. Inside some of the enclosures were low circles of walling, up to 4 metres in diameter, which were presumably the lower walling of houses (Summers 1958).

The nature of the relationship between the villages and their forts is unclear. It seems improbable that the forts were places of refuge to which the villagers fled while under attack, for then the elaborate protective architecture of the villages themselves would have been unnecessary. The forts could have housed regional leaders, bearing a

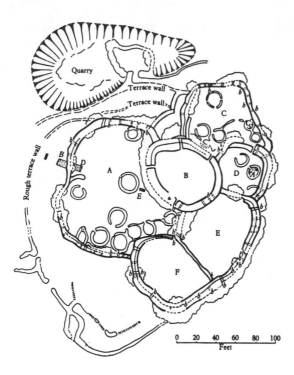

Nyangwe, built on a high outcrop in the eastern highlands of Zimbabwe. Originally described by MacIver, the settlement consists of six internal enclosures, protected by perimeter walls in which are set lintelled doorways and numerous loopholes. (From the original plan published by Roger Summers in 1958.)

similar relationship to the cluster of villages around them as the smaller *madzimbahwe* to the houses outside their walls in the Zimbabwe state. If this is the case, then the poverty of these communities is further emphasised, for excavations in midden deposits against the enclosure walls at Nyangwe yielded only a few glass beads and none of the more exotic imports that came the way of the leaders of the earlier states (Summers 1958).

Thus the people who lived in the Inyanga area in the seventeenth and eighteenth centuries, who have been identified from traditions and documentary sources as Tonga originally from the Lower Zambezi valley (Beach 1980), seem to have been constantly threatened by the war lords who were competing for power all around them. They were forced to practise an intensive form of agriculture, from which the yields must have been low, to protect their grain and small stock from raiders and to build structures that could withstand attack. As David Beach has commented, this was a 'culture of losers' (Beach 1980: 186).

The south

Competition between chiefs and kings in the south-eastern subcontinent for access to trade through Delagoa Bay was as pronounced as the rivalry between different factions in and around the Zambezi valley. Attempts to control trade with visiting vessels in Delagoa Bay rapidly militarised the chiefdoms of southern Mozambique, and Dingiswayo himself entered this confrontation, sending porters directly to the bay to trade. One of Dingiswayo's first problems was with the Qwabe chiefdom which 'had refused to surrender a pretender to the Mthethwa chieftaincy. Perhaps uncertain of his own power, Dingiswayo concluded an alliance with the Maputo [at Delagoa Bay]. In return for the aid of musket-carrying soldiers, Dingiswayo agreed to exchange all of his goods through Maputo. With the support of the soldiers and firearms from Maputo, the Mthethwa were easily able to overcome the Qwabe. Dingiswayo had found another way to turn the trade and politics of Delagoa Bay to his own advantage.' (Smith 1969)

Once the core area of the state was secure, the Zulu kings were able to use their regiments, the *amabutho*, to carry out raids over a wider area. Although it is often stated that slavery was an unknown institution in these southern areas, it is clear that the Zulu broke down the established political and social structures of the chiefdoms on the expanding frontiers of the new state, incorporating the men from these chiefdoms into regiments and the women into new lineages in a fashion that fits easily within the definition of slavery (Lovejoy 1983). The particular success of the Zulu kings was in moving the frontier well away from the core area of the kingdom, allowing the development of stable institutions that continued until the state was dismembered by British and colonial authorities (Guy 1982).

That the early Zulu kingdom was a product of warrior leaders is underlined by patterns of settlement. Unlike the Mapungubwe and Zimbabwe states, with their established capitals and regional centres, the power of the Zulu kingdom rested on a set of large military towns that were imposed on the existing network of similar villages. Thus settlement patterns in the Lower Mfolozi River valley remained much the same throughout the second millennium, despite the fact that this was the area from which the Mthethwa began to build up their power (Hall 1981). Similarly, the villages that Nathaniel Isaacs encountered as he travelled across the kingdom to appear before Shaka were

136

much the same in composition and size, and it was only the king's capital that was of a different order (Herman 1936).

Although the locations of several of these military towns are known, only one has been partially excavated and described. Mgungundlovu was built by Shaka's successor Dingane in 1829 and occupied until 1838. The town was visited by a number of traders and travellers, who left descriptions of its plan and structure, and to these have been added the results of excavation (Parkington and Cronin 1979). At the head of the town was the *isigodlo*, housing the king and his personal retinue. At least one house within the *isigodlo* was specially designed for storing weapons. The barracks were to the left and right of the *isigodlo*, extending down the gentle slope of the hill to form the oval shape of the town as a whole. Excavation has shown that the houses within the barracks were densely packed and standard in design, perhaps numbering about 800 in all, and housing some 5 000 warriors. Although large herds of cattle were certainly brought to Mgungundlovu from time to time, there is no evidence for the range of domestic activities that took place in the outer towns of centres such as Great Zimbabwe and Khami. Mgungundlovu was undoubtedly provisioned directly from distant villages (Parkington and Cronin 1979) and did not have its own immediate economic hinterland with the full range of domestic functions needed to support its large population.

Not all the chiefdoms that fell across the widening frontier of the Zulu kingdom succumbed to incorporation, and some leaders moved away with their followers to seek their own fortunes. Thus in about 1821 Soshangane moved away from Zululand, establishing control, in a little more than fifteen years, over a large area between the Zambezi River and Delagoa Bay (Liesegang 1975). It is probable that the Gaza state, as it became known, was established so rapidly and successfully by

Mgungundlovu. The plan shows the king's residence (the isigodlo*) where the royal wives lived, and part of the arc of military housing which formed a circular town. (From Parkington* et al. *1979.)*

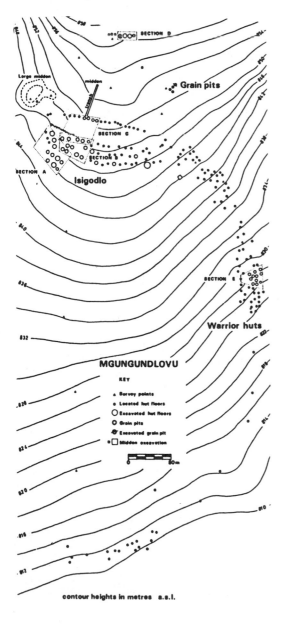

A detail of the tightly packed warrior houses at Mgungundlovu (from Parkington et al. *1979).*

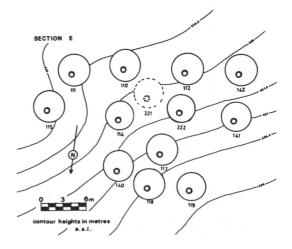

Mgungundlovu: a house used for storing beer, after excavation. Large clay pots were set into the plaster floor. (Photograph by courtesy of John Parkington.)

A house at Mgungundlovu specially equipped for storing shields. Racks were set into the floor of the house, enabling the leather shields to be kept away from the ground and thus protected from insect damage. The postholes which once supported the racks can be clearly seen in the photograph. (Photograph by courtesy of John Parkington.)

means of slavery. In the early nineteenth century there was a considerable demand for male slaves for the expanding plantation economies outside Africa, and traders collected their cargoes at, among other ports, Delagoa Bay and Inhambane, both of which had hinterlands controlled by Gaza. Female slaves were retained on the mainland and used to build the Gaza lineages rapidly, expanding on the small core that had moved away from the Zulu frontier. After 1836 the demand for slaves at the Mozambique coast declined and the Gaza rulers retained their captives within the state and traded ivory to the Portuguese instead (Harries 1981).

A second example of a group that moved away were two *amabutho* under the leadership of Mzilikazi, a member of the ruling lineage of the kwaKhumalo chiefdom that occupied the high land between the Mfolozi and Thukela rivers. It has been shown in Chapter 5 that the Khumalo communities probably occupied the Type B style of settlements, the ruins of which are today scattered widely across the grasslands of the Babanango plateau. It is also probable that the Khumalo were in economic crisis by the early nineteenth century, as their holdings in livestock exceeded the carrying capacity of their territory (Hall and Mack 1983), and this may have contributed to Mzilikazi's decision to move away with his regiments.

The Ndebele, as they became known, crossed the Drakensberg in about 1822 and eventually settled in the south-western part of the Zimbabwean plateau between 1837 and 1842 (Cobbing 1974), defeating the Rozvi dynasties (Beach 1980). Although, as Julian Cobbing has pointed out, earlier accounts have substantially exaggerated the military nature and regimentation of the Ndebele state, and although only a small proportion of the population was mobilised at any one time, the *amabutho* still had a central role in the society. Regiments were housed in temporary settlements, the men returning to their villages to help with the harvest and other economic activities. After between four and eight years of service, the members of a particular *ibutho* would bring wives back to their barracks, around which they would build their own villages under a local chief, forming an administrative unit known as the *isigaba* (Cobbing 1974).

Thus the *amabutho* were centres around which the Ndebele state grew, and the senior members of the regiments enjoyed high status: 'The mature warrior (*iqawe*) with several wives, a village of his own (*umusi zamathanga*) and many children, occupied a central position in Ndebele society. His family grew with the addition of captives (*abafuyiweyo*) taken in war, distributed to him by the king or by the chief and distributed by him amongst his wives. In an analogous way a brave man could become wealthy in cattle. His status within the *isigaba* increased if he married the daughter or other female relative of the chief. If he caught the king's eye he might be given the command of an *ibutho* . . . and raise himself to chiefly rank. Only at certain points along this tortuous path was a man a purely military figure: his means may have been the exploitation of his martial abilities, but his aims were control of people, cattle and territory, the major standards by which others judged him.' (Cobbing 1974: 630)

But although the Ndebele and Zulu *amabutho* were powerful forces that enabled the rulers of such polities to build up large followings over short periods, there were inherent limitations in their military capabilities. Members of regiments had to return periodically to their villages in order to take part in agricultural activities – a factor which was decisive in Cetshwayo's defeat by the British in 1879 (Guy 1982) – and there was often the tendency for regiments to break away: the 'centrifugal tensions' of the Ndebele (Cobbing 1974). In addition, the *amabutho* were mostly dependent on force of numbers, for muskets and rifles were only occasionally available in the first part of the nineteenth century.

These weaknesses became particularly evident when the Zulu and Ndebele and other communities were attacked by small, highly mobile groups armed with vastly superior weapons. Through the late eighteenth and early nineteenth centuries Afrikaner pastoralists had moved inland from the Cape in search of new grazing lands, and after 1835 this steady diffusion was transformed into a migration as thousands of families moved across the interior grasslands and to the east and south-east of the Drakensberg (Lye and Murray 1980). Both the Ndebele and the Zulu clashed with these Voortrekkers, and Dingane set fire to Mgungundlovu as he retreated in the face of the Afrikaner advance.

Although to some extent the Afrikaner communities were seeking to escape colonial control from the Cape, they were also attempting to strengthen their economic base. Individual families had little capital, so that expansion was preferable to intensification: 'as long as the frontier was still open, it was more economical for the fron-

Carriages, waggons and horsemen, depicted by San artists in the western Cape. (After a drawing of a rock painting at Stompiesfontein by H. C. Woodhouse.)

The 'Great Trek': the expansion of pastoralists north-eastwards from the Cape Colony in the early nineteenth century in search of grazing land and new commercial outlets.

'Louis Trichardt crossing the Drakensberg', an etching by W. H. Coetzer. (Reproduced by kind permission of the Africana Museum, Johannesburg.)

tiersmen to expand production by enlarging the size of their grazing lands than by using the already occupied area more intensively' (Giliomee 1981). Families were also small and so slavery was essential if power was to be secured. Armed commandos retrieved cattle and captured children for service, and labourers were indentured to their masters (Giliomee 1981). But as with the slaves who served the *prazeros* the rate of deaths and desertions was high, and it was constantly necessary for the commandos to replenish the labour supply, generating continuing turmoil in the frontier zone.

The Afrikaner leaders were as anxious as other war lords to gain access to the profitable trade routes, and from 1845 commandos were used to

considerable effect to the east of the Drakensberg to procure ivory for export through the Portuguese at Delagoa Bay. In Peter Delius's words, 'these Trekboers were not the peripatetic subsistence-orientated pastoralists of popular account. They were the products of a society in the Cape which had been partially formed under the dominance of merchant capital. Their early history in the Transvaal was shaped by their attempts to forge independent links with the world economy, not to escape from it.' (Delius 1983)

Diamonds and gold

Although the trekkers were successful in claiming large tracts of grassland for their use, they did not conquer southern Africa, and by the middle of the nineteenth century there was an uneasy balance between several major power blocs. The Mutapa state could still prevent incursions into its reduced territory on the Zambezi (Beach 1980), while lower down the river *prazeros*, albeit not on the same scale as the vast estates of the seventeenth century, were still established (Newitt 1973). To the south, the Ndebele controlled the former Torwa lands, and the Gaza state was dominant in the lowlands of Mozambique. The Zulu kingdom, under Mpande, had retained its autonomy within reduced borders (Guy 1982). In most of these cases, power had been gained in an environment of acute competition, and rulers had built up strength through various forms of slavery and had succeeded in establishing stability behind frontiers that had again become more definite.

But from the 1860s, this general pattern changed, for the discovery of diamonds and new and substantial goldfields began the process of transition from a predominantly farming economy to industrial centralisation, and the essential features of contemporary southern African society began to take shape (Bundy 1979). Instead of providing a basis of power for different war lords, individuals were now drawn into the industrial areas as labourers, creating an unfolding contrast between the wealth of the cities and the poverty of the rural areas: 'the relationship between the industrial core and the rural periphery is one of fundamental imbalance. Capital accumulation has taken place in the core areas at the expense of the peripheral areas. In simple terms, this means that spectacular economic growth in 'white' South Africa has been accompanied by increasing poverty in the

'Missionary arriving at a kraal' in the late nineteenth century. (From the South African Museum photographic collection.)

black periphery. The standard of living of inhabitants of the periphery has steadily declined in the
last hundred years, a process which may be described as *underdevelopment*. At different periods in
different areas, a largely self-sufficient peasantry
was transformed into a rural proletariat.' (Lye and
Murray 1980: 135)

Thus in the end the war lords themselves were
defeated by a new element in the commercial relationship between southern Africa and the outside
world – the massive amounts of capital that were
used to take advantage of the new-found wealth of
the subcontinent.

Mass housing in Soweto, near Johannesburg.
(Photograph by Martin West.)

12

Transformations in southern Africa

Beyond the Iron Age

In an earlier chapter the conventional categories in which the southern African past has been ordered have been criticised. It was suggested that terms such as 'Stone Age', 'Early Iron Age', 'Bambata Culture' and 'Moloko Tradition' have little real value because they are devices to describe categories of artefacts, such as pots or settlement designs, rather than reflections of what people were actually *doing* in the past.

Now that the evidence, tenuous and incomplete as it is, for the way people were living has been set out, a different scheme can be suggested for encapsulating the past. In this the aim is to emphasise phases of significant change – 'transformations' – when aspects of society were rearranged, with implications that affected everyone.

Again, the concept of the mode of production, which was discussed in Chapter 6 and which has been used to considerable effect by historians and archaeologists in other parts of the world, can be used to define what can be expected of such transformations. Rearrangements in the manner in which people made a living – the 'means of production' – are likely to have happened frequently in the past as farmers adjusted to changes in their environment. To elevate shifts from, for example, small stock-keeping to cattle herding, or sorghum cultivation to a heavier dependency on maize, to the status of transformations is to imply economic or ecological determinism, in which all aspects of a society are seen as dependent on the nature of an 'economic base'. For major change to take place, a shift in the means of production must be accompanied by new 'relations of production' – the manner in which the product of forest, field or herd is distributed in the community and which serves to define the nature of social relations.

There were at least two such transformations during the centuries covered in the chapters of this book. The periods between them were not equal, and the transformations did not happen over the whole of southern Africa at the same time. Indeed, in some areas only one occurred. Thus transformations do not mark the beginnings and ends of fixed periods or 'ages', although implications were often wide enough to give the impression of a simultaneous event. Together, these changes have formed and re- formed southern African society.

Gathering, hunting and farming

At the beginning of the first millennium A.D. the gathering and hunting way of life, which had been established in one form or another in southern Africa for perhaps several million years, began to give way to the cultivation of crops and, to a more limited extent, the husbandry of domestic animals. The actual process of domestication took place well to the north, but this does not necessarily mean that new people arrived, for it is equally possible that knowledge of farming, along with the plants and animals needed for the new way of life, were passed from community to community. There was probably extensive demographic rearrangement, with some people moving into the subcontinent and others joining them and the new way of life, but within the areas which they and their ancestors had always occupied.

But did the advent of crop cultivation and animal husbandry south of the Zambezi necessarily lead to a change in the mode of production? Certainly, domestic plants and animals were new sources of food that had to be propagated and husbanded, while iron technology was far more expensive in labour than working stone tools. Certainly, crop cultivation demanded a degree of sedentarism if fields were to be prepared, protected and harvested. But on the other hand, gatherer-hunters in southern Africa also propagated food supplies by burning vegetation to encourage plant growth and attract grazing prey (Schrire 1980; Hall 1984c), had adequate leisure time (Lee and DeVore 1968), and returned regularly to the same rock shelters, coastal and other locations.

Thus although adoption of domestic crops and animals was by definition a transition in means of production, the use of the new resources did not necessarily demand a concomitant change in the relations of production. The crucial issue would seem to be the pattern of distribution – was the produce of farming shared out differently to the plant foods gathered from the veld or to the prey snared or hunted? Certainly, crop cultivation and animal husbandry demand investment for future yield, and this in turn is usually accompanied by some sort of 'ownership' of resources, either on an individual or on a corporate basis. But on the other hand, it has been argued in an earlier chapter that the uncertainty of agricultural production would have demanded carefully maintained networks of reciprocal obligation, in which the surplus produced by one household was shared with others in order to ensure a livelihood when such good for-

tune was reversed. Such a pattern of distribution would, of course, be equivalent to the sharing so characteristic of gatherer-hunter societies, indicating that farming had not brought about the changes in the relations of production essential for a major transformation of society.

Therefore on balance it would seem best to disregard the conventional distinction between Late Stone Age and Early Iron Age in southern Africa, and think instead of a period of transition, lasting several centuries, in which immigrants with new ways of living interacted with established communities and introduced new resources and technology without necessarily transforming the social fabric – the classic pattern, in fact, existing at the 'open frontier'.

Livestock, the key to change

Although the early centuries of the first millennium may not have seen a change in the mode of production dominant in the summer-rainfall regions of south-eastern Africa, farming did initiate a change in the relationship between communities and their environment that was to have a marked effect on the form of society. For in clearing fields and gardens in the forests and savannas that mantled the lower-lying areas of south-eastern Africa, the farmer began the process of changing closed forests into a mosaic of open woodland and secondary grasslands. This in turn allowed communities to keep more livestock – a case of 'positive feedback' that was to lead to a definite transformation in mode of production.

Archaeological evidence shows that, although the very first farmers in the south-east may not have kept domestic animals, the generations that followed after them always had a few head of stock. While the woodlands were still pressing closely around the villages the possibilities for animal husbandry were limited, for grazing was in short supply and insect-borne diseases and parasites made the woods an unhealthy home for domestic animals. But as more fields were cleared through the decades of the first millennium, so domestic livestock came to play an increasingly important part in the economy. Between about A.D. 700 and 1200 (the date of the transition varied from area to area) communities reached a critical point in the economies that sustained them – a time of decision when it was possible to base a livelihood principally on livestock rather than on cultivated crops.

Once taken, such a decision cast the southern

African environment in a new light, for the high grasslands – an economic desert for a cultivator – offered unbounded possibilities for livestock husbandry. By A.D. 1400 much of the southern highveld and the high south-eastern watershed grasslands, which had been eschewed for a thousand years, were colonised by agro-pastoralist communities.

In the south-western part of the subcontinent – the drylands and winter-rainfall areas that did not have environments suited to the cultivation of the African domestic plant species – animal husbandry had, of course, been established for many centuries before agro-pastoralists began to build their distinctive stone enclosures on the high grasslands of southern Africa's interior basin. But in this case, there is every reason to believe that the open frontier was *not* sustained, and that the advent of pastoralism in the south-west was accompanied by a new mode of production.

This conclusion is based on the different options available in the south-east and the south-west for dealing with risk. For whereas the south-eastern cultivators could not accumulate resources and could best manage the uncertainties of the future by sharing, south-western pastoralists could not afford to lose their breeding herds and the secondary products that they yielded, and could best

Small-tailed sheep, with characteristic ears, drawn on the walls of Ruchero Cave, Mtoko, Zimbabwe. (After the original tracing by Goodall (1946), by courtesy of Tony Manhire, Spatial Archaeology Research Unit, University of Cape Town.)

anticipate future needs by keeping resources within the community. In turn, this would necessitate relations of production that were radically different from the communal ethic of gatherer-hunters, and therefore a new mode of production.

Thus domestic livestock seem to have been the key to the emergence of a new mode of production in southern Africa, in which an emphasis on the dispersal and sharing of surplus production was replaced by accumulation and by the political and economic transactions that have been described in earlier chapters. The transformation leading to this new mode took place in different places at different times: in northern Botswana sometime in the last millennium B.C., in Namibia and the south-western Cape some centuries later, and in south-eastern Africa towards the end of the first millennium A.D., after a long period of transition. Again, this pattern of change underlines the point that the conventional archaeological periods, based only on particular technological characteristics, can be misleading.

From chief to tributary, from subject to slave

Although it is probably dangerous to substitute one system of categories for another and to group pastoralist and agro-pastoralist societies in southern Africa together as chiefdoms, there is one apparent thread of continuity that does seem to run through all the cases considered in earlier chapters: the tendency for accumulation of livestock to be balanced by fission. Although holdings in domes-

tic stock allowed the heads of some households and villages to gain power over other people, their subordinates retained the right of desertion, thus placing a sanction on overreaching central authority.

By the twelfth century this balance had been broken in the Limpopo valley, as the occupants of a few major centres succeeded in retaining considerable power for a sustained period. This was clearly a qualitative difference, indicating the emergence of a different form of society which has justifiably been called the state. Early Mapungubwe was followed by Zimbabwe, Torwa, Mutapa and other centralised polities which thrived before the first stage of European colonialism.

Although the results of this transformation are clearly evident in the archaeological record, it has proved more difficult to explain the transition which rendered the formerly independent chief the tributary of a king, and which introduced a class distinction between ruler and ruled.

It has been suggested here that for a chief to perpetuate his power and attain the status of kingship it would be necessary for him to acquire control over a new form of wealth that, unlike domestic livestock, was not readily available to subordinates as a basis for usurping power for themselves. The archaeological evidence shows that, in southern Africa, this wealth took the form of cloth, beads and other trade items that had little use value. For this reason, power in these early states must have been based on the common acceptance of a system of signification - tokens mutually acceptable to those who, together, provided the coercion necessary to prevent the state from fragmenting.

The transformation to statehood in southern Africa linked the rulers of Mapungubwe and Zimbabwe to the international world of commerce through the Islamic cities such as Kilwa which grew up and thrived on the East African coast. But early in the sixteenth century, the style in which trade was conducted came to be disrupted by fleets of 'infidels' from Europe. The Portuguese were driven to Africa and the East by different economic needs, and in their attempts to maximise the profits of trade and deprive their Muslim competitors of their hinterland, they soon thrust into the interior, establishing markets and hegemony over vast estates.

Although the Portuguese had only limited success in the southern African interior, their direct intervention had a cataclysmic effect, for networks of kinship and marriage, which had been the basis of alliance and power from the earliest years of farming, were replaced by coerced support. Men and women were removed from their own areas of habitation and forced to become members of the conquerors' armies and households – in a word, slaves.

Thus for many people in southern Africa, the intervention of foreign traders in their history meant the change from subject to slave, as for three centuries different groups competed for control of wealth in land, cattle and commodities. Fortunes varied. For some slaves, capture meant physical abuse and a high risk of death, while others were soon integrated and gained wealth and status in their new societies. Similarly, the style of the war lords varied considerably, from Calvinistic Afrikaners who preferred clear lines of separation between themselves and their subjects, to military leaders such as the Rozvi Changamire and the early Zulu and Ndebele kings, to the Africanised Catholicism of the Portuguese estate owners.

None of these leaders, however, had the resources to achieve a complete dominance of southern Africa, and although there were many shifts in power, southern Africa in the middle of the nineteenth century was a diverse political and economic arena. But change came again as the result of a shift in southern Africa's status in the international economy. The discovery of new mineral resources meant commercial possibilities far beyond the profits of conventional trade, and large capital investments from outside the region marked the beginning of industrialisation in what was to become the economic core of southern Africa. In turn, such industrialisation created a heavy demand for a workforce, and people were drawn, in a transformation that shaped the basic form of modern southern Africa, towards the mines and fast-growing cities as labourers, separated now from the land and working for wages in a new economy.

Thus, from the social perspective advocated in this book, the crucial transformations in southern African society appear not as the replacement of stone technology by iron-working, or even the substitution of farming for gatherer-hunter economies, but rather the fundamental changes in mode of production in which, firstly, accumulation replaced distribution and, secondly, centralisation replaced fission.

Transformations in interpretation

But there is a second way in which the societies

in southern Africa have undergone transformation, and that is in the nature of the interpretations that later communities have placed on the history of the subcontinent. For just as Nathaniel Isaacs, standing on the deck of the *Mary* in 1825, brought his preconceptions and expectations to bear on the Zulu kingdom, so other chroniclers, historians and archaeologists have brought differing tones to the reading of the past.

It was suggested in an earlier chapter that a crucial watershed in the perception of the past came in 1929, when Gertrude Caton-Thompson began work at Great Zimbabwe which was to set the standard for subsequent professional research. Before her research, southern Africa had been an open field for the fictions constructed by the ethnohistorians. The publication of her results provided the foundation for a series of carefully conducted research projects that have transformed understanding of the chronology, distribution and nature of farming communities in southern Africa.

But it has also been pointed out that such professional research cannot be regarded as value-free. Indeed it seems unlikely that an objective truth about the past can exist. It has been argued that archaeologists have been influenced by the structure of southern African society, emphasising ethnicity and diversity while championing the cause of African antiquity. Such bias is not peculiar to southern African studies, and has been seen as intrinsic to historical disciplines everywhere (Hodder 1983).

If it is accepted that the social context of the archaeologist has affected interpretation of the past in contemporary as well as early research, then it must be anticipated that the tone of conclusions will shift again in the years to come, particularly in the volatile social and political environment of southern Africa. Indeed, there are strong indications that such changes are already taking place.

It is perhaps appropriate that one of the barometers of new opinion should be Great Zimbabwe, a site which attracted the attention of Cecil Rhodes, Caton-Thompson, Roger Summers, Keith Robinson, Peter Garlake, Tom Huffman and the romantic popularisers who still find publishers, and therefore presumably markets, for their favoured visions. But through Zimbabwe's liberation war, and particularly after that country's independence in 1980, Great Zimbabwe has become a symbol of nationalism, leading to its re-interpretation by the Director of Museums and Monuments in Zimbabwe, as the centre of a classless, socialist society (Mufuka 1983).

Mufuka's understanding of Great Zimbabwe is, in the least, idiosyncratic and has been shown to be without substance (Garlake 1984). Nevertheless, the suspicion that earlier archaeologies of southern Africa may have imposed capitalist beliefs in the inevitability of class division is evident in post-colonial consideration of Mozambique's prehistory as well. Thus Joao Morais (1984: 113, 124) has written that 'independence brought about a radical transformation of the concept of the past' and that 'it was independence and, above all, the struggle to forge a new nation, that determined the nature of the propositions that are shaping the development of archaeology in Mozambique. . . . New forms of expression of scientific knowledge are being produced and will eventually link up with popular consciousness and with history.'

In South Africa, professional archaeology is still completely dominated by the liberal academic tradition. Nevertheless, a perception of the past clearly plays an important part in the Black Consciousness ideology which first developed in the 1960s and which has become an inherent part of the liberation movement. Thus Kelwyn Sole has pointed out that the urban-based poetry and literature of Soweto and elsewhere has stressed the need to revive the values of pre-colonial African society, which is often seen as classless and unchanging, in this way, ironically, mimicking the prejudices of nineteenth-century ethnohistorians. Thus 'while trying to counter the European degradation of all things African, some African nationalists have nevertheless maintained the fiction of humanistic, natural and spontaneous African political systems and values existing in pre-colonial times. Such systems are then compared favourably to the exploitative European system of colonialism.' (Sole 1983: 40-1)

In future years the debate in southern African archaeology will probably be between those who employ the past as a social and political charter for the present, and those who would contest that there is some 'archaeological reality' that transcends the specific context of the analyst. Arguing for this last position, Nicholas David has contested that 'archaeology's primary role is not . . . that of a purveyor of satisfying pasts and identities to ethnic, national and social groups; rather it is a comparative discipline, operating on a world scale to better our understanding of hominid evolution and cultural development' (David 1984: 1).

References

Alexander, J. 1977. The 'frontier' concept in prehistory: the end of the moving frontier. In J. V. Megaw (ed.) *Hunters, gatherers and first farmers beyond Europe.* Leicester: University Press

Alexander, J. 1984. Early frontiers in southern Africa. In M. Hall, G. Avery, D. M. Avery, M. L. Wilson and A. J. B. Humphreys (eds.) *Frontiers: southern African archaeology today*, pp. 12–23. Oxford: British Archaeological Reports

Alphers, E. 1975. *Ivory and slaves in east Central Africa. Changing patterns of international trade in the later nineteenth century.* London: Heinemann

Ambrose, S. H. 1984. The introduction of pastoral adaptations to the highlands of East Africa. In J. D. Clark and S. A. Brandt (eds.) *From hunters to farmers. The causes and consequences of food production in Africa*, pp. 212–239. Berkeley: University of California Press

Ammerman, A. J. and Cavelli-Sforza, L. L. 1973. A population model for the diffusion of early farming in Europe. In C. Renfrew (ed.) *The explanation of culture change: models in prehistory*, pp. 343–357. London: Duckworth

Angas, G. F. 1849. *The Kafirs illustrated.* London: Hogarth

Assad, T. 1979. Equality in nomadic social systems? Notes towards the dissolution of an anthropological category. In Equipe écologie et anthropologie des sociétés pastorales (eds.) *Pastoral production and society*, pp. 419–428. Cambridge: Cambridge University Press

Avery, D. H. and Schmidt, P. 1979. A metallurgical study of the iron bloomery, particularly as practised in Buhaya. *Journal of Metals* 31(10): 14–20

Axelson, E. 1960. *Portuguese in south-east Africa 1600–1700.* Johannesburg: Witwatersrand University Press

Axelson, E. 1973. *Portuguese in south-east Africa 1488–1600.* Cape Town: Struik

Baines, T. 1864. *Explorations in south-west Africa.* London: Longmans, Green

Baker, P. T. 1967. The biological race concept as a research tool. *American Journal of Physical Anthropology* 27(1): 21–26

Barker, G. 1978. Economic models for the Manekweni zimbabwe, Mozambique. *Azania* 13: 71–100

Beach, D. N. 1980. *The Shona and Zimbabwe 900–1850. An outline of Shona history.* London: Heinemann

Bender, B. 1978. Gatherer-hunter to farmer: a social perspective. *World Archaeology* 10(2): 204–222

Bent, J. T. 1892. *The ruined cities of Mashonaland.* London: Longmans, Green

Bernhard, F. O. 1971. *Karl Mauch. African explorer.* Cape Town: Struik

Binford, L. R. and Sabloff, J. A. 1982. Paradigms, systematics and archaeology. *Journal of Anthropological Research* 38(2): 137–153

Bonner, P. 1981. The dynamics of late eighteenth century northern Nguni society: some hypotheses. In J. Peires (ed.) *Before and after Shaka. Papers in Nguni history*, pp. 74–81. Grahamstown: Rhodes University, Institute for Social and Economic Research

Bonner, P. 1982. *Kings, commoners and concessionaires.* Cambridge: Cambridge University Press Borland, C. H. 1982. How basic is 'basic' vocabulary? *Current Anthropology* 23(3): 315–316

Borland, C. H. 1986. The linguistic reconstruction of prehistoric pastoralist vocabulary. *South African Archaeological Society, Goodwin Series* 5: 31–35

Bourdieu, P. 1977. *Outline of a theory of practice.* Cambridge: Cambridge University Press

Boxer, C. R. 1961. *Four centuries of Portuguese expansion, 1415–1825: a succinct survey.* Johannesburg: Witwatersrand University Press

Brain, C. K. 1974. Human food remains from the Iron Age at Zimbabwe. *South African Journal of Science* 70: 303–309

Braudel, F. 1973. *Capitalism and material life, 1400–1800.* London: Weidenfeld and Nicolson

Braudel, F. 1981. *Civilization and capitalism 15th-18th century*, volume 1. London: Collins

Bronson, B. 1975. The earliest farming: demography as cause and consequence. In S. Polgar (ed.) *Population, ecology and social evolution*, pp. 53–78. The Hague: Mouton

Brown, R. 1892. *Africa and its explorers.* London: Cassell

Bryant, A. 1929. *Olden times in Zululand and Natal.* London: Longmans

Bundy, C. 1979. *The rise and fall of the South African peasantry.* London: Heinemann

Burke, E. E. 1969. *The journals of Carl Mauch.* Salisbury: National Archives of Rhodesia

Bushnell, G. H. S. 1969. Woven textiles and cords from Ingombe Ilede. In B. M. Fagan, D. W. Phillipson and S. G. Daniels (eds.) *Iron Age cultures in Zambia*, volume 2, pp. 243–246. London: Chatto and Windus

Calvocoressi, D. and David, N. 1979. A new survey of radiocarbon and thermoluminescence dates for West Africa. *Journal of African History* 20(1): 1–29

Campbell, A. C. 1982. Notes on the prehistoric background to 1840. In R. R. Hitchcock and M. R. Smith (eds.) *Settlement in Botswana*, pp. 13–22. Johannesburg: Heinemann

Carneiro, R. L. 1982. The chiefdom; precursor of the state. In G. D. Jones and R. R. Kautz (eds.) *The transition to statehood in the New World.* Cambridge: Cambridge University Press

Caton-Thompson, G. 1931. *The Zimbabwe culture. Ruins and reactions.* Oxford: Clarendon Press

Childe, V. G. 1929. *The Danube in prehistory.* Oxford: Clarendon Press

Chittick, H. N. 1965. The 'Shirazi' colonization of East Africa. *Journal of African History* 6(3): 275–294

Chittick, H. N. 1971. The coast of East Africa. In P. L. Shinnie (ed.) *The African Iron Age*, pp. 108–141. Oxford: Clarendon Press

Chittick, H. N. 1974. *Kilwa: an Islamic trading city on the East African coast.* Nairobi: British Institute in Eastern Africa

Chittick, H. N. 1975. The peopling of the East African coast. In H. N. Chittick and R. Rotberg (eds.) *East Africa and the Orient*, pp. 16–43. New York: Africana Publishing Company

Clark, J. D. 1971. A re-examination of the evidence for agricultural origins in the Nile Valley. *Proceedings of the Prehistoric Society* 37(2): 34–79

Clark, J. D. 1980. Human populations and cultural adaptations in the Sahara and Nile during prehistoric times. In M. A. J. Williams and H. Faure (eds.) *The Sahara and the Nile. Quaternary environments and prehistoric occupation in northern Africa*, pp. 527–582. Rotterdam: Balkema

Clark, J. D. 1984. Prehistoric cultural continuity and economic change in the central Sudan in the early Holocene. In J. D. Clark and S. A. Brandt (eds.) *From hunters to farmers. The causes and consequences of food production in Africa*, pp. 113–126. Berkeley: University of California Press

Clarke, D. L. 1968. *Analytical archaeology.* London: Methuen

Clarke, D. L. 1972. Models and paradigms in contemporary archaeology. In D. L. Clarke (ed.) *Models in archaeology*, pp. 1–60. London: Methuen

Close, A. E. (ed.) 1984. *Cattle-keepers of the eastern Sahara: the Neolithic of Bir Kiseiba.* Dallas: Southern Methodist University Department of Anthropology

Cobbing, J. 1974. The evolution of the Ndebele amabutho. *Journal of African History* 15(4): 607–631

Cobbing, J. 1983. The case against the Mfecane. Paper presented to the Africa Seminar, Centre for African Studies, University of Cape Town

Cohen, R. 1978. Introduction. In R. Cohen and E. R. Service

(eds.) *Origins of the state: the anthropology of political evolution.* Philadelphia: Institute for the Study of Human Issues

Collett, D. P. 1982. Models of the spread of the Early Iron Age. In C. Ehret and M. Posnansky (eds.) *The archaeological and linguistic reconstruction of African history*, pp. 182–198. Berkeley: University of California Press

Connah, G. 1981. *Three thousand years in Africa. Man and his environment in the Lake Chad region of Nigeria.* Cambridge: Cambridge University Press

Cooke, C. K. 1965. Evidence of human migrations from the rock art of Southern Rhodesia. *Africa* 35(3): 263–285

Cooke, H. J. 1982. The physical environment of Botswana. In R. R. Hitchcock and M. R. Smith (eds.) *Settlement in Botswana*, pp. 1–12. Johannesburg: Heinemann

Cooper, F. 1977. *Plantation slavery on the east coast of Africa.* New Haven: Yale University Press

Cornevin, M. 1980. *Apartheid: power and historical falsification.* Paris: Unesco

Curtin, P. D. 1968. Field techniques for collecting and processing oral data. *Journal of African History* 9(3): 367–385.

Daniel, G. 1975. *A hundred and fifty years of archaeology.* London: Duckworth

Dapper, O. 1668. *Naukeurige beschryvinge der Afrikaensche gewesten.* Amsterdam: Jacob van Meurs

Dart, R. A. 1923. Boskop remains from the south-east African coast. *Nature* 112: 623–625

David, N. 1984. Editorial. *African Archaeological Review* 2: 1–3

Davidson, B. 1959. *Old Africa rediscovered.* London: Gollancz

Davies, O. 1975. Excavations at Shongweni South Cave: the oldest evidence to date for cultigens in southern Africa. *Annals of the Natal Museum* 22(2): 627–662

Davison, P. and Harries, P. 1980. Cotton weaving in south-east Africa: its history and technology. *Textile History* 11: 175–192

De Castilho, A. 1891. *Relatorio da guerra da Zambesia.* Lisbon: Elvas Typographia Progresso

De Jager, J. M. and Schulze, R. E. 1977. The broad geographic distribution in Natal of climatological factors important to agricultural planning. *Agrochemophysica* 9: 81–91

Deacon, H. J., Deacon, J., Brooker, M. and Wilson, M. L. 1978. The evidence for herding at Boomplaas Cave in the southern Cape, South Africa. *South African Archaeological Bulletin* 33: 39–65

Deacon, J. 1984. Later Stone Age people and their descendants in southern Africa. In R. G. Klein (ed.) *Southern African prehistory and palaeoenvironments*, pp. 221–238. Rotterdam: Balkema

Deetz, J. 1977. *In small things forgotten. The archaeology of early American life.* New York: Anchor Press

Delius, P. 1983. *The land belongs to us. The Pedi polity, the boers and the British in the nineteenth century Transvaal.* Johannesburg: Ravan Press

Denbow, J. R. 1979. Cenchrus ciliaris: an ecological indicator of Iron Age middens using aerial photography in eastern Botswana. *South African Journal of Science* 75: 405–408

Denbow, J. R. 1982. The Toutswe Tradition, a study in socio-economic change. In R. R. Hitchcock and M. R. Smith (eds.) *Settlement in Botswana*, pp. 73–86. Johannesburg: Heinemann

Denbow, J. R. 1984a. Prehistoric herders and foragers of the Kalahari: the evidence for 1 500 years of interaction. In C. Schrire (ed.) *Past and present in hunter gatherer studies*, pp. 175–193. New York: Academic Press

Denbow, J. R. 1984b. Cows and kings: a spatial and economic analysis of a hierarchical Early Iron Age settlement system in eastern Botswana. In M. Hall, G. Avery, D. M. Avery, M. L. Wilson and A. J. B. Humphreys (eds.) *Frontiers: southern African archaeology today*, pp. 24–39. Oxford: British Archaeological Reports

Denbow, J. R. 1985. Preliminary report on an archaeological reconnaissance of the BP Soda Ash Lease, Makgadikgadi Pans, Botswana. Unpublished report, Gaborone

Denbow, J. R. and Wilmsen, E. N. 1983. Iron Age pastoralist settlements in Botswana. *South African Journal of Science* 79: 405–407

De Villiers, H. 1968. *The skull of the South African Negro: a biometrical and morphological study.* Johannesburg: Witwatersrand University Press

De Villiers, H. and Fatti, L. P. 1982. The antiquity of the Negro. *South African Journal of Science* 78: 321–332

Ehret, C. 1973. Patterns of Bantu and Central Sudanic settlement in central and southern Africa (ca. 1000 B.C.–500 A.D.). *Transafrican Journal of History* 3: 1–71

Ehret, C. 1982a. Linguistic inferences about early Bantu history. In C. Ehret and M. Posnansky (eds.) *The archaeological and linguistic reconstruction of African history*, pp. 57–65. Berkeley: University of California Press

Ehret, C. 1982b. The first spread of food production to southern Africa. In C. Ehret and M. Posnansky (eds.) *The archaeological and linguistic reconstruction of African history*, pp. 158–181. Berkeley: University of California Press

Ehret, C. 1984. Historical/linguistic evidence for early African food production. In J. D. Clark and S. A. Brandt (eds.) *From hunters to farmers. The causes and consequences of food production in Africa*, pp. 26–35. Berkeley: University of California Press

Eloff, J. F. and Meyer, A. 1981. The Greefswald sites. In E. A. Voigt (ed.) *Guide to archaeological sites in the northern and eastern Transvaal*, pp. 7–22. Pretoria: Southern African Association of Archaeologists

Elphick, R. 1985. *Khoikhoi and the founding of white South Africa.* Johannesburg: Ravan Press

Evers, T. M. 1979. Salt and soapstone bowl factories at Harmony, Letaba district, north-east Transvaal. *South African Archaeological Society, Goodwin Series* 3: 94–107

Evers, T. M. 1981. The Iron Age in the eastern Transvaal, South Africa. In E. A. Voigt (ed.) *Guide to archaeological sites in the northern and eastern Transvaal*, pp. 64–109. Pretoria: Southern African Association of Archaeologists

Evers, T. M. 1982. Excavations at the Lydenburg Heads site, eastern Transvaal, South Africa. *South African Archaeological Bulletin* 37: 16–33

Evers, T. M. 1983. Mr Evers replies. *South African Journal of Science* 79(7): 261–264

Fagan, B. M. 1969. Excavations at Ingombe Ilede, 1960–62. In B. M. Fagan, D. W. Phillipson and S. G. Daniels (eds.) *Iron Age cultures in Zambia*, volume 2, pp. 55–161. London: Chatto and Windus

Frederikse, J. 1982. *None but ourselves: masses vs media in the making of Zimbabwe.* Johannesburg: Ravan Press

Freeman-Grenville, G. P. S. 1962. *The East African coast. Select documents from the first to the earlier nineteenth century.* Oxford: Clarendon Press

Fried, M. 1967. *The evolution of political society.* New York: Random House

Galloway, A. 1937. Man in Africa in the light of recent discoveries. *South African Journal of Science* 34: 89–120

Garbett, G. K. 1966. Religious aspects of political succession among the valley Korekore (N. Shona). In E. Stokes and R. Brown (eds.) *The Zambezian past: studies in Central African history*, pp. 137–170. Manchester: Manchester University Press

Garbett, G. K. 1977. Disparate regional cults and a unitary field in Zimbabwe. In R. P. Werbner (ed.) *Regional cults*, pp. 55–92. London: Academic Press

Garlake, P. S. 1966. *The early Islamic architecture of the East African coast.* Oxford: Oxford University Press

Garlake, P. S. 1968. The value of imported ceramics in the dating and interpretation of the Rhodesian Iron Age. *Journal of African History* 9(1): 13–34

Garlake, P. S. 1970. Rhodesian ruins: a preliminary assessment of their styles and chronology. *Journal of African History* 11(4): 495–513

Garlake, P. S. 1973a. *Great Zimbabwe.* London: Thames and Hudson

Garlake, P. S. 1973b. Excavations at the Nhunguza and Ruanga Ruins in northern Mashonaland. *South African Archaeological Bulletin* 27: 107–143

Garlake, P. S. 1976. An investigation of Manekweni, Mozambique. *Azania* 11: 25–47

Garlake, P. S. 1978. Pastoralism and Zimbabwe. *Journal of African History* 19(4): 479–493

Garlake, P. S. 1982a. Prehistory and ideology in Zimbabwe. *Africa* 52(3): 1–19

Garlake, P. S. 1982b. *Great Zimbabwe described and explained.* Harare: Zimbabwe Publishing House

Garlake, P. S. 1982c. *Life at Great Zimbabwe.* Harare: Mambo Press

Garlake, P. S. 1984. Ken Mufuka and Great Zimbabwe. *Antiquity* 58: 121–123

Gayre, R. 1973. *Origin of the Zimbabwean civilization.* Harare: Galaxie Press

Giddens, A. 1981. *A contemporary critique of historical materialism.* London: Macmillan

Giddens, A. 1984. *The constitution of society. Outline of the theory of structuration.* Cambridge: Polity Press

Giliomee, H. 1981. Processes in development of the southern African frontier. In H. Lamar and L. Thompson (eds.) *The frontier in history. North America and southern Africa compared,* pp. 76–119. New Haven: Yale University Press

Godelier, M. 1975. Modes of production, kinship and demographic structures. In M. Bloch (ed.) *Marxist analyses and social anthropology,* pp. 3–28. London: Malaby Press

Goldschmidt, W. 1979. A general model for pastoral social systems. In Equipe écologie et anthropologie des sociétés pastorales (eds.) *Pastoral production and society,* pp. 15–27. Cambridge: Cambridge University Press

Goodall, E. 1946. Domestic animals in rock art. *Transactions of the Rhodesian Scientific Association* 41: 57–62

Gould, S. J. 1981. *The mismeasure of man.* New York: W. W. Norton

Granger, J. E. 1984. Fire in forest. In P. de V. Booysen and N. M. Tainton (eds.) *Ecological effects of fire in South African ecosystems,* pp. 177–198. Berlin: Springer-Verlag

Granger, J. E., Hall, M., McKenzie, B. and Feely, J. M. 1985. Archaeological research on plant and animal husbandry in Transkei. *South African Journal of Science* 81: 12–15

Grebenart, D. 1983. Les métallurgies du cuivre et du fer autour d'Agadez (Niger), des origines au début de la période médiévale. *Mémoires de la Société des Africanistes* 9: 109–125

Greenberg, J. 1963. *The languages of Africa.* Bloomington: Indiana University Press

Guthrie, M. 1962. Some developments in the prehistory of the Bantu languages. *Journal of African History* 3: 273–282

Guy, J. 1978. Production and exchange in the Zulu Kingdom. *Mohlomi: Journal of southern African Studies* 2: 96–106

Guy, J. 1982. *The destruction of the Zulu kingdom.* Johannesburg: Ravan Press

Haas, J. 1982. *The evolution of the prehistoric state.* New York: Columbia University Press

Habermas, J. 1972. *Knowledge and human interests.* London: Heinemann

Hall, M. 1976. Dendroclimatology, rainfall and human adaptation in the later Iron Age of Natal and Zululand. *Annals of the Natal Museum* 22(3): 693–703

Hall, M. 1980. The ecology of the Iron Age in Zululand. Unpublished Ph.D. thesis, University of Cambridge

Hall, M. 1981. *Settlement patterns in the Iron Age of Zululand.* Oxford: British Archaeological Reports

Hall, M. 1983. Tribes, traditions and numbers: the American model in southern African Iron Age studies. *South African Archaeological Bulletin* 38: 51–61

Hall, M. 1984a. The burden of tribalism: the social context of southern African Iron Age studies. *American Antiquity* 49(3): 455–467

Hall, M. 1984b. Pots and politics: ceramic interpretations in southern Africa. *World Archaeology* 15(3): 262–273

Hall, M. 1984c. Man's historical and traditional use of fire in southern Africa. In P. de V. Booysen and N. M. Tainton (eds.) *Ecological effects of fire in South African ecosystems,* pp. 39–52. Berlin: Springer-Verlag

Hall, M. 1984d. The myth of the Zulu homestead: archaeology and ethnography. *Africa* 54(1): 65–79

Hall, M. 1985a. The early household in southern Africa: the signification of relations of power between domestic groups. Paper presented to the Africa Seminar, Centre for African Studies, University of Cape Town

Hall, M. 1985b. Beyond the mode of production: power and signification in southern African pre-colonial archaeology. Paper presented at the conference of the Southern African Association of Archaeologists, Grahamstown

Hall, M. 1986. The role of cattle in southern African agropastoral societies: more than bones alone can tell. *South African Archaeological Society, Goodwin Series* 5: 83–87

Hall, M. and Mack, K. 1983. The outline of an eighteenth century economic system in south-east Africa. *Annals of the South African Museum* 91(2): 163–194

Hall, M. and Maggs, T. 1979. Nqabeni, a Later Iron Age site in Zululand. *South African Archaeological Society, Goodwin Series* 3: 159–176

Hall, M. and Morris, A. 1983. Race and Iron Age human skeletal remains from southern Africa: an assessment. *Social Dynamics* 9(2): 29–36

Hall, M. and Vogel, J.C. 1978. Enkwazini, fourth century Iron Age site on the Zululand coast. *South African Journal of Science* 74: 70–71

Hall, M. and Vogel, J. C. 1980. Some recent radiocarbon dates from southern Africa. *Journal of African History* 21(4): 431–455

Hall, R. N. 1905. *Great Zimbabwe.* London: Methuen

Hall, R. N. and Neal, W. G. 1904. *The ancient ruins of Rhodesia.* London: Methuen

Hallett, R. 1970. *Africa to 1875: a modern history.* Ann Arbor: University of Michigan Press

Hammond-Tooke, D. 1984. In search of the lineage: the Cape Nguni case. *Man* 19(1): 77–93

Hanisch, E. O. M. 1981. Schroda: a Zhizo site in the northern Transvaal. In E. A. Voigt (ed.) *Guide to archaeological sites in the northern and eastern Transvaal,* pp. 37–54. Pretoria: Southern African Association of Archaeologists

Hannan, M. 1974. *Standard Shona dictionary.* Salisbury: Rhodesia Literature Bureau

Harries, P. 1981. Slavery, social incorporation and surplus extraction: the nature of free and unfree labour in south-east Africa. *Journal of African History* 22(3): 309–330

Hedges, D. W. 1978. Trade and politics in southern Mozambique and Zululand in the eighteenth and early nineteenth centuries. Unpublished Ph.D. dissertation, University of London

Heine, B. 1973. Zur genetischen Gliederung der Bantusprachen. *Afrika und Übersee* 56: 164–85

Henige, D. P. 1971. Oral tradition and chronology. *Journal of African History* 12(3): 371–389

Henrici, A. 1973. Numerical classification of Bantu languages. *African Language Studies* 14: 82–104

Herman, L. (ed.) 1936. *Travels and adventures in eastern Africa by Nathaniel Isaacs.* Cape Town: Van Riebeeck Society

Hindess, B. and Hirst, P. Q. 1975. *Precapitalist modes of production.* London: Routledge and Kegan Paul

Hitzeroth, H. W. 1972. *Fisiese anthropologie van die inheemse mense in Suidelike Afrika.* Pretoria: Africa Institute

Hodder, I. 1982. *Symbols in action. Ethnoarchaeological studies of material culture.* Cambridge: Cambridge University Press

Hodder, I. 1983. Archaeology, ideology and contemporary society. *Royal Anthropological Institute News* 56: 6–7

Hodder, I. 1984. Ideology and power: the archaeological debate. *Environment and Planning D: Society and Space* 2: 347–353

Holt, P. M., Lambton, A. K. S. and Lewis, B. (eds.) 1970. *The Cambridge history of Islam. Volume 2. The further Islamic lands, Islamic society and civilization.* Cambridge: Cambridge University Press

Houser, T. 1975. A survey of Chipukuswi Ruin, Matibi, Rhodesia. *Rhodesian Prehistory* 7(14): 25–26

Hromnik, C. A. 1981. *Indo-Africa: towards a new understanding of the history of sub-Saharan Africa.* Cape Town: Juta

Huffman, T. N. 1970. The Early Iron Age and the spread of the Bantu. *South African Archaeological Bulletin* 25: 3–21

Huffman, T. N. 1971. Cloth from the Iron Age in Rhodesia. *Arnoldia (Rhodesia)* 5(14): 1–19

Huffman, T. N. 1972. An Arab coin from Zimbabwe. *Arnoldia (Rhodesia)* 5(32): 1–7

Huffman, T. N. 1974. The Leopard's Kopje Tradition. *National*

Museums and Monuments of Rhodesia, Museum Memoir 6: 1–150

Huffman, T. N. 1975. Cattle from Mabveni. *South African Archaeological Bulletin* 30: 23–24

Huffman, T. N. 1977. Zimbabwe: southern Africa's first town. *Rhodesian Prehistory* 7(15): 9–14

Huffman, T. N. 1978a. The origins of Leopard's Kopje: an 11th century difaqane. *Arnoldia (Rhodesia)* 7(7): 1–12

Huffman, T. N. 1978b. The Iron Age of the Buhwa district, Rhodesia. *Occasional Papers of the National Museums and Monuments of Rhodesia, Series A* 4(3): 81–100

Huffman, T. N. 1979a. African origins. *South African Journal of Science* 75: 233–237

Huffman, T. N. 1979b. Test excavations at Chamabvevfa, southern Mashonaland. *South African Archaeological Bulletin* 34: 57–70

Huffman, T. N. 1981. Snakes and birds: expressive space at Great Zimbabwe. *African Studies* 40(2): 131–150

Huffman, T. N. 1982. Archaeology and ethnohistory of the African Iron Age. *Annual Review of Anthropology* 11: 133–150

Huffman, T. N. 1984. Where you are the girls gather to play: the Great Enclosure at Great Zimbabwe. In M. Hall, G. Avery, D. M. Avery, M. L. Wilson and A. J. B. Humphreys (eds.) *Frontiers: southern African archaeology today*, pp. 252–265. Oxford: British Archaeological Reports

Huffman, T. N. 1985a. Cognitive studies of the Iron Age in southern Africa. Paper presented at the conference of the Southern African Association of Archaeologists, Grahamstown

Huffman, T. N. 1985b. The soapstone birds from Great Zimbabwe. *African Arts* 18(3): 68–73

Huffman, T. N. 1986a. Iron Age settlement patterns and the origins of class distinction in southern Africa. *Advances in World Archaeology* 5: 291–338

Huffman, T. N. 1986b. In press. Great Zimbabwe and the politics of space. In M. Posnansky and D. Brokenshaw (eds.) *The indigenous African town*. London: Heinemann

Huffman, T. N. and Vogel, J. C. 1979. The controversial lintels from Great Zimbabwe. *Antiquity* 53: 55–57

Huffman, T. N. and Vogel, J. C. 1986. The chronology of Great Zimbabwe. Unpublished manuscript

Humphreys, A. J. B. 1973. A report on excavations carried out on a Type R settlement unit (Khartoum 1) in the Jacobsdal district, O.F.S. *Annals of the Cape Provincial Museums* 9: 123–157

Humphreys, A. J. B. and Maggs, T. 1970. Further graves and cultural material from the banks of the Riet River. *South African Archaeological Bulletin* 25: 116–126

Humphreys, A. J. B. and Thackeray, A. I. 1984. *Ghaap and Gariep. Later Stone Age studies in the northern Cape*. Cape Town: South African Archaeological Society

Huntley, B. J. 1984. Characteristics of South African biomes. In P. de V. Booysen and N. M. Tainton (eds.) *Ecological effects of fire in South African ecosystems*, pp. 1–18. Berlin: Springer-Verlag

Hymes, D. 1960. Lexicostatistics so far. *Current Anthropology* 1: 5–44

Inskeep, R. R. and Maggs, T. M. 1975. Unique art objects in the Iron Age of the Transvaal. *South African Archaeological Bulletin* 30: 114–138

Isaacman, A. 1972. *Mozambique: the Africanization of a European institution. The Zambezi prazos*. Madison: University of Wisconsin Press

Isaacman, A. and Isaacman, B. 1975. The prazeros as transfrontiersmen: a study in social and cultural change. *International Journal of African Historical Studies* 8(1): 1–39

Jacobson, L. 1984. Hunting versus gathering in an arid ecosystem: the evidence from the Namib Desert. In M. Hall, G. Avery, D. M. Avery, M. L. Wilson and A. J. B. Humphreys (eds.) *Frontiers: southern African archaeology today*, pp. 75–79. Oxford: British Archaeological Reports

Johnson, G. A. 1972. A test of the utility of Central Place Theory in archaeology. In P. J. Ucko, R. Tringham and G. W. Dimbleby (eds.) *Man, settlement and urbanism*, pp. 769–785. London: Duckworth

Jones, J. S. 1981. How different are human races? *Nature* 293:
188–190

King, J. C. 1981. *The biology of race*. Berkeley: University of California Press

King, L. 1982. *The Natal Monocline*. Pietermaritzburg: University of Natal Press

Knight, D. 1981. *Ordering the world. A history of classifying man*. London: Burnett Books

Kolb, P. 1719. *Caput Bonae Spei Hodiernum*. Nurenberg: Peter Conrad

Kopytoff, I. and Miers, S. 1977. African slavery as an institution of marginality. In S. Miers and I. Kopytoff (eds.) *Slavery in Africa. Historical and anthropological perspectives*, pp. 3–84. Madison: Wisconsin University Press

Kruger, F. J. and Bigalke, R. C. 1984. Fire in fynbos. In P. de V. Booysen and N. M. Tainton (eds.) *Ecological effects of fire in South African ecosystems*, pp. 67–114. Berlin: Springer-Verlag

Kuhn, T. S. 1970. *The structure of scientific revolutions*. Chicago: Chicago University Press

Kuper, A. 1980. Symbolic dimensions of the southern Bantu homestead. *Africa* 50(1): 8–23

Kuper, A. 1982a. *Wives for cattle. Bridewealth and marriage in southern Africa*. London: Routledge and Kegan Paul

Kuper, A. 1982b. Lineage theory: a critical retrospect. *Annual Review of Anthropology* 11: 71–95

Laidler, P. W. 1938. South African native ceramics: their characteristics and classification. *Transactions of the Royal Society of South Africa* 26: 93–172

Landstrom, B. 1961. *The Ship*. London: Allen and Unwin

Latter, B. D. H. 1980. Genetic differences within and between populations of the major human subgroups. *American Naturalist* 116(2): 220–237

Law, R. C. C. 1978. North Africa in the period of Phoenician and Greek colonization, c.800 to 323 B.C. In J.D. Fage (ed.) *The Cambridge history of Africa*, volume 2, pp. 87–147. Cambridge: Cambridge University Press

Lee, R. B. and Devore, I. (eds.) 1968. *Man the hunter*. Chicago: Aldine

Lepionka, L. 1978. Excavations at Tautswemogala. *Botswana Notes and Records* 9: 1–16

Lewis-Williams, J. D. 1980. Ethnography and iconography: aspects of southern San thought and art. *Man* 15: 467–482

Lewis-Williams, J. D. 1981. *Believing and seeing: symbolic meanings in southern San rock paintings*. London: Academic Press

Lewis-Williams, J. D. 1982. The social and economic context of southern San rock art. *Current Anthropology* 23: 429–449

Lewis-Williams, J. D. 1983. Introductory essay. Science and rock art. *South African Archaeological Society, Goodwin Series* 4: 3–13

Lewis-Williams, J. D. 1984a. The empiricist impasse in southern African rock art studies. *South African Archaeological Bulletin* 39: 58–66

Lewis-Williams, J. D. 1984b. Ideological continuities in prehistoric southern Africa: the evidence of rock art. In C. Schrire (ed.) *Past and present in hunter gatherer studies*, pp. 225–252. New York: Academic Press

Lewis-Williams, J. D. 1985. Social theory in southern African archaeology. Paper presented at the conference of the Southern African Association of Archaeologists, Grahamstown

Liesegang, G. 1975. Aspects of Gaza Nguni history 1821–1897. *Rhodesian History* 6: 1–14

Lovejoy, P. 1983. *Transformations in slavery. A history of slavery in Africa*. Cambridge: Cambridge University Press

Lye, W. and Murray, C. 1980. *Transformations on the highveld; the Tswana and Southern Sotho*. Cape Town: David Philip

MacIver, D. R. 1906. *Medieval Rhodesia*. London: Macmillan

Maggs, T. 1971. Pastoral settlements on the Riet River. *South African Archaeological Bulletin* 26: 37–63

Maggs, T. 1973. The NC3 Iron Age tradition. *South African Journal of Science* 69: 326

Maggs, T. 1976a. *Iron Age communities of the southern highveld*. Pietermaritzburg: Natal Museum

Maggs, T. 1976b. Iron Age patterns and Sotho history on the southern highveld, South Africa. *World Archaeology* 7(3): 318–332

Maggs, T. 1977. Some recent radiocarbon dates from eastern and southern Africa. *Journal of African History* 18(2): 161–191

Maggs, T. 1980a. The Iron Age sequence south of the Vaal and Pongola rivers: some historical implications. *Journal of African History* 21(1): 1–15

Maggs, T. 1980b. Mzonjani and the beginnings of the Iron Age in Natal. *Annals of the Natal Museum* 24(1): 71–96

Maggs, T. 1980c. Msuluzi Confluence: a seventh century Early Iron Age site on the Tugela River. *Annals of the Natal Museum* 24(1): 111–145

Maggs, T. 1982. Mabhija: pre-colonial industrial development in the Tugela basin. *Annals of the Natal Museum* 25(1): 123–141

Maggs, T. 1984a. The Iron Age south of the Zambezi. In R. G. Klein (ed.) *Southern African prehistory and palaeoenvironments,* pp. 329–360. Rotterdam: Balkema

Maggs, T. 1984b. Ndondondwane: a preliminary report on an Early Iron Age site on the Lower Tugela River. *Annals of the Natal Museum* 26(1): 71–93

Maggs, T. and Michael, M. 1976. Ntshekane, an Early Iron Age site in the Tugela basin, Natal. *Annals of the Natal Museum* 22(3): 705–739

Maggs, T. and Ward, V. 1984. Early Iron Age sites in the Muden area of Natal. *Annals of the Natal Museum* 26(1): 105–140

Mallows, W. 1984. *The mystery of the Great Zimbabwe.* New York: W. W. Norton

Manhire, A. 1984. Stone tools and sandveld settlement. Unpublished M.Sc. thesis, University of Cape Town

Manhire, A., Parkington, J. E. and Robey, T. S. 1984. Stone tools and sandveld settlement. In M. Hall, G. Avery, D. M. Avery, M. L. Wilson and A. J. B. Humphreys (eds.) *Frontiers: southern African archaeology today,* pp. 111–120. Oxford: British Archaeological Reports

Marker, M. and Evers, T. M. 1976. Iron Age settlement and soil erosion in the eastern Transvaal, South Africa. *South African Archaeological Bulletin* 31: 153–165

Marks, S. 1967. The rise of the Zulu kingdom. In R. Oliver (ed.) *The Middle Age of African history,* pp. 85–91. London: Oxford University Press

Mason, R. 1951. The excavation of four caves near Johannesburg. *South African Archaeological Bulletin* 6: 71–79

Mason, R. 1962. *Prehistory of the Transvaal: a record of human activity.* Johannesburg: Witwatersrand University Press

Mason, R. 1968. Transvaal and Natal Iron Age settlement revealed by aerial photographs and excavation. *African Studies* 27(4): 167–180

Mason, R. 1981. Early Iron Age settlement at Broederstroom 24/73, Transvaal, South Africa. *South African Journal of Science* 77: 401–416

Mason, R. 1983. 'Oori' or 'Moloko'? The origins of the Sotho-Tswana on the evidence of the Iron Age of the Transvaal. *South African Journal of Science* 79(7): 261

Mauny, R. 1971. The western Sudan. In P. L. Shinnie (ed.) *The African Iron Age,* pp. 66–88. Oxford: Clarendon Press

McKenzie, B. 1984. Utilization of the Transkeian landscape: an ecological interpretation. *Annals of the Natal Museum* 26(1): 165–172

Meillassoux, C. 1972. From reproduction to production. A Marxist approach to economic anthropology. *Economy and Society* 1(1): 93–105

Miller, D. and Tilley, C. 1984. Ideology, power and prehistory: an introduction. In D. Miller and C. Tilley (eds.) *Ideology, power and prehistory,* pp. 1–15. Cambridge: Cambridge University Press

Monod, T. 1975. Introduction. In T. Monod (ed.) *Pastoralism in tropical Africa,* pp. 99–183. London: Oxford University Press

Monro, D. F. and Spies, C. W. 1975. Excavations at Musimbira, Bikita district, Rhodesia. *Arnoldia (Rhodesia)* 7(22): 1–11

Morais, J. 1984. Mozambican archaeology: past and present. *African Archaeological Review* 2: 113–128

Morais, J. and Sinclair, P. 1980. Manyikeni, a zimbabwe in southern Mozambique. In R. E. Leakey and B. A. Ogot (eds.) *Proceedings of the 8th Pan African Congress of Prehistory and Quaternary Studies,* pp. 351–354. Nairobi: International Leakey Memorial Institute for African Prehistory

Mufuka, K. N. 1983. *Dzimbahwe: life and politics in the Golden Age 1100–1500 A.D.* Harare: Harare Publishing House

Newitt, M. D. D. 1973. *Portuguese settlement on the Zambezi. Exploration, land tenure and colonial rule in East Africa.* London: Longman

Newitt, M. D. D. and Garlake, P. S. 1967. The 'aringa' at Massangano. *Journal of African History* 8(1): 133–156

Nott, J. C. and Gliddon, G. R. 1868. *Indigenous races of the earth.* Philadelphia

Nurse, D. 1982. Bantu expansion into East Africa: linguistic evidence. In C. Ehret and M. Posnansky (eds.) *The archaeological and linguistic reconstruction of African history,* pp. 199–222. Berkeley: University of California Press

Nurse, G. T. 1983. Population movement around the northern Kalahari. *African Studies* 42(2): 153–163

Oliver, R. 1966. The problem of the Bantu expansion. *Journal of African History* 6: 361–376

Oliver, R. and Fagan, B. M. 1975. *Africa in the Iron Age, c.500 B.C. to A.D. 1400.* London: Cambridge University Press

Omer-Cooper, J. D. 1966. *The Zulu aftermath: a nineteenth-century revolution in Bantu Africa.* London: Longmans

Parkington, J. E. 1984. Soaqua and Bushman: hunters and robbers. In C. Schrire (ed.) *Past and present in hunter gatherer studies,* pp. 151–174. New York: Academic Press

Parkington, J. E. and Cronin, M. 1979. The size and layout of Mgungundlovu 1829–1838. *South African Archaeological Society, Goodwin Series* 3: 133–148

Parkington, J. E. and Hall, M. 1986. In press. Patterning in recent radiocarbon dates from southern Africa as a reflection of prehistoric settlement and interaction. *Journal of African History*

Peires, J. B. 1981. *The house of Phalo: a history of the Xhosa people in the days of their independence.* Johannesburg: Ravan Press

Phillipson, D. W. 1977. *The later prehistory of eastern and southern Africa.* London: Heinemann

Phillipson, D. W. 1985. *African archaeology.* Cambridge: Cambridge University Press

Phillipson, D. W. and Fagan, B. M. 1969. The date of the Ingombe Ilede burials. *Journal of African History* 10(2): 199–204

Phimister, I. R. 1976. Pre-colonial gold mining in southern Zambezia: a reassessment. *African Social Research* 21: 1–30

Puzo, B. 1978. Patterns of man–land relations. In M. J. A. Werger (ed.) *Biogeography and ecology of southern Africa,* pp. 1049–1112. The Hague: W. Junk

Robertshaw, P. T. 1978a. The origin of pastoralism in the Cape. *South African Historical Journal* 10: 117–133

Robertshaw, P. T. 1978b. The archaeology of an abandoned pastoralist camp-site. *South African Journal of Science* 74: 29–31

Robins, P. A. and Whitty, A. 1966. Excavations at Harleigh Farm, near Rusape, Rhodesia, 1958–62. *South African Archaeological Bulletin* 21: 61–81

Robinson, K. R. 1959. *Khami ruins.* Cambridge: Cambridge University Press

Robinson, K. R. 1961a. An Early Iron Age site from the Chibi district, Southern Rhodesia. *South African Archaeological Bulletin* 16: 75–102

Robinson, K. R. 1961b. Excavations on the Acropolis Hill. *Occasional Papers of the National Museums of Southern Rhodesia* 23a: 159–192

Robinson, K. R., Summers, R. and Whitty, A. 1961. Some general conclusions. *Occasional Papers of the National Museums of Southern Rhodesia* 23a: 326–330

Rudd, S. 1968. Preliminary report of excavations, 1963–66, at Lekkerwater Ruins, Tsindi Hill, Theydon, Rhodesia. *Proceedings and Transactions of the Rhodesia Scientific Association* 52(5): 38–50

Rudd, S. 1984. Excavations at Lekkerwater Ruins, Tsindi Hill, Theydon, Zimbabwe. *South African Archaeological Bulletin* 39: 83–105

Sahlins, M. 1972. *Stone Age economics.* Chicago: Aldine

Sansom, B. 1974. Traditional economic systems. In W. D. Hammond-Tooke (ed.) *The Bantu-speaking peoples of southern Africa,* pp. 135–176. London: Routledge and Kegan Paul

Schmidt, P. R. 1978. *Historical archaeology. A structural approach in an African culture.* Westport: Greenwood Press

Schofield, J. F. 1926. Zimbabwe: a critical examination of the building methods employed. *South African Journal of Science* 23: 971–986

Schofield, J. F. 1937. The pottery of the Mapungubwe district. In L. Fouché (ed.) *Mapungubwe: ancient Bantu civilization on the Limpopo*, pp. 32–60. Cambridge: Cambridge University Press

Schofield, J. F. 1948. *Primitive pottery. An introduction to South African ceramics, prehistoric and protohistoric.* Cape Town: South African Archaeological Society

Schrire, C. 1980. An inquiry into the evolutionary status and apparent identity of San hunter-gatherers. *Human Ecology* 8(1): 9–32

Scully, R. T. K. 1978. Phalaborwa oral tradition. Unpublished Ph.D. thesis, State University of New York

Seligman, C. G. 1930. *Races of Africa.* London: Thornton, Butterworth

Service, E. R. 1980. *Origins of the state and civilization.* New York: W. W. Norton

Shinnie, P. L. 1967. *Meroe. A civilization of the Sudan.* London: Thames and Hudson

Shinnie, P. L. 1971. The Sudan. In P. L. Shinnie (ed.) *The African Iron Age*, pp. 89–107. Oxford: Clarendon Press

Sinclair, P. 1982. Chibuene: an early trading site in southern Mozambique. *Paideuma* 28: 150–64

Sinclair, P. 1984. Some aspects of the economic level of the Zimbabwe state. *Zimbabwea* 1(1): 48–53

Skalnik, P. 1983. Questioning the concept of the state in indigenous Africa. *Social Dynamics* 9(2): 11–28

Slater, H. 1976. Transitions in the political economy of southeast Africa before 1840. Unpublished Ph.D. dissertation, University of Sussex

Smith, A. 1969. The trade of Delagoa Bay as a factor in Nguni politics 1750–1835. In L. Thompson (ed.) *African societies in southern Africa*, pp. 171–189. London: Heinemann

Smith, A. 1970. The struggle for control of southern Mozambique, 1720–1835. Unpublished Ph.D. dissertation, University of California, Los Angeles

Smith, A. B. 1979. Biogeographical considerations of colonization of the Lower Tilemsi valley in the second millennium B.C. *Journal of Arid Environments* 2: 355–361

Smith, A. B. 1980a. The Neolithic tradition in the Sahara. In M. A. J. Williams and H. Faure (eds.) *The Sahara and the Nile. Quaternary environments and prehistoric occupation in northern Africa*, pp. 451–465. Rotterdam: Balkema

Smith, A. B. 1980b. Domesticated cattle in the Sahara and their introduction into West Africa. In M. A. J. Williams and H. Faure (eds.) *The Sahara and the Nile. Quaternary environments and prehistoric occupation in northern Africa*, pp. 489–501. Rotterdam: Balkema

Smith, A. B. 1983. Prehistoric pastoralism in the southwestern Cape, South Africa. *World Archaeology* 15(1): 79–89

Smith, A. B. 1984a. Origins of the Neolithic in the Sahara. In J. D. Clark and S. A. Brandt (eds.) *From hunters to farmers. The causes and consequences of food production in Africa*, pp. 84–92. Berkeley: University of California Press

Smith, A. B. 1984b. Environmental limitations on prehistoric pastoralism in Africa. *African Archaeological Review* 2: 99–111

Smith, A. B. 1984c. Adaptive strategies of prehistoric pastoralism in the south-western Cape. In M. Hall, G. Avery, D. M. Avery, M. L. Wilson and A. J. B. Humphreys (eds.) *Frontiers: southern African archaeology today*, pp. 131–142. Oxford: British Archaeological Reports

Smith, A. B. 1985. Colonial interaction in the southwestern Cape: hunters, herders and settlers. Paper presented at the Conference of the Southern African Association of Archaeologists, Grahamstown

Smith, A. B. 1986. Excavations at Plettenberg Bay, South Africa, of the camp site of the survivors of the wreck *Sao Goncalo*, 1630. *International Journal of Nautical Archaeology and Underwater Exploration* 15(1): 53–63

Sole, K. 1983. Culture, politics and the black writer: a critical look at prevailing assumptions. *English in Africa* 10(1): 37–83

Soper, R. 1982. Bantu expansion into eastern Africa: archaeological evidence. In C. Ehret and M. Posnansky (eds.) *The archaeological and linguistic reconstruction of African history*, pp. 223–238. Berkeley: University of California Press

South Africa. 1978. *Official yearbook of the Republic of South Africa.* Johannesburg: Department of Information

Stahl, A. B. 1984. A history and critique of investigations into early African agriculture. In J. D. Clark and S. A. Brandt (eds.) *From hunters to farmers. The causes and consequences of food production in Africa*, pp. 9–21. Berkeley: University of California Press

Stemler, A. B. L. 1980. Origins of plant domestication in the Sahara and the Nile valley. In M. A. J. Williams and H. Faure (eds.) *The Sahara and the Nile. Quaternary environments and prehistoric occupation in northern Africa*, pp. 503–526. Rotterdam: Balkema

Stemler, A. B. L. 1984. The transition from food collecting to food production in northern Africa. In J. D. Clark and S. A. Brandt (eds.) *From hunters to farmers. The causes and consequences of food production in Africa*, pp. 127–131. Berkeley: University of California Press

Stow, G. W. 1905. *The native races of South Africa.* London: Sonnenschein

Summers, R. 1950. Iron Age cultures in Southern Rhodesia. *South African Journal of Science* 47: 95–107

Summers, R. 1955. The dating of the Zimbabwe ruins. *Antiquity* 29: 107–11

Summers, R. 1958. *Inyanga. Prehistoric settlements in Southern Rhodesia.* Cambridge: Cambridge University Press

Summers, R. 1961. Excavations in the Great Enclosure. *Occasional Papers of the National Museums of Southern Rhodesia* 23a: 236–288

Summers, R. 1963. *Zimbabwe. A Rhodesian mystery.* Cape Town: Don Nelson

Summers, R. 1967. Iron Age industries of southern Africa, with notes on their chronology, terminology and economic status. In W. W. Bishop and J. D. Clark (eds.) *Background to evolution in Africa*, pp. 687–700. Chicago: University of Chicago Press

Summers, R. 1969. *Ancient mining in Rhodesia and adjacent areas.* Salisbury: National Museums of Rhodesia

Summers, R. 1970. Forty years' progress in Iron Age studies in Rhodesia, 1929–1969. *South African Archaeological Bulletin* 25: 95–103

Summers, R. 1971. *Ancient ruins and vanished civilizations of southern Africa.* Cape Town: Bulpin

Summers, R. 1986. A note on the bead trade in southern and south-eastern Africa. Unpublished manuscript

Summers, R. and Whitty, A. 1961. The development of the Great Enclosure. *Occasional Papers of the National Museums of Southern Rhodesia* 23a: 306–325

Tainton, N. M. and Mentis, M. T. 1984. Fire in grasslands. In P. de V. Booysen and N. M. Tainton (eds.) *Ecological effects of fire in South African ecosystems*, pp. 115–148. Berlin: Springer-Verlag

Tamplin, M. J. 1977. Preliminary report on an archaeological survey of the Republic of Botswana. Trent University Department of Anthropology

Theal, G. M. 1907. *History and ethnography of Africa south of the Zambezi.* London: Sonnenschein

Thornton, R. 1982. Modelling of spatial relations in a boundary marking ritual of the Iraqw of Tanzania. *Man* 17: 528–545

Thorp, C. 1979. Cattle from the Early Iron Age of Zimbabwe–Rhodesia. *South African Journal of Science* 75: 461

Thorp, C. 1984. A cultural interpretation of the faunal assemblage from Khami Hill Ruin. In M. Hall, G. Avery, D. M. Avery, M. L. Wilson and A. J. B. Humphreys (eds.) *Frontiers: southern African archaeology today*, pp. 266–276. Oxford: British Archaeological Reports

Tobias, P. V. 1955. Physical anthropology and somatic origins of the Hottentots. *African Studies* 14: 1–22

Tobias, P. V. 1966. The peoples of Africa south of the Sahara. In P. T. Baker and J. S. Weiner (eds.) *The biology of human adaptability.* Oxford: Clarendon Press

Tobias, P. V. 1974. The biology of the southern African Negro. In W. D. Hammond-Tooke (ed.) *The Bantu-speaking peoples of southern Africa*, pp. 3–45. London: Routledge and Kegan

Paul

Trevor-Roper, H. 1965. *The rise of Christian Europe*. London: Thames and Hudson

Trigger, B. G. 1969. The myth of Meroe and the African Iron Age. *African Historical Studies* 2(1): 23–50

Trigger, B. G. 1980. *Gordon Childe: revolutions in archaeology*. London: Thames and Hudson

Trimingham, J. S. 1975. The Arab geographers and the East African coast. In H. N. Chittick and R. I. Rotberg (eds.) *East Africa and the Orient*, pp. 115–146. New York: Africana Publishing Company

Tylecote, R. F. 1975. The origin of iron smelting in Africa. *West African Journal of Archaeology* 5: 1–9

Tylecote, R. F. 1982. Early copper slags and copper-base metal from the Agadez region of Niger. *Historical Metallurgy* 16(2): 58–64

Tyson, P. D., Dyer, T. G. J. and Mametse, M. N. 1975. Secular changes in South African rainfall: 1910 to 1972. *Quarterly Journal of the Royal Meteorological Society* 101: 817–833

Van der Merwe, N. J. 1980a. The advent of iron in Africa. In A. Wertime and J. D. Muhly (eds.) *The coming of the age of iron*, pp. 463–506. New Haven: Yale University Press

Van der Merwe, N. J. 1980b. Production of high carbon steel in the African Iron Age: the direct steel process. In R. E. Leakey and B. A. Ogot (eds.) *Proceedings of the 8th Pan African Congress of Prehistory and Quaternary Studies*, pp. 331–334. Nairobi: International Leakey Memorial Institute for African Prehistory

Van der Merwe, N. J. and Killick, D. J. 1979. Square: an iron smelting site near Phalaborwa. *South African Archaeological Society, Goodwin Series* 3: 86–93

Van der Merwe, N. J. and Scully, R. 1971. The Phalaborwa story: archaeological and ethnographic investigation of a South African Iron Age group. *World Archaeology* 3(2): 178–196

Vansina, J. 1965. *Oral tradition: a study in historical methodology*. London: Routledge and Kegan Paul

Vansina, J. 1979. Bantu in the crystal ball I. *History in Africa* 6: 287–333

Vansina, J. 1980. Bantu in the crystal ball II. *History in Africa* 7: 293–325

Van Warmelo, N. J. 1935. *A preliminary survey of the Bantu tribes of South Africa*. Pretoria: Government Printer

Voigt, E. A. 1980. Reconstructing Iron Age economies of the northern Transvaal: a preliminary report. *South African Archaeological Bulletin* 35: 39–45

Voigt, E. A. 1981. The faunal remains from Schroda. In E. A. Voigt (ed.) *Guide to archaeological sites in the northern and eastern Transvaal*, pp. 54–62. Pretoria: Southern African Association of Archaeologists

Voigt, E. A. 1983. *Mapungubwe: an archaeo-zoological interpretation of an Iron Age community*. Pretoria: Transvaal Museum

Voigt, E. A. 1984. The faunal remains from Magogo and Mhlopeni: small stock herding in the Early Iron Age of Natal. *Annals of the Natal Museum* 26(1): 141–163

Voigt, E. A. and Plug, I. 1981. Early Iron Age herders of the Limpopo valley. Unpublished report, Transvaal Museum, Pretoria

Voigt, E. A. and Von den Driesch, A. 1984. Preliminary report on the faunal assemblage from Ndondondwane, Natal. *Annals of the Natal Museum* 26(1): 95–104

Walker, N. J. 1983. The significance of an early date for pottery and sheep in Zimbabwe. *South African Archaeological Bulletin* 38: 88–92

Webb, C. de B. and Wright J. B. 1976. *The James Stuart archive of recorded oral evidence relating to the history of the Zulu and neighbouring peoples*, volume 1. Pietermaritzburg: Natal University Press

Webb, C. de B. and Wright J. B. 1979. *The James Stuart archive of recorded oral evidence relating to the history of the Zulu and neighbouring peoples*, volume 2. Pietermaritzburg: Natal University Press

Weiss, K. M. and Maruyama, T. 1976. Archaeology, population genetics and studies of human racial ancestry. *American Journal of Physical Anthropology* 44: 31–50

Welbourn, A. 1984. Endo ceramics and power strategies. In D. Miller and C. Tilley (eds.) *Ideology, power and prehistory*, pp. 17–24. Cambridge: Cambridge University Press

Wellington, J. H. 1955. *Southern Africa, a geographical study*. Vol. 1, Physical geography. London: Cambridge University Press

Wendorf, F. and Schild, R. 1984. Conclusions. In A. E. Close (ed.) *Cattle keepers of the eastern Sahara: the Neolithic of Bir Kiseiba*, pp. 404–428. Dallas: Southern Methodist University Department of Anthropology

Westphal, E. O. J. 1963. The linguistic prehistory of southern Africa: Bush, Kwadi, Hottentot, and Bantu linguistic relationships. *Africa* 33(3): 237–265

Whitty, A. 1961. Architectural style at Zimbabwe. *Occasional Papers of the National Museums of Southern Rhodesia* 23a: 289–305

Wiessner, P. 1982. Risk, reciprocity and social influences on !Kung San economics. In E. Leacock and R. Lee (eds.) *Politics and history in band societies*, pp. 61–84. Cambridge: Cambridge University Press

Willcox, A. R. 1956. *Rock paintings of the Drakensberg*. London: Parrish

Willey, G. R. and Sabloff, J. A. 1980. *A history of American archaeology*. London: Thames and Hudson

Williams, M. A. J. 1984. Late Quaternary prehistoric environments in the Sahara. In J. D. Clark and S. A. Brandt (eds.) *From hunters to farmers. The causes and consequences of food production in Africa*, pp. 74–83. Berkeley: University of California Press

Wilmot, A. 1896. *Monomotapa. Its monuments and its history from the most ancient times to the present century*. London: Fisher Unwin

Wilson, M. and Thompson, L. (eds.) 1969. *The Oxford History of South Africa. Volume 1. South Africa to 1870*. Oxford: Clarendon Press

Wolf, E. R. 1982. *Europe and the people without history*. Berkeley: University of California Press

Wolpert, J. 1964. The decision process in spatial context. *Annals of the Association of American Geographers* 54: 537–58

Yellen, J. E. 1984. The integration of herding into prehistoric hunting and gathering economies. In M. Hall, G. Avery, D. M. Avery, M. L. Wilson and A. J. B. Humphreys (eds.) *Frontiers: southern African archaeology today*, pp. 53–64. Oxford: British Archaeological Reports

Index

concept of, 8, 10, 16–17, 21, 22*,
31–2, 34–5, 143–4; Early Iron Age
/Late Iron Age transition, 14, 14*,
15, 23–4; and race, 19
iron production: see metallurgy
Isaacs, Nathaniel, 2–5, 136, 147
Islam, spread of, 78, 91, 99–101,
122–4, 133, 146
isotopic analysis, 12, 12*, 68
ivory: see crafts, elephant hunting
Jabasta: see Chibuene
K2 (Transvaal, South Africa), 77,
79–83, 89
Kalahari Desert, 19, 44, 71, 85,
88–90, 92, 102
Kalambo Falls (Zambia), 10
Karanga: see Mutapa
Karoo, 35
Karoo series, 47, 55
Kasteelberg (Cape, South Africa),
58, 59*
Katanga (Zaire), 20*
Katuruka (Tanzania), 28, 28*
Kenya, 13
Kenyon, Kathleen, 7
Kgatla lineage, 53, 65
Khami (Zimbabwe), 14, 119–22,
120*, 137
Khami River, 118*, 119
Khoikhoin: communities, 35, 44,
58–60, 59, 64, 64*, 67, 72, 74–5,
125; languages (see also Tshu-khwe),
22*, 23
Khumalo: see kwaKhumalo
Kilwa (Tanzania), 76*, 78, 81, 91,
99–102, 100*, 101*, 117, 122–4,
133, 146
King, James Saunders, 2–3
kings: see state
kinship, 61, 132–3, 146
Klip River, 49, 51
! Kung: see San
Kuper, Adam, 72–3, 96, 114
Kutama Tradition, 14–15, 14*
kwaButhelezi, 57, 57*, 64, 74–5
kwaKhumalo, 57, 57*, 64, 74–5,
139
Kwekwena: see Khoikhoin
Kwena lineage, 53, 65
Laidler, P. W., 8
language: Bantu languages, origins
of, 20–1, 20*, 21*, 22*, 23–4,
30–1; classification, 20–1, 20*,
21*, 23; concept of, 20; Cushitic,
21; Eastern Highland group, 23;
glottochronology, 23, 34–5; Khoikhoi (see also Tshu-khwe language
group), 22*, 23; loanwords, 23;
Nguni, 23; Niger-Congo family,
20, 20*; and race, 20, 24; Shona,
origins of, 14, 23; Sotho–Tswana,
origins of, 14–15, 23, 53; Sudanic,
23; Tshu-khwe group, 34–5, 47,
58; Western Highlands group, 22*,
23
Latter, B. D. H., 18

Lechana (Botswana), 87
Leopard's Kopje Tradition, 14
Letaba River, 66
Lewis-Williams, David, 62–3, 71
Limpopo River, 13, 15, 38–9, 43,
53, 74–80, 76*, 82, 85, 88–9,
91–2, 94, 99, 102, 119, 146
lineage, concept of, 65
lineage mode of production: see
mode of production
Linnaeus, Carl, 17
Lisbon, 123
Little Muck (Transvaal, South
Africa), 77, 88
Lovejoy, Paul, 129, 132
Luenha River, 131
Lundi River, 92, 119, 122
Lydenburg, Iron Age sites (Trans-
vaal, South Africa), 14, 38*, 41–2,
41*, 44
'Lydenburg heads', 2*, 41–2, 41*, 53
Lydenburg Tradition, 13–15, 13*,
15*, 42, 42*
Lydenburg valley, 40, 41*, 43
Mabhija (Natal, South Africa), 66*,
68, 69*, 80
Mabveni (Zimbabwe), 38–40, 38*
MacIver, D. R., 7, 103, 136
Madeira, Diogo Simoes, 130
madzimbahwe: see *dzimbahwe*
Magalies Mountains, 10
Magalies River, 39, 43
Maggs, Tim, 10, 12, 14–15, 17, 43–4,
48–9, 50–1, 53, 55, 64–5, 68
Magogo (Natal, South Africa), 43
Maiphetwane (Botswana), 87
Makgadikgadi Pans, 92, 96
Makgwareng (Orange Free State,
South Africa), 48*, 51–3, 52*, 64
Makhutswi River, 66
Malawi, 23, 29
Maleme Dam Shelter (Zimbabwe),
35
Mali, 26
Mamazapi River, 66
Mamba (Natal, South Africa), 42*
Mambula (Natal, South Africa), 42*
Manhire, Tony, 44
Manyika, 134
Manyikeni (Mozambique), 92–3,
92*, 95
Mapela (Zimbabwe), 76*, 77–8, 82
Mapungubwe (Transvaal, South
Africa), 43, 76*, 77–85, 77*, 80*,
81*, 83*, 84*, 85*, 88–9, 91, 96,
98, 116, 121
Mapungubwe state, 77–9, 82–3, 85,
88–92, 94, 96, 102, 118, 124, 128,
136, 146
Maputo, 136
Mary (brig), 2–3, 147
Mashonaland (Zimbabwe), 5
Mason, Revil, 8, 10, 15, 39–40
Massangano (Zimbabwe), 130*,
131*
Matloang (Orange Free State, South

Africa), 48*, 53, 54*, 64
Matola, Iron Age site (Mozambique), 38, 38*
Matola (Silverleaves) Tradition,
13–15, 13*, 15*
Mauch, Carl, 7, 103
'Maund Ruins' (Great Zimbabwe),
110–11, 110*, 111*
McKenzie, Bruce, 126
medicine men, 62, 71; see also San
Meroe (Sudan), 24, 27, 28*
metallurgy: copper smelting, 28–9,
67–8, 79, 98–9, 99*; forging, 68,
68*, 79; gold, 27, 88, 91, 93,
96–102, 122–4, 127, 129–31; iron-
smelting, 10, 11*, 24, 28–9, 29*,
36–7, 40–2, 56, 65, 67–9, 68*,
69*, 73, 79, 93, 99, 144; origins
of, 27–31, 28*, 29*; see also
mining
metal-working: see metallurgy
Mfolozi River, 55, 57*, 136, 139
Mgungundlovu (Natal, South Africa),
4, 79, 137–9, 137*, 138*
military power, 75, 89, 94–5, 125,
128, 128*, 129–41, 137*,
138*, 146
mining: for gold, 96–7, 97*, 118,
133, 141; for iron-ore, 68, 68*,
69*
missionaries, 130, 141*
Mmamgwa Hill (Botswana), 77, 82,
88
mode of production, concept of,
64–5, 74–5, 88–9, 125, 143–6
Moloko Tradition, 14–15, 14*, 143
Monod, T., 26
Monomotapa: see Mutapa
Montevideo Ranch (Zimbabwe), 93,
95–6
Mooi River, 42
Morais, Joao, 147
moran, 70
Mosetse River, 92, 96
Mozambique, 13, 15, 23, 38
Mozambique Island, 118*, 124, 127
Mpande, 141
Msuluzi Confluence (Natal, South
Africa), 42–4
Msuluzi River, 42
Mthethwa: see Zulu kingdom
Mufuka, Ken, 147
Musimbira (Zimbabwe), 94–5
Mutapa state, 118–19, 118*, 121–2,
124, 127–8, 130, 133–5, 141, 146
Mzilikazi, 139
Mzonjani (Natal, South Africa), 15*,
37*, 38*
Nalatale (Zimbabwe), 7*, 118*, 122*
Nama, 35; see also Khoikhoin
Namaqualand, 35
Namibia, 19, 23, 34–5
Natal coastal (NC) pottery: see
ceramics
Ndebele, 139, 141, 146
Ndondondwane (Natal, South

Acknowledgements

Grateful acknowledgement is made to the following for photographs or illustrations supplied, or for permission to reproduce previously published illustrations in part or in whole, on the pages indicated:

Academic Press for reproduction from C. Schrire (ed.), *Past and present in hunter gatherer studies,* 63; Africana Museum, Johannesburg, 140 bottom; British Institute in Eastern Africa, 100, 101 top; Cambridge University Press for reproductions from *Journal of African History,* 8 (1967), 131, and from R. Summers, *Inyanga. Prehistoric settlements in Southern Rhodesia,* 135, 136; Brian Fagan for reproduction from B. M. Fagan *et al.* (eds.), *Iron Age cultures in Zambia* (vol. 2), 98 top right; Tim Maggs, 47, 51, and for reproductions from T. Maggs, *Iron Age communities of the southern highveld,* 49, 52, 54; Natal Museum, Pietermaritzburg, for reproductions from *Annals of the Natal Museum,* 26 (1984), 42 top left, *Annals of the Natal Museum,* 22 (1976), 42 top right, and *Annals of the Natal Museum,* 25 (1982), 69 top left; National Cultural History and Open Air Museum, Pretoria, 76 bottom, 82; John Parkington for reproductions from J. E. Parkington and M. Cronin, 'The size and layout of Mgungundlovu', 137 bottom left and right; Keith Robinson for reproductions from K. R. Robinson, 'Excavations on the Acropolis Hill', 105, and from K. R. Robinson, *Khami Ruins,* 120; Routledge and Kegan Paul for reproductions from W. D. Hammond-Tooke (ed.), *The Bantu-speaking peoples of southern Africa,* 19 top right, and from *World Archaeology,* 7 (1976), 48 bottom; South African Museum, Cape Town, 2, 45 bottom, 112, 141, and for reproduction from *Annals of the South African Museum,* 91 (1983), 57 bottom; South African Archaeological Society for reproductions from J. F. Schofield, *Primitive pottery,* 8, and from *South African Archaeological Bulletin,* 38 (1983), 35 top left, and *Goodwin Series,* 4 (1983), 62, and *Goodwin Series,* 3 (1979), 137 top and bottom; Transvaal Museum, Pretoria, 80 top, 81 top; University of California Press for reproduction from J. D. Clark and S. A. Brandt (eds.), *From hunters to farmers,* 26 top left; University of Pretoria, 77, 83, 84, 85; University of Wisconsin Press for reproduction from A. Isaacman, *Mozambique: the Africanization of a European institution,* 132; Bert Woodhouse, 140 top right.